The Evolution of the Single European Market

The Evolution of the Single European Market

Edited by
David G. Mayes

Reserve Bank of New Zealand, University of Waikato and National Institute of Economic and Social Research, London.

Edward Elgar
Cheltenham, UK • Lyme, US

© David G. Mayes 1997

Published by
Edward Elgar Publishing Limited
8 Lansdown Place
Cheltenham
Glos GL50 2HU
UK

Edward Elgar Publishing, Inc.
1 Pinnacle Hill Road
Lyme
NH 03768
US

A catalogue record for this book
is available from the British Library

Library of Congress Cataloguing in Publication Data

The evolution of the single European market / edited by David G. Mayes.
    Includes index.
        1. Europe—Economic integration—History. I. Mayes, David G.
    HC241.E96 1997
    337.1'4—dc21   97–14362
                                                                        CIP

ISBN 1 85898 649 4

Printed and bound in Great Britain by Bookcraft (Bath) Ltd

Contents

Figures

Tables

Contributors

Christopher Brewin is Lecturer in Politics at the University of Keele.

Simon Bulmer is Professor of Government at the University of Manchester.

Andrew Cox is a Professor at the University of Birmingham

Keith Hartley is Professor of Economics at the University of York and Director of the Institute of Defence Economics.

Robert M. Lindley is Professor of Economics at the University of Warwick and Director of the Centre for Employment Research.

Giandomenico Majone is a Professor at the European University Institute in Florence.

Duncan Matthews, formerly of the National Institute of Economic and Social Research in London, is a Lecturer at the University of Warwick.

David G. Mayes, formerly Senior Research Fellow at the National Institute of Economic and Social Research in London, is Chief Manager, Economics Department, Reserve Bank of New Zealand and Adjunct Professor at the University of Waikato.

John A. Usher is Professor of Law at the University of Exeter.

Albert Weale is Professor of Government at the University of Essex.

Stephen Woolcock, formerly of the Royal Institute of International Affairs, is at the London School of Economics.

Preface

This book draws on the work of over one hundred researchers, mainly located in the United Kingdom but also spread over the rest of Europe, who participated in the Economic and Social Research Council's *Single European Market* research programme, entitled 'The Evolution of Rules for a Single European Market'. While the authors, who all played a leading role in the research themselves, have done their best to acknowledge where they have drawn on the ideas of others, it is inevitable that much of this painstaking work has gone unsung and we take this opportunity to express our appreciation. The principal researchers are listed in Table 1.1 and all of them have made substantial contributions to the programme. Without this initiative by the ESRC and their extensive funding of the work there would be no book. However, other organisations, listed in Chapter 1, also played their part in financing and encouraging the work. While it is no doubt invidious to single out just some of them for comment, I am particularly grateful for the help of the successive Research Directors at the Anglo–German Foundation for the Advancement of an Industrial Society and to Michael White of the British Council in Madrid.

The international collaboration was greatly assisted by the creation of an Action under the COST framework of co-operation among official funders of research in Europe. I take this opportunity to thank the members of the Management Committee, particularly those like Kirsti Rissanen (Finnish Justice Ministry), Janos Kovacs (Hungarian Academy of Sciences), Per Kongshof Madsen (University of Copenhagen), Per Halstrom (University of Stockholm), Iris Bohnet (University of Zurich), Eddy Wymeersch (University of Gent), Eugene du Puy (NWO-ECOZOEK in Den Haag) and Pekka Kosonen (University of Helsinki) who helped organise meetings and Tuija Partonen the Secretary from the European Commission. Our Dutch colleagues were particularly active in setting up this network.

The ESRC organised an active Steering Committee and I owe a lot to the careful advice of the members and successive Chairmen, Michael Bichard (Gloucester County Council and the Benefits Agency) and Richard Freeman (ICI) as well as to the ESRC staff. The National Institute of Economic and Social Research provided a very effective home for the research and the initiative would have fallen apart without the guiding hand of my PA, Sarah Leeming. It was Sarah who organised the major conference at the University of Exeter at which the initial drafts of these chapters were presented and discussed. Finally, my thanks are due to Debbie May, my PA in New Zealand, who put the final product together and to all those among my family, friends and colleagues, who have suffered while I concentrated on this work.

DAVID G. MAYES

1. Introduction

David G. Mayes

The rapid development of the integration of Europe since the mid-1980s has been the focus of considerable political debate and academic research. However, the political process has outstripped the research achievements for much of the period. The so-called 'completion' of the internal market was agreed following the publication of the Commission's White Paper in 1985 and enacted with the Single European Act of 1986, which came into force in 1987. The first attempts to quantify what this might mean in practice appeared in 1988, with the Cecchini Report, *The Economics of 1992* (published in *European Economy* and subsequently as Emerson *et al.* 1989) and the 17 volumes of background papers entitled *'The Costs of Non-Europe'*. The member states of the European Community were thus signing up to the most significant changes in the regulatory structure of the European economy since the first enlargement of the EC in 1973 on the basis of generalised economic, social and political beliefs rather than hard evidence. Indeed the benefits appeared so self-evident that such research was not felt to be immediately relevant.

Not only were the expected results of this closer integration not forecast with anything but the most cursory precision but the mechanisms to be employed in achieving this change were themselves relatively untested, or, where tested, were of mixed success. One might be tempted to criticise the political process for running ahead too fast. It would, however, be more realistic to criticise academic research for moving too slowly. After all academics should be a major source of the production and development of new ideas.

Prior to the agreements on enlargement there were estimates of their consequence and a considerable debate about these projected outcomes. When I wrote my survey article on this research area shortly after the first enlargement (Mayes, 1977) it was possible to point to considerable theoretical and empirical development over the preceding two decades. When Alan Winters extended the survey a decade later (Winters, 1987), although the single market programme was well under way, there had been no equivalent progress. Estimates of the likely progress of integration had become much rarer and the theory was little developed.

Indeed, when we held a conference at Exeter University in September 1986 on European industry and integration (Macmillen, Mayes and van Veen, 1987) it was very difficult to raise any interest in the subject despite an excellent introduction to the single market issues by Jacques Pelkmans. Indeed, his book with Alan Winters (Pelkmans and Winters, 1988) had to go far outside the available information to try to sort out the issues involved.

Much of the interesting tale in that research was the nature of the mechanisms that would be applied to reach a single market. These included the idea that agreements at the official level on European standards would relate only to minimum conditions for health, safety and the environment and that the detailed agreements would emanate from the voluntary decisions of the market players. Since only minimum standards were to be agreed, different national systems would co-exist. Goods and services produced under these different national regulatory systems, provided they complied with the minima, would have to be accepted under a process of mutual recognition. This would apply particularly in areas such as type approval, so that items accepted as complying with the rules in one part of the market would automatically be deemed to comply with them in the rest.

These procedures generated the thought-provoking idea that instead of looking at the behaviour of firms competing under a common set of rules that there would be competition among the very rule systems themselves, in the sense that firms might gain an advantage from being subject to one system rather than another. In a single market transnational firms could move their operations so as to be subject to the most favourable system. Authorities would then react as they saw this migration, encouraging it where it led to a reduction in costs and trying to block it by eliminating the differences where it increased them.

However, the economics of this sort of behaviour, as relating just to firms, usually represented by game theory, is itself only recently developed. The twist of endogenising the rule system took it beyond where theory had then reached.

The poverty of research on this important subject was aided by the strong divisions which existed between the different subject approaches to integration. The issues in economics were fairly clearly set out in terms of much traditional trade theory and relatively ill put together until more recently in their industrial and spatial counterparts. Political scientists had at the same time been pursuing theories of integration but the whole conceptual base of this was completely different with discussions of neo-functionalism and intergovernmentalism totally bemusing the economists. Indeed I was disappointed to see at the conference of the European Community Studies Association in Washington in 1993 that this separation of approach still existed and that the new synthesis being advanced ignored the contribution of other disciplines.

Even by late 1993 research on the impact of the single market was still very limited (Mayes and Burridge, 1993) and it is no surprise that the

Commission is undertaking a major programme of research to ascertain progress.

1 THE NEED FOR A RESEARCH INITIATIVE

It is in this context of the obvious failure of academics either to keep up to speed with policy making or to transcend the subject barriers effectively that the Economic and Social Research Council in the UK (ESRC) decided to intervene. Unlike the research councils or other bodies organising the allocation of public funds to research in some other European countries the ESRC is able to be pro-active. It can identify research deficiencies and channel funds towards remedying them. Several routes are available, such as the funding of a research centre on the subject but the principal mechanism used has been to develop a co-ordinated research programme. The committees of the ESRC are composed of prominent academics and other experts, not officials, so researchers themselves are effectively responsible to a large extent for determining the focus of funding.

In general the ESRC does not support institutions or research groups but funds research projects or groups of such projects in programmes where each funding decision has been made on the base of open peer review. It is thus not a matter of picking on an individual or an institution and asking them to get on with organising research in an area but of inviting bids from individual academics, singly or in teams, to put forward ideas which lie within a designated specialised research area. However, to ensure that the research is focused and that the individual researchers benefit from the activities of others funded under the same programme such initiatives are co-ordinated.

The Single European Market Programme, which I co-ordinated and whose work forms the basis of this book, is one such initiative. It was developed as the result of recognition of the research gap – initially by the committee concerned with political and social issues but then also by that concerned with economic, industrial and environmental issues. Projects were selected as the result of a widely publicised open competition. The response was so great that only about 10 per cent of ideas could be funded.

Before going on to discuss the various projects within the research programme I want to make a few more remarks about the form of the programme as a whole.

The ESRC was very keen to make sure that the programme added value to the research process and did not merely duplicate what was happening elsewhere or follow what would have happened anyway without the initiative. It therefore stressed two aspects of the single market:

- its multidisciplinary character; and
- the need to focus on the future policy issues.

The first of these headings therefore concentrated on a traditional area of weakness in social science research in the UK, while the second in looking forward ensured that the research would continue to be of value. Two routes are used by the ESRC to ensure this value is attained by research programmes. One is to require that co-ordinators raise finance from other sources – other nearer market funders must also think the research is well directed. The second is that the researchers must develop a working relationship with policy makers and ensure that the results of their work are widely disseminated. This book is part of that process as was the closely focused conference at which the earlier versions of the chapters were discussed.

The Single Market programme was quite successful in raising cofinance and considerable thanks are due to the major cofunders which included: the UK government through the Departments of Employment and Trade and Industry; the British Council; the Bank of England; and industry itself, both through trade associations like the Finance and Leasing Association; and individual firms such as ICI. Other research funders, such as the Anglo–German Foundation for the Study of Industrial Society, have joined the initiative both with separate projects and with joint funding. There has also been very welcome support both from other countries, including the Spanish government and the Finnish food industry and from international organisations particularly the European Parliament, the European Commission, who helped sponsor the conference at Exeter where these chapters were discussed, the European Foundation for Living and Working Conditions and the Association for the Monetary Union of Europe.

Rather than looking backwards at what had been done or what might have been done, the research programme has been looking at the single market as a dynamic process. The research teams have not been of the opinion that the single market was a simple transition from one state to another which would be completed in a relatively limited number of years following the decision to implement the 1985 White Paper. They have regarded it as a much more evolutionary process that began well before the White Paper and will continue well into the next century even without further changes such as economic and monetary union or the widening of the EU to contain further members.

What the programme has sought to do is understand that evolutionary process, its impact and how it might develop. For example in the early years of the research a prime concern was that the process might be too inward looking, focusing on the needs of the member states without regard to the impact that it might have on the wider world. The worry was that the potential adverse consequences would generate a reaction leading to retaliation or the creation of competing trading blocs (Mayes, 1993b). A second focus was on the question of whether this process of deepening the EC might be at the expense of widening it. We now know that the two questions are related. The negotiations for the European Economic Area were so one-sided, with the EC virtually dictating the conditions under which the other states could join, that it helped propel several of them into applying for full membership of the EU. In that case they would at least have a voice in the future development of the system.

One obvious characteristic of the single market, and indeed the whole process of integration stemming from the Treaties of Paris and Rome, is that it is rule driven. Unlike free trade agreements which tend to focus on 'negative' integration, the removal of barriers, the SEM has a strong positive element to it, seeking to harmonise behaviour across a wide front. However, also unlike free trade agreements – as exemplified by NAFTA – the treaty embodying the agreement, the Single European Act, is quite short and largely composed of non-specific general statements. The NAFTA agreement is massive, packed with detailed exceptions and provisions. The detailed negotiation and determination of the SEM was to follow the treaty, not precede it, as is the more traditional case for international agreements. It is a framework enabling change, not the full prescription of the change itself.

That framework has many innovative features. It is not simply laying out a series of areas where the contracting parties have to come to specific detailed agreements. It offers a whole range of approaches, strongly influenced by the unique institutional structure of the European Community. Some agreements would indeed involve traditional negotiation but the European Commission plays a key role in initiating policy and does not merely act as some facilitating secretariat. Secondly, in many areas the process of harmonisation was deliberately intended to be incomplete at the governmental level. Agreements were to cover minimum requirements, mainly relating to health, safety and the environment. Beyond that, agreement would be voluntary, in some cases through negotiation, such as for standards, or in others by simple operation of markets. In this second instance different approaches would compete, permitted by the principle of 'mutual recognition'.

The sorts of rules themselves vary enormously in character and affect behaviour at all levels of society (Shipman and Mayes, 1989). While there is a basic international treaty, it is augmented by directives and regulations emanating from the Commission, national law, other official legal instruments, international agreements, self-regulatory arrangements in industries and professions, down to codes of behaviour and informal rules applied by individual firms and households. The single market not only introduces a whole range of new rules but it brings people into contact with other rules, and indeed rule systems, that they would not normally have experienced. Exporting firms have to cope with domestic rules in the destination country, migrants have to handle different social benefit and taxation systems as well as having to adjust to different cultural norms. Not only do people have to adjust to new rules but the rules themselves need to adjust to the new environment.

The framers of the research programme therefore lighted on this aspect of the 'rules' as being a characteristic which not merely differentiated the single market from most other attempts at voluntary integration among countries but also one which raised a whole host of issues running right across the social sciences. Political scientists may have studied regulatory institutions, economists have explored how regulatory systems operate and estimated their impact, while lawyers have explored the content of the rules themselves. There is a long list. However, there has been relatively little co-ordination among these groups. Indeed there are several instances where similarly entitled concepts have been developed which have little in common with each other. In combination, therefore, this research programme very clearly meets the objectives the ESRC set out.

Formulating the Rules

The generalised format of the programme has been to look at the stages of the evolutionary process, beginning with how rules are formed in the first place. Rule formation raises some obvious issues for research:

- who decides on whether there is a need for a rule?
- how do they go about making that decision?
- who influences it?
- how do they decide upon the content of the rule?
- how can that content be amended?

The results from this first aspect of the research have been fascinating, revealing how important the particular institutional arrangements of the EU are. Two features stand out. One is the role of experts. Given the width of its policy mandate, the Commission is a lightly staffed organisation compared with those of the member states and must therefore seek outside advice on many issues, particularly since the measures have to cope with the variation across twelve countries. Individual officials have to see through dossiers till the completion of the process. Help, while it may come from an invitation to tender, is nevertheless likely to have a national flavour to it as most experts are firmly rooted in one or a few member states. As in all tendering, there is also a tendency to opt for advisors who are known quantities, thus restricting the scope somewhat – as members of the research programme have found both to their advantage and disadvantage in their own contributions to the Commission. Hence the form of the proposed rules emanating from an expert may have the structure of the system in one particular country rather more heavily embedded in it than those from the others.

This can mean for the UK that, although it provides at least its fair share of experts, since its regulatory system and policy approach often differ from that of its partners, the chances of its approach being reflected in draft legislation is relatively small. This, therefore, increases the chance that UK officials will be vociferous in pointing out that proposals do not take account of the specific features of the UK system.

This chance of developing legislation with an apparently 'foreign' flavour to it is exacerbated by the second finding that once a proposal is drafted it is very difficult to alter it. Positions become entrenched. Hence if private sector organisations only come across prospective legislation after it has been drafted and is circulated for comment, they have much less chance of influencing it than if they had been involved in the previous stage when nothing was published. As most large companies and trade associations have realised, this means the need for effective representation in Brussels.

Implementing the Rules

I could go on with the issues here, including the detailed findings emanating from my own work on the legislation relating to the leasing industry with Duncan Matthews (Matthews and Mayes, 1994a). However, I shall turn to the next part of the evolutionary process which is the implementation of the rules. In the initial stage the rule may have changed markedly from the initial concept which motivated the process. Some will have been dropped altogether. Even when it has got through the process of consultation within the Commission and then through the other institutions until final approval by the Council, it still has a long way to go before it takes effect. (There is an important distinction between regulations and directives and I want to restrict myself here to the more complicated case of directives.)

A directive has to be transposed into national law. Ignoring the delay that this can involve, which may in itself permit pre-emptive response, this can involve substantially different processes within the various member states so that the effect is not particularly similar. In any case just having a rule does not ensure that it is complied with. A member state has to detect infringements and take action to enforce compliance. Here again a variety of methods can be applied. Harsh penalties may be more effective in achieving compliance than an active programme of advice on how to comply. From my own point of view a particularly interesting concept arose from a seminar which Terence Daintith organised at the Institute of Advanced Legal Studies in 1992.

Economists typically view compliance in simple terms. They suggest that firms weigh up the costs of compliance against those of non-compliance. The former include the capital, training and production costs involved, while the latter are the product of the chance of detection, the chance of prosecution, the likely penalty and subsequent costs. These latter may be substantial as repairing a reputation after successful prosecution for inadequate health standards may take years of hard effort and persuasion. Doreen McBarnett and Chris Whelan however came up with a different 'socio-legal' concept namely the idea of 'creative compliance'. According to this view firms dislike disobeying the law, they therefore seek a means of complying with the law which minimises their costs. In some cases this will involve complying with the letter rather than the spirit of the law. In these circumstances the rule will be achieving a rather different outcome from that intended – increasing the chance of subsequent amendment and hence evolution of the system.

The Impact of Rules

The third stage of the evolution of the system relates to the impact of the rule. Although, rules are intended to achieve a particular outcome, such as open competition in an industry, they can only facilitate it, they cannot compel it. Hence, although the rule may exist, the resultant behaviour may be rather different from that intended. Thus, for example, prices for a particular product may still continue to vary widely across the EU, say, because producers can successfully differentiate their products. Public procurement may follow all the required rules yet nevertheless the proportion of domestic suppliers may be much larger than that supplying the private sector with similar goods or services. Not surprisingly then one might expect a further round of change in order to get closer to the desired outcome.

Changing the Rules

Lastly, one can consider how the rules are changed. In our work we have made a basic distinction between the formal rule system, laid down by legislation, and that derived either formally or informally within companies or markets. We have hijacked the expression 'soft law' (Matthews and Mayes, 1994b) to cover this second category – it is normally applied less widely to non-enforceable international agreements and to codes of practice such as those under health and safety legislation. The procedures for change in the two areas are markedly different. In the case of 'hard' law a legislative process is required. For legislation just applying in a member state this can be a relatively rapid process. When laws are seen to fail in their prime purpose they can be amended relatively easily. Indeed, in some cases this can be obtained by administrative interpretation or instrument without having to do more than report the action to parliament. The same is not so true for European legislation. In that case the problem needing rectification has to be observed in a number of countries or at least recognised by a sufficient number of them to initiate action. The progress through Council and the Commission with appropriate consultation means that change is a slow and difficult prospect.

To an extent member states can act rather faster by either failing to enforce existing law or enacting new legislation and persisting until action is taken against them by which time the prevailing view may have changed. However, the European Court of Justice has itself been a force for accelerating change and, indeed, in averting the occurrence of some of the more anomalous pieces of legislation.

When it comes to soft law, however, change can be much more rapid. Providing there is no clash with hard law, it is largely up to the bodies themselves to determine their own rules. In the case of firms this may be a relatively straightforward process, which management can decide for itself. The Reserve Bank of New Zealand, in which I now work, has very publicly been through just that process. The restructuring of the external framework took place in 1989 with the Reserve Bank Act which set up the objectives, terms of reference, etc. However, in order to respond to that changed focus, the bank itself had to undergo major reorganisation, which resulted in widespread changes in internal and external procedures and in the general philosophy of operation. Some of these involve rewriting internal procedures. For example, we have recodified what should be done in the case of 'failure to settle' and how 'the lender of last resort' function should be exercised. Our powers under the Act are enormous but the market needs to understand how they will be exercised.

In the European case we have looked at a number of examples, particularly in the retailing and leasing industries, the legal profession and general practice. Again there is a distinction between the national associations or member firms altering their behaviour or the derivation of new international agreements. In the case of leasing, for example, there was a basic discrepancy between what could be described as the Anglo-Saxon and Continental regimes, particularly in the case of accounting standards. After toying with compromises which involved largely adopting one or other system with caveats to allow for the problems of the other group, the eventual outcome has been to duck the issue and allow the two systems to coexist, with enough extra information to permit a comparison.

2   THE ESRC RESEARCH PROGRAMME

The 27 projects that have formed the ESRC-led research programme are listed in Table 1.1. The programme lasts from 1991 to 1996 and is divided into two phases. The first phase ended at the end of September 1994 and 17 of the projects were entirely in that phase. The last four projects in the list are solely in phase 2 which will end in late 1996. Six projects span both phases of the research programme, although four of have wound down leaving a core of six projects for phase 2.

The projects approach the issues from two main directions: vertically – looking at a particular part of the process of the evolution of the system and horizontally where they have looked at particular industries or regions running right across a swathe of the issues.

Two projects look directly at the process of rule formation: that by Chris Brewin and that by Jeremy Richardson and Sonia Mazey. Both are concerned with aspects of the process of influence, the latter through lobbying and the former by non-member states. Indeed, I referred to both of them earlier. In the former case several different categories of non-members are distinguished: the EFTA countries, central European countries, associated states, favoured developing countries, large unrelated countries and the rest. As it is my purpose here to discuss the structure of the research programme rather than the results themselves, as that is the principal purpose of the subsequent chapters, I shall restrict myself only to a few passing remarks on some of the projects. A third project considering rule setting is that between Geoffrey Pridham and Albert Weale, on 'the politics of expertise'. Here taking some examples from the environmental field and looking at a cross section of member states in 'northern' and 'southern' Europe they explore how the particular proposals arise and the principles which are invoked to implement them. They too provide part of the basis for the study of conflicts among objectives in the single market, as having harsher environmental regulatory conditions, to which employers adhere, may impose extra costs which harm their international competitiveness.

Table 1.1 Projects in the ESRC research programme

Title	Project Leader (Institution)
European Cohesion: competition, technology and the regions	Dr Ash Amin, University of Newcastle-upon-Tyne
Participation of Non-Member States in Shaping the Rules of the EC's Single Market	Dr Christopher Brewin, University of Keele
Competition Between Metropolitan Regions in the Single European Market	Professor Paul Cheshire, University of Reading
The Legal Implementation of the Single European Market at National Level	Professor Terence Daintith, Institute of Advanced Legal Studies, London
The Future of Public Procurement in Europe: rules, public choice and the single European market	Professor Keith Hartley, University of York
The Interaction of Trade, Competition and Technology Policy in the Single Market	Dr Peter Holmes, University of Sussex
Human Resource Regimes and the Single European Market	Professor Robert Lindley, University of Warwick
A New Strategy for Social and Economic Cohesion After 1992	David Mayes, NIESR
1992: the Stimulus for Change in British and West German Industry	David Mayes, NIESR
The Implications of the Evolution of European Integration for the UK Labour Market	David Mayes, NIESR
The Harmonisation of EC Securities Market Regulations	Dr George McKenzie, University of Southampton
Regulatory Institutions and Practices in the Single European Market	Professor Michael Moran, University of Manchester
The Free Movement of Workers and the Single European Market	Professor David O'Keeffe, University College London

Table 1.1 continued

Title	Project Leader (Institution)
Environmental Standards and the Politics of Expertise in the Single European Market	Dr Geoffrey Pridham, University of Bristol, Professor Albert Weale, University of Essex
Lobbying in the EC: a comparative study	Professor Jeremy Richardson, University of Warwick
Regulation and Competition in the European Air Transport Industry	Dr Paul Seabright, University of Cambridge
Rules for Energy Taxation in the Single European Market	Stephen Smith, Institute for Fiscal Studies, London
The Consequences of Finnish Membership of the EC for the Finnish Food Industries	Professor Henri Vartiainen, The Helsinki Research Institute for Business Administration
Comparative Competition Policy	Professor Stephen Wilks, University of Exeter
The Evolution of Rules for a Single European Market	Stephen Woolcock, London School of Economics
The Competitiveness of Spanish Industry in the 1990s: Unleashing the Potential	Professor Manuel Ahijado, Universidad Nacional de Educacion a Distancia, Madrid
The Role of the Firm in the Evolution of Rules for a Single European Market	David Mayes, NIESR
The Implications for Firms and Industry of the Adoption of the ECU as the Single Currency of the EC	David Mayes, NIESR
Institutions, Local Economic Development and European Integration	Dr Ash Amin, University of Newcastle-upon-Tyne
The Completion of the Single European Market and European Labour Markets: bargaining, wages, employment and growth	Professor John Driffill, University of Southampton
National Budgetary Procedures and the Avoidance of 'Excessive Deficits'	Ian Harden, University of Sheffield
Balancing Public and Private Interests Under Duress	Professor Helen Wallace, University of Sussex

There are two main studies on implementation of the rules, one looking at a specific aspect, namely public procurement, and the other looking at some specific sectors, particularly in the food and drink sectors. The study of public procurement is particularly important as this is one of the areas which is crucial to the credibility of the single market programme. If one looks at the list of the 40 sensitive sectors outlined by Pierre Buigues and colleagues in the 1991 Special Edition of *European Economy/Social Europe* a substantial portion show prior distortion because of the impact of public purchasing which favours local suppliers. There is however a general disbelief that the patterns will change and, indeed, a fear by suppliers that procurement will, indeed, be opened up in their own countries but will remain closed elsewhere.

In addition to their work on public procurement within the ESRC research programme, Andrew Cox and Keith Hartley have been involved in a number of projects with the Commission, one of which includes the development of indicators for the surveillance of progress in Germany, the Netherlands and UK. Ingo Albrecht and I completed an application of the same methodology to Sweden and Iceland. Iceland is also included within the framework because of its participation in the European Economic Area.

The project on legal implementation by Terence Daintith and a wide range of lawyers is notable because it does actually achieve the aim of comparative research with parallel teams in other member states addressing the same problems. However, many of the results turned out to be not as directly comparable as was initially intended.

The largest single group of projects considers the issues from a more horizontal point of view, taking individual sectors and exploring the whole range of issues (rather than taking a single issue and applying it across the whole range of sectors). George McKenzie and Richard Dale have picked the case of securities markets, Paul Seabright and Francis McGowan are tackling the air transport industry, Stephen Smith has looked at energy taxation. These three studies are interestingly different in character. The case of securities markets exposes that Europe is only part of a global market and, in determining its framework, it has to be compatible with the international markets, particularly in the US and to a lesser extent in Japan. The idea that Europe might be able to gain an edge over foreign suppliers by setting different standards or rules has been shown to have only a negligible applicability. In general it is necessary to follow the international lead.

The work by Seabright and McGowan, on the other hand, explores the failure of the member states to tackle the question of air transport because of the extent of the domestic political feelings that it arouses. State supported national carriers tend to continue even when the drain on resources is considerable. And, as the subsidies to Air France and Olympic show, the subject is far from resolved, much to the disappointment of the privately owned airlines.

Stephen Smith's work on energy taxation has been very influential, explaining the principles and the problems of reconciling environmental and fiscal objectives. This work came to a head at the time of the Rio Summit and the SEM programme organised a seminar to help brief delegates before they left.

We were also lucky in attracting a project from outside the UK, which was also funded externally (by the Finnish Food Industries). Henry Vartiainen has tackled a problem which increased in importance as Finland came to decide whether it would become a full member of the EU. Its harsh climate means that domestic agriculture has been heavily subsidised even compared with EU levels because of the greater costs of keeping animals alive and the shortness of the growing season. A fall in output will have a knock on effect on food processing, to say nothing on the impact on rural communities and on the already high unemployment. Were it not for the security issues, the debate over membership might have been much fiercer in Finland.

Lastly, my own project with Duncan Matthews on the role of the firm in the process of the evolution of rules includes several case studies. We have completed those on leasing, machine tools, retailing and most recently construction services. Our focus in this study has been how firms singly and jointly actually implement or frustrate the single market. Much of the single market literature follows the paradigm that as barriers are reduced so firms will be thrust into fiercer competition as opportunities for price differentiation and inefficiency will diminish. Not surprisingly, firms act vigorously to protect their market share and successful competition can come from deliberate product differentiation. We also explore the role of trade associations, which can seek regulatory compromise rather than a single market through successful competition.

Three further projects have been looking at the social dimension and the impact on labour markets in particular. David O'Keeffe has been focused on the free movement of workers and has revealed a picture less complete and more anomalous than was planned. My own work with Duncan Matthews and Michael Gold looks at a range of measures, particularly in health and safety, running from how policy is derived right through to their impact and assessment. I want to return to this project later as our work also relates to the theme of *conflict among rules*. Our work has a strong policy focus, exploring how policy should respond to the experience thus far and alter the balance of action from issues of workers rights towards unemployment.

Robert Lindley and his colleagues at Warwick have been exploring a series of different scenarios for the impact of the single market on human resources. However, the nature of the process of change has been tackled directly. First of all by Steve Woolcock and colleagues at Chatham House who have been exploring how some of the main mechanisms of market creation are actually working in practice. They have thus looked in detail into how competition among rules is working. This is extended by a study of mutual recognition but here the evidence has proved much harder to come by.

Michael Moran, Simon Bulmer and their colleagues at Manchester have looked not merely at the regulatory structures which existed before the single market, as in the case of doctors and lawyers, but explored the way these are changing both as the new European rules come into force and as the individual professional groups see how they can manage to extract a relative benefit, effectively increasing some of the other barriers to movement or competition. The strongest theme, however, is the tendency towards voluntary institutional convergence.

In the same way as there was a set of sectoral horizontal studies, my work with Peter Hart (Mayes and Hart, 1994), comparing the impact on the UK and Germany, extends that analysis to the spatial dimension. Our work focuses on the extent of the institutional differences in the two countries which lead their markets to respond remarkably differently to the process of integration.

This leaves us with a group of five projects which are characterised by questions of competition and conflict among instruments and objectives. In an associated project, Stephen Wilks is exploring the institutions of competition policy across the EU (and further afield) and finding fascinating differences based on the different cultures of operation of the firms involved. At a more specific level, Paul Cheshire and Ian Gordon have been exploring how major and secondary European cities compete as institutions. While some aspects of this competitive process may represent a zero sum game, others show that there can indeed be positive benefits from focused policies. (Iain Begg and I have developed this sort of approach explicitly in an unrelated project for the ESRC on decentralised industrial policies (Begg, Lansbury and Mayes. 1995).) The single market eliminates the opportunity to pursue traditional national industrial policies through the restrictions on state aids. However, the reinstatement of such powers in disadvantaged regions is positively encouraged to try to raise their competitive potential.

These possible policy conflicts are made much more explicit in work by Peter Holmes on the contradictions between trade, competition and technology policy. Competition policy is seeking to remove internal barriers, while technology policy encourages collaboration and trade policy has a clear element of external protection despite the GATT round. Ash Amin and Tim Frazer, in a separate project, have looked at the conflict between competition policy, technology and the regions, arguing strongly that many of the tendencies unleashed, particularly towards globalisation, will tend to militate against less favoured regions and against smaller firms. Iain Begg and I have followed this up more comprehensively in terms of the impact on disadvantaged regions in our work for the European parliament (NIESR, 1991).

The extent of these conflicts is non-trivial. We do not see the least-favoured regions being able to integrate into the single market on anything like an equal basis unless there is a major development in the instruments used to assist them. In the same way Gold, Matthews and Mayes (1994) argue that a serious impact on cohesion cannot be achieved without an extension of social policy to its more traditional coverage of the disadvantaged and the disabled, whether or not in the labourforce. The major distinction between these two pieces of work lies in the attempt (in NIESR, 1991) to suggest how existing resources can be used rather better with a focus on what will make the greatest progress towards the objectives rather than the existing requirement that the projects should occur in the right region. (There is a danger, in some respects, that the incidence of the transfer mechanisms in the EU tends to be from the less well off in the higher income member states to the better off in the low income. Revenue comes from higher food prices and VAT while spending frequently goes on projects and equipment suppliers, not into the hands of the least well off.)

Much of the rest of the work has been looking further forward including at the relations between the single market and economic and monetary union and with enlargement. Although much of this latter task is in Phase 2 of the research, we have already undertaken a moderate amount of work on how monetary union should function, particularly on the role of the ECU (Burridge and Mayes, 1992; Britton and Mayes, 1993, Ernst and Young and NIESR, 1990). Indeed, I was a member of the Commission's expert group on the implementation of the ECU as the single currency, chaired by Cees Maas.

Phase 2 itself has four new projects. I will not dwell on them as this book focuses on Phase 1. Two of them clearly follow from the previous work. That by Ash Amin will look more closely at the structures that will encourage local economic recovery under the SEM, while Helen Wallace is looking at the balance of public and private interests. She has already organised a most thought-provoking seminar which looked at the styles of regulation in the EU and the EEA. Some limited progress was made in this area in Phase 1 with the publication of *Public Interest and Market Pressures* (Mayes *et al.*, 1993) which dealt primarily with problems of cohesion.

Two further projects by people new to the research programme – John Driffill at Southampton and Ian Harden at Sheffield – are striking at the key problems in integration over the coming few years. The first deals with the labour market and the second with the fiscal requirements of EMU. Both of these are areas of considerable tension at present, the scope for whose release is not yet clear.

3 BEYOND THE RESEARCH PROJECTS

In setting up research programmes the ESRC gives a much broader brief to the co-ordinator than just the co-ordination of the financed projects. One of the main purposes of the ESRC research programmes is to encourage research in the chosen area. It is impossible for the ESRC to contemplate funding all the research itself.

In the instance of the single market programme this endeavour has been assisted by the surge of interest in teaching and research in the field, aided *inter alia* by the creation of the Jean Monnet 'chairs' and other EU initiatives such as the Erasmus programme. I want in particular to refer to UACES, the University Association for Contemporary European Studies, and its sister European Community Studies Associations across the world. These associations have helped foster the links between researchers both nationally and internationally. The association in the US is particularly strong and some of its members have been collaborating in our research.

UACES has put on a variety of focused conferences over the years, many of which have involved researchers within the ESRC programme. We organised a joint conference on standards which focused on the extent of technical harmonisation and the strong role that major players, including the larger standards organisations, are playing in shaping the single market. The *Journal of Common Market Studies,* which the UACES fosters, has also been very valuable in disseminating the results of research in the area and documenting the progress of the process of integration in Europe through its annual reviews.

The programme has followed a strategic approach to collaborating with others and in encouraging international networks of researchers in the field. In part we have tried to get into contact with individuals through a newsletter and have deliberately encouraged researchers outside the programme to participate in our events.

In establishing links with other countries we have followed a sequential strategy, initially trying to establish bilateral links and then moving on to the multilateral. Our first links were with Dutch and French researchers, in both cases organised through their equivalents of the ESRC – the NWO and its component bodies ECOZOEK and NESRO in the Dutch case and the CNRS in the French. It is worth making a couple of remarks about this as it illustrates at first hand the problem of achieving a single market and the way institutional rules can hinder or aid the process. The exchange with the Dutch has been both successful in the sense of having four annual meetings to date and, more importantly, in setting up and developing research links and co-operation subsequently. This process will continue over coming years. NWO can focus its research efforts and devote funds to particular purposes, which has meant that we could quickly come to decisions about what to do and act upon them.

Dealing with the CNRS has been much more difficult because the structure of research support in the two countries is so different. In the French case it is institution based rather than project or topic based. Thus despite the existence of the Programme Franco–Britannique and consider-able good will we have managed to organise just one substantial meeting in the UK and two smaller highly focused seminars, one in each country. We have made eight attempts to organise joint research, all of which have failed because we could never get the approval mechanisms in the two countries to coincide. If CNRS approved we could guarantee that the ESRC would turn the project down. This must be very frustrating for the French because once a CNRS institute is prepared to include the collaborative project in its agreed research programme then the work will go ahead. In the UK case we have to apply for funding in open competition, with a very considerable time lag. There is a clear need for a single international scientific committee which decides upon such collaborative efforts in the light of reports from independent referees.

It is not that France presents an especially difficult set of problems; the rest of our bilateral arrangements have either been more limited or faced their own difficulties. The best arrangement has been with German colleagues, not because we have developed a good relationship with the Deutsche Forschungsgemeinschaft, the equivalent of the ESRC, but because there is an explicit organisation to finance collaborative research, financed by the two governments, the Anglo–German Foundation for the Study of an Industrial Society. They have been enormously helpful, financing several meetings and joint research projects – my own project on the Single Market Programme as a Stimulus to Change in the two countries is a case in point (Mayes and Hart, 1994). They financed a further joint meeting in Berlin in 1995 on lessons that the two countries can learn from each other for the approach to problems in their new Objective One regions.

The British Council and the European University Institute helped finance a joint meeting in Italy but the finance for the joint research proposed came through nearly a year after the team was disbanded. The British Council did a splendid job in collaboration with the Spanish Education ministry in financing and helping with the organisation of a joint meeting in Castellon and at least two collaborative projects have emerged from this in addition to the project that Iain Begg and I have undertaken with Manuel Ahijado on a strategy for Spanish industry in the face of the challenge of the single market and economic and monetary union.

However, our principal focus has been to move to the level of multilateral rather than bilateral collaboration as there are a number of organisations which finance research and co-operation at that level. Fairly typically, we have been more successful at collaboration than joint research and, indeed, the fact that the conference discussing the chapters of this book was held jointly with COST reflects that success. After a number of years of negotiation led by our Dutch colleagues, COST adopted an 'Action' for collaboration with the same title as our own research programme 'The Evolution of Rules for a Single European Market'. However, the outline of the project was a little different and the focus agreed by the management committee very different, as explained below.

I should explain what COST is. The word itself is the acronym from the French. It is an organisation, administered through the European Commission, set up by the official research funders in almost all the western European countries and more recently the central European countries, to encourage co-operation in science and technology. Most of the collaboration is in the natural sciences but there are six agreements (labelled 'actions') in the social sciences. Countries decide which actions to support and there are fifteen in the present action which is a little above average. Each action lasts three years and this one is due to expire at the end of 1995, although it can be extended.

These actions are intended to stimulate collaborations which then endure after the COST funding expires. I expect that to be the case in our instance. Although the ultimate aim is collaborative research, COST does not actually finance that research (with an exception I shall mention in a moment). It finances scientific meetings, the dissemination of information and, more recently, research secondments. The initial sums assigned to this action were 3 million ECU and with the increase in the number of participating countries these have grown to 5–6 million ECU. However, this allocation in the main does not represent new money. The budget for the action assigned to the Management Committee was only 65,000 ECU in 1994 and less in 1995. (Each COST action is organised by a management committee composed of one or two representatives from the signatory countries.)

The large majority of the funding is what the signatories already intend to contribute to research in this area. Thus the UK's contribution is principally its Single European Market research programme. While there are several plans to set up joint projects by researchers from the signatory countries, the funding for those projects will come from elsewhere.

I mentioned an exception.   The exception is research by the central European members.   Here there is a small opportunity and within the A7 action there was one such project, directed by Professor Kovacs at the Institute of Economics in Budapest, on the problems of transforming the knowledge and research base in central Europe for the process of transition to a modern advanced western style economy.   It was possible to set this up relatively quickly because it renewed a longstanding link with the NIESR.

The COST action has five other foci in addition to the problems of transition for central and eastern European countries:

the role of democracy in setting and legitimating rules;
environmental concerns;
the relation between the single market process and globalisation;
implications for the social dimension and welfare;
deregulation and reregulation.

There are enough funds for each participating country to organise one scientific meeting provided that there is also a domestic contribution to the costs.   The conference at Exeter was the UK's scientific meeting under the action.   Some progress on collaborative comparative research is being made, but I have to say that the effort which has gone into the organisation of these collaborations thus far, and its cost, are very high compared with the size of the resultant research projects.   Nevertheless, there have been some very successful meetings with results published in Faure *et al.* (1995) and Mayes (1993a), for example.

Other attempts at multilateral collaboration have been more difficult. We have had some success in projects with both the Commission and the European Parliament and after an immense amount of effort have a project under the co-operation programme with central Europe, ACE, on Competition Policy and Cohesion.   Much of this work revolves round the question of whether the economies in transition should also have transitional institutions focused on facilitating the process of transition or whether they should progress directly to the institutions required by the single market. As part of that discussion we looked at the lessons which could be learned from the New Zealand experience (Bollard and Mayes, 1993).   There, indeed, the emphasis has been on creating the correct framework, but 10 years down the track there are still some changes to make.   Although some regard the New Zealand of the 1960s and 1970s as an honorary member of the CMEA because of the extent of its regulation of the economy, it clearly had a much easier job to do.   It endured a decade of very slow growth, a rise in unemployment towards the OECD average and, while it now appears to be reaping the benefits with stable prices and growth of over 6 per cent of GDP in the last two years, the real proof is still to come and we must wait to see what is sustainable. Furthermore, most OECD countries are not prepared to change this fast and the New Zealand experience is viewed very much as the 'cold turkey' approach to structural reform (see Harris in Mayes 1996). In that context the transition experience of the better managed of the economies in transition has actually been rather favourable.

It has been the ESRC's hope that the Fourth Framework Programme will at last provide the funding to enable decent collaborative research to take place at the European level in the social sciences. The description of the Programme is not particularly promising for achieving this. It is not clear that it is the appropriate framework for academic research, which is often at its best when it challenges accepted wisdom and policy. The European Science Foundation remains a further possibility.

4   THE STRUCTURE OF THE BOOK

The structure of this book very much follows the form of the research that I have outlined and the scope of the COST programme. What we have done is divide up the evolutionary process into eight segments:

setting and influencing the rules;
implementing the rules;
competition and conflict among rules;
the impact of the rules;
rules under different visions of economy and society;
the evolution of rules;
political legitimacy; and
the external impact.

Between them they cover the whole range of the research. Although there is inevitably some overlap, the research relating to each segment is summarised in a chapter written by a member of the research team. These chapters are not necessarily comprehensive and inevitably reflect the author's own interests and research. They set the work in its wider context.

Simon Bulmer opens the discussion in the next chapter by exploring how the EU expanded its governance capacity in order to be able to cope with the demands of the single market for rule making. He views the SEM and the enabling Single European Act of 1986 as giving the means and motivation to achieve what were already long-standing goals for integration. It is itself part of the evolution of the rule making process in the EU. The Single European Act signalled progress on a wide front for the *aims* of the

Community including the environment, competition policy and economic and social cohesion as well as the single market as narrowly defined. The existence of this wide front was one of the essential features which enabled the process to be so successful, along with having a clear agenda in the White Paper and the motivating deadline of 1992. It helped provide 'something for everybody' in the process of change.

While qualified majority voting was probably the biggest single contributor to enabling the SEM legislation to progress, the growth of the importance of the Commission and the need for non-governmental institutions, particularly lobbyists, to participate closely enhanced the ability to change. The Maastricht Treaty by contrast involved much more limited change in this regard.

Chapter 3 is a considerable contrast. While Simon Bulmer examined the issues of rule setting from a political science viewpoint, John Usher's chapter on implementation strongly reflects his position as a lawyer. Rather than dealing with all aspects of Community legislation he concentrates on competition law. This is an area where the Commission has considerable direct ability to enforce conformity. On the whole the Commission cannot decide on individual cases, it is necessary for them or national governments to approach the European Court of Justice to get the matter resolved. Competition policy is an exception. However, even in this case the Commission tries to encourage complainants to use the national courts.

Usher goes on to point out that much of the success of the single market comes from the unofficial means of implementation and enforcement, through organising exemplary Court cases and even obtaining damages. Unlike the US, for example, there is not a wide range of agencies involved in monitoring or enforcement at a supranational level. This remains the responsibility of each national government within its own territory. (This is developed more extensively by Duncan Matthews in Chapter 7.) In his conclusions John Usher raises the key point about the existence of a dichotomy between the legal framework and the market performance. It is one thing to observe that the intended framework has been implemented. It is another to observe that the market which has eventuated has the characteristics that its 'single' epithet might imply.

Stephen Woolcock focuses in Chapter 4 on one of the major 'new' mechanisms employed under the Single European Act to help speed the process of integration towards a single market, namely 'competition among rules'. This particular mechanism has the advantage that it removes the need to seek detailed agreement and go through the process of negotiating 'compensating' features for those states which may lose out. However, there is no guarantee that the results of this process will be effective nor that the resulting rules will be in some sense optimal. There may be 'a race to the bottom' whereby national authorities or self-regulatory bodies try to ease the requirements on business in a competitive spiral of deregulation to the detriment of consumers, employees, etc. Indeed, there is not even a guarantee that rules will converge. 'Competition among rules' may permit diversity rather than providing a market-driven mechanism towards harmonisation. The competitive process itself may in part be reflected in movement by those affected to jurisdictions where the rule systems are more congenial (this does not necessarily involve changes in physical location as it is possible in some cases to change, say, the regulatory group under which one is classified) or for the rule makers to change, perhaps by emulating others.

This chapter provides one of the first attempts to illustrate the extent of the progress in practice in competition among rules by looking at the evidence produced by a range of sectoral and horizontal studies within the ESRC research programme and outside it. He points to the problem of transparency – it is difficult to harmonise if a rule is not clearly specified, particularly when it is how it is implemented in practice which is the prime concern. Similarly mutual recognition can only progress effectively when the parties to it are convinced that each other is following similar objectives effectively. On balance, the evidence shows the restraints there are on this particular route to achieving a single market although he concludes that in most cases the worries about the rush to the bottom are misplaced. On the contrary there is clear evidence of moves to improve conditions in a number of areas such as social policy and financial markets. It seems unlikely that this process of competition will always come to a stable conclusion and the question of needing European level regulatory agencies will not be avoided.

The next two chapters – by Keith Hartley, Andrew Cox and myself and by Robert Lindley – consider the impact of the single market but from two very different perspectives. Hartley *et al.* follow the more traditional, sectoral route exploring how changes in various sectors have an impact. The principal focus is on the impact of the new public purchasing rules. This focus is particularly appropriate as public purchasing is one of the areas which provide a harsh test of whether the single market will be a reality. Public procurement has typically favoured local suppliers and attempts at widening it face local political opposition. Hartley *et al.* explore how the new measures are intended to operate, explaining how difficult it is to monitor in practice because, for example, foreign suppliers will use domestic agents to help secure the contract. Rather than remaining at the descriptive level, Hartley *et al.* embed their analysis in public choice theory.

Robert Lindley's chapter on the other hand is much more ambitious. It explores how the whole social economic context impinges on rule making and is in turn altered by it. Taking the case of labour market policy he explores four different scenarios which would embrace the policy frame-work, labelling them:

efficiency;
cost-cutting;
economic and social cohesion; and
quality.

These four are, in turn, embedded in an exploration of the global environ-ment of socio-economic change, with advent of globalisation and other features which characterise the pattern of development. Globalisation is an overused term and can itself reflect some very different scenarios of behaviour, ranging from a European success story where co-operation and increased scale leads to an effective competitive response through to competitive failure where the continuing emergence of new competitors from the developing world leads to economic decay in much of the OECD.

The importance of these scenarios is that they are not merely economic in character but have major social implications. Hence Lindley's chapter focuses on the 'social dimension' of the single market and the key role that this plays in the overall success or failure of the process of integration. Under the 'efficiency' scenario Europe responds to the global challenge by loosening some of the rigidities in the labour market and becoming an efficient competitor. However, this drive for efficiency could degenerate into a drive for 'cutting costs' where the focus on price competitiveness crowds out the ability to develop high value added products and attempts (un-successfully) to compete against the developing countries head on. Much of the philosophy behind the Single European Act suggests there should be a deliberate counter to this in European labour market policy seeking to provide strong rights and benefits for the workforce. That, however, does not necessarily offer an effective competitive strategy and Lindley's last 'quality' scenario describes how a virtuous circle of development based on high human capital can develop, with high productivity, high wages, profits, investment and innovation.

Transnational companies are the major force in developing the economies and they are doing so in the context of wide variation in the labour market regimes across the EU. To some extent this can result in the emphasising of the core–periphery dichotomy as firms concentrate on those with the highest skills and the locations with the best facilities and access to markets.

In this context Lindley goes on to analyse the main features of labour market policy and how it can be used to develop a coherent strategy, following the quality rather than the other scenarios. More active labour market policies both facilitate the necessary improvement in competitiveness and constrain it to avoid having a detrimental effect on working conditions.

An attempt to summarise the range of policies explored would involve effectively repeating the chapter here. The various measures seek to make markets work better, promoting flexibility not just in changing employment but in adapting the new challenges. However, others seek to alter the characteristics of labour supply, both reducing the demand for employment and trying to increase the employability of disadvantaged groups. Lindley concludes by exploring how a European social policy can be developed to try to improve the convergence and cohesion of the economy. The key process in trying to move forward in this manner is 'experimental variation'.

Circumstances and the labour market framework vary substantially across the EU. Implementing increased social cohesion, therefore, involves a variety of approaches as success will vary. The advantage the EU offers is the ability to obtain and exchange a wide variety of evidence and experience so that it is possible to learn, innovate and improve the socio-economic environment. (These conclusions dovetail well with those of Gold, Matthews and Mayes, 1994, discussed above.)

Chapter 7 by Duncan Matthews continues the broader view of the work of the research programme by discussing the whole process of the evolution of rules in the single market. It tackles the fundamental question of what is meant by 'evolution' in this context. To some extent the process represents the survival of the fittest but much of the evolutionary process occurs not in the rules themselves but in the way they are applied and interpreted. Duncan Matthews therefore explores not just the role of the regulatory institutions and the different processes such as 'competition among rules' and the voluntary harmonisation through the standards setting bodies but he runs through the role of each of the main groups in the market: firms, consumers, trade unions, interest groups and finally individuals. This chapter hence plays a key role in bringing together the ideas which have been discussed in those which precede it. It is particularly helpful in that it illustrates each of the mechanisms described with examples drawn from the other projects in the research programme and hence provides a unification of much of the work.

The major issue which is focused on towards the end of the chapter is whether this process of evolution is in fact convergent. In general he comes out with a very positive answer but there is a large questionmark over the operation of subsidiarity which could readily be a means of promoting divergence. Furthermore, there are areas like leasing where positions have been polarised into Anglo-Saxon and 'continental' camps, actually reversing a drift towards common international standards.

While Duncan Matthews' chapter provides a unification of what has gone before, Albert Weale tackles what became the leading political issue after Denmark's narrow rejection of ratification of the Maastricht Treaty, namely, legitimacy. He explores two views of the subject – one based on the works of Locke and the other on those of Hume. In the Lockean tradition legitimacy is obtained through consent. The Humean approach, on the other hand, rests on acquiescence based on the recognition of benefit. These may not sound far apart but the Humean approach might give a good explanation of why there was a crisis in popular support for deeper integration at a time when economic progress was at a low ebb. Nevertheless, at the same time governments and economies were moving towards closer integration. However, failure to implement the single market effectively may represent a lack of conviction over its legitimacy. The rise in interest in environmental and social policies to help offset some of the adverse impacts of the main single market measures might be thought of as a means of trying to restore legitimacy but Weale suggests the evidence makes this uncertain.

The 'democratic' deficit is clear but dealing with it poses further problems. It may indeed require an unacceptable degree of centralisation in the operation of the system. The interesting question that Albert Weale poses at the end, is whether in fact legitimacy could be increased by a change in the process of international agreement. Perhaps it could be more open and democratic on the next occasion.

In Chapter 9 Christopher Brewin also looks to wider issues, in this case he looks outward to the external impact of the single market. The simplest measure of this impact is the fact that it was extended en bloc to the EFTA countries bar Switzerland, when the agreement was rejected in a referendum. Furthermore, it acted as a stimulus for Austria, Finland and Sweden to join the EU as full members, the agreement with Norway having also failed to find ratification in the November 1994 referendum.

Christopher Brewin explores the development of external relations concerning the single market, distinguishing between the impact on and involvement of the EFTA countries, Turkey and other 'southern' aspirant members, Hungary and the rest of central Europe, and finally the US and Japan. Although there were clear routes of influence for EFTA countries both governmentally and for firms and other lobbyists, the form of agreement for expansion was how the single market legislation could be adopted by EFTA as whole, not how it might be amended to suit their particular interests. The EC made it clear that deepening came before widening and that the single market would be put in place first.

The associated countries played only a limited role, although provisions of personnel to assist transition helped frame institutions and policy in a complementary manner for the SEM. However, US firms and the US government played a vigorous role in shaping the SEM, particularly from the inside of the consultation process, in contrast to the Japanese who were prepared to follow a much more low key role. What is clear is that this development in international trade relations was much more one-sided than previous agreements, reflecting the power of the single market as an attraction to others.

The final chapter is provided by Giandomenico Majone from the European University Institute in Florence, who, although not a participant in the ESRC research programme, pulled together some of the main threads of the analysis. In his chapter he considers how countries can work together to establish the mutual trust that, despite delegating control to others, they will still achieve a fair and intended outcome and the benefits of co-operation. He concludes from the Maastricht Treaty that the member states have called a halt to increasing centralisation and see greater effective integration coming from greater co-operation and joint action at the various levels of government. However, for this to work well he argues that there needs to be delegation to independent regulatory bodies at both the national and European level so that member states can feel comfortable that the designated job is being done fairly, effectively and efficiently. The planned European Central Bank and the approach to monetary union is a clear example.

The heavy legislative programme implemented to 'complete' the internal market reflects an attempt to set up an effective system of binding the member states in circumstances of mistrust. While such an approach encourages centralisation, indeed over-centralisation in Majone's opinion it does not of itself entail adequate compliance, even with the good offices of the European Court of Justice. The worry remains that other states are not conforming as completely to the regulations, which in turn provides an incentive for weaker compliance.

The structure of the EU itself encourages complex and, indeed, inconsistent regulation. The small European level budget means the Commission must rely on national governments for implementation. The small size of the Commission and the independence of the various Directorates general means that legislation relies on separated technical experts and hence may have less regard for cost effectiveness or practical implementation.

Mutual recognition ought to cut through some of these requirements but it also imposes very harsh burdens itself as it requires not just conformity with the agreed common approach to an area of regulation but the acceptance within each member state that the regulations of others do actually conform. Lengthy and detailed dispute over this can effectively frustrate the operation of mutual recognition. Confidence would be enhanced by having agencies, independent of political influence, that have clear objectives and accountability. Majone also offers a 'second best' solution of having agencies which audit the existing national regulatory bodies.

However, the most important feature of Majone's proposals is that they are forward-looking. They cover part of the agenda for the 1996 Inter-governmental Conference on institutional reform. The whole of the experience analysed in this book should be taken in a forward looking framework. The experience thus far with the Single Market programme provides some clear lessons for the development of the process over the coming years. Indeed the most obvious message is that the process is not by any means complete, nor is it likely to be for many years to come.

To some extent the incompleteness of the market depends upon whether regulation has gone far enough. However, that is only part of the problem. Some of the existing rules have yet to be fully implemented. The standardisation process has years to run and mechanisms such as competition among rules and mutual recognition are too new for a clear impression to be formed of how they will turn out.

None of this detracts from the size of the step forward in European integration that the Single Market programme represents. It has collapsed into a decade changes which might otherwise have taken several times as long to achieve. It is not surprising therefore that it takes time for firms and consumers to adjust to changes on such a scale. Development will continue and the evolution of rules for a single European market is far from complete. The 1996 intergovernmental conference and stage 3 of Economic and Monetary Union will be steps in that process but evolution will continue well into the next century.

REFERENCES

Begg, I.G., Lansbury, M. and Mayes, D.G. (1995), 'The case for decentralised industrial policy', ch. 9 in P. Cheshire and I. Gordon (eds) *Territorial Competition in an Integrating Europe*, Aldershot: Avebury, pp. 179–206.

Bollard, A.E. and Mayes, D.G. (1993), 'Lessons from New Zealand's Liberalisation Experience', *National Institute Economic Review*, no 143, February.

Britton, A. and Mayes, D.G. (1993), *Achieving Monetary Union*, London: Sage.

Burridge, M. and Mayes, D.G. (1992), *The Implications for Firms and Industry of the Adoption of the ECU as the Single Currency of the EC*, Brussels: European Commission.

Emerson, M., Aujean, M., Catinat, N., Goybet, P. and Jacquemin, A. (1989), *The Economics of 1992*, Oxford: Oxford University Press.

Ernst and Young and NIESR (1990), *A Strategy for the ECU*, London: Kogan Page.

Faure, M., Vervaele, J. and Weale, A. (eds) (1995), *Environmental Standards in the European Union*

Gold, M., Matthews, D. and Mayes, D.G. (1994), *A New Strategy for Social Policy in Europe*, Bund Verlag (forthcoming) (with I. Albrecht).

Macmillen, M., Mayes, D.G. and van Veen, P. (1987), *European Integration and Industry*, Tilburg University Press.

Matthews, D. and Mayes, D.G. (1994a), 'Towards a Single European Market? The Leasing Industry' *Journal of the Economics of Business*, 1 (2), 179–98.

Matthews, D. and Mayes, D.G. (1994b), 'The Role of Soft Law in the Evolution of Rules for a Single European Market: the Case of Retailing', *National Institute Discussion Paper*, no. 61.

Mayes, D.G. (1977), 'The Effects of Economic Integration on Trade', *Journal of Common Market Studies*, 17 (1), 1–25.

Mayes, D.G. (1993a), *Aspects of European Integration: Environment, Regulation and Social Dimensions*, National Institute Report no. 5.

Mayes, D.G. (1993b), *External Implications of European Integration*, Hemel Hempstead: Harvester-Wheatsheaf.

Mayes, D.G. (1996), *Sources of Productivity Growth*, Cambridge: Cambridge University Press.

Mayes, D.G. and Burridge, M. (1993), *The Impact of the Internal Market Programme on European Economic Structure and Performance*, Strasbourg: European Parliament, Economic Series E-2.

Mayes, D.G. and Hart P.E. (1994), *The Single European Market as a Stimulus to Change in Britain and Germany*, Cambridge: Cambridge University Press.

Mayes, D.G., Hager, W., Knight, Sir A., Streeck, W. (1993), *Public Interest and Market Pressure: problems posed by EC 1992*, London: Macmillan.

NIESR (1991), *A New Strategy for Economic and Social Cohesion after 1992*, (D. Mayes, I. Begg, with M. Levitt and A. Shipman), European Parliament Research Paper, 19.

Pelkmans, J. and Winters, L.A. (1988), *Europe's Domestic Market*, London: Pinter for RIIA.

Shipman, A. and Mayes, D.G. (1989), *Changing the Rules: a framework for examining government and company responses to 1992*, National Institute Discussion Paper no. 199.

Winters, L.A. (1987), 'Britain in Europe: A Survey of Quantitative Trade Studies', *Journal of Common Market Studies*, 25 (4), 315–35.

2. Setting and Influencing the Rules[1]

Simon Bulmer

1   INTRODUCTION

This chapter is concerned with reviewing the research conducted within the ESRC's research programme on the Single European Market (SEM) from the perspective of 'setting and influencing the rules'.   As this chapter could potentially review almost all the projects in the programme, a selective, illustrative approach is adopted.

But what exactly delineates *setting and influencing the rules*? The project within the ESRC programme which I was engaged on in conjunction with Kenneth Armstrong was, indeed, concerned with the 'rule-making process'.[2] However, we were conscious of the fact that our central concern with rule-making should not lead us to ignore other phases and aspects of rule development. None of our six case studies involved the regulation of a subject matter entirely new to the EC. All entailed reform of existing regulatory arrangements.

Similarly, the completion of the single market itself may be seen as an expression of continuity: and in two senses. In one sense it was a reaction against what had gone before. Much of its contents had been set out – explicitly or implicitly – in the 1957 EEC Treaty, in other political declarations and in judgements of the European Court of Justice (ECJ). The record in achieving the original objective of a common market had been poor, so the single market programme represented a re-launching and re-definition of pre-existing goals. Thus, the SEM programme may be seen as the 'evolution of rules' and *not* the creation of rules 'from scratch'. This situation applies, with variation on details, whether one refers to the core single market issues of standards or to associated measures like health and safety regulation, environmental policy, merger control or air transport liberalisation. So, even if the idea of removing border controls was new, most of the broad and specific objectives did not suddenly confront

---

[1] I am grateful to Emil Kirchner, Sir Arthur Knight and Niels Thygesen, discussants of this paper at the Exeter conference, for their comments. The usual disclaimer applies.

[2] The research was part of a wider project on regulatory institutions and practices in the single market, conducted at Manchester University under ESRC award no. W113251014. The general observations regarding governance derive from this research, which is published in K. Armstrong and S. Bulmer, *The Governance of the Single European Market* (Manchester: Manchester University Press, 1995).

governments after the 1985 agreement to complete the single market. Put another way, the SEM essentially reformulated existing objectives and created, through the inseparable Single European Act (SEA), a new institutional dynamic designed to see their achievement. This dynamic comprised changes to the institutional arrangements of supranational rule-making. It also entailed a shift in the expectations and norms of policy-makers.

To present a balanced picture of the SEM initiative, however, it must also be seen in another light. The economic integration objectives of the late 1950s, i.e. the creation of a common market, were defined in a quite different context from those of the 1980s. In the latter case the issue of global competitiveness in the context of the international economic triad superseded the original, Euro-centric concerns of integration. Hence we may see the SEM project as arising from a new international economic and political context. In this second sense, therefore, the SEM project entailed putting *existing* goals and institutions into the service of new motivations.

In accordance with these two views, and reflecting the situation in respect of many of the component parts of the SEM project, the question must be asked whether it really is possible to identify a stage of 'setting and influencing the rules' that is specific to the period from 1985. Rather, there is much evidence to see the SEM project as part of a continuing regulatory process. In this continuing process objectives are re-defined, there are changes in the level of regulation, and the regulatory capacity of the EU institutions has been reformed.

In order not to commence a rules-based analysis of the SEM by undermining the very structure of that analysis, I will leave these comments as a health warning. In what follows I will consider how the SEM/SEA transformed the governance of the European Union, thereby facilitating the setting and influencing of rules.

The poor performance of the EC – as it then was – in achieving the goal of a common market was attributable to deficiencies in the policy-making arrangements and the lack of political will on the part of national governments. For the SEM objective to succeed, the EC's governance capacity had to be enhanced and given new purpose. Moreover, these changes had to be achieved both in general terms and in the many specialised issue areas comprising, or linked to, the single market. The latter was essential to ensure that the necessary rules for the creation of the SEM were put in place. Thus, it is important to be able to conceptualise what governance capacity is comprised of in the EC/EU context, and then examine how it changed at the systemic and sub-systemic levels. These tasks will enable us to see how the setting and influencing of rules was transformed in the context of the SEM programme.

2   ANALYSING GOVERNANCE CAPACITY

Two well established ways of assessing governmental capability are in terms of democratic rule and policy outputs (see survey in Weaver and Rockman, 1993a). Under the former criterion the concern is with the responsiveness of government to the will of the people. This criterion is particularly problematic for measuring supranational governance, since accountability structures are largely indirect, through national governments, with the problem of the (direct) democratic deficit remaining unresolved (see, for instance, Wallace, 1994; Featherstone, 1994). This theme is explored in more detail by Albert Weale in Chapter 8. Under the latter criterion we are concerned with the policy outputs of the particular system of government. These outputs can be measured quantitatively and qualitatively. They can also, with profit, be compared with those of other systems of government (on the EC see the study by Scharpf, 1988; more generally, Weaver and Rockman, 1993b). Furthermore, it is possible to make comparisons over time within the one system of government. Such comparative perspectives are an important corrective against short-term, snapshot judgements, as well as against the unhelpful tendency to regard European integration as a *sui generis* phenomenon.

Our concern with 'setting and influencing the rules' of the SEM means that we are chiefly concerned with the output capacity of the EC/EU rather than with democratic accountability. However, it should be clear from both the subsidiarity debate and the problems with ratifying the (Maastricht) Treaty on European Union (TEU) that the member governments' prioritisation of the policy output criterion over that of accountability and legitimacy may simply have stored up problems for later.

What determines governance capacity as measured by policy output? Three component parts can be identified: the constitutive goals of the system of government; the institutional structure for achieving those goals; and the 'toolkit' for putting policies into operation. Each of these is examined in turn.

2.1   Constitutive Goals

What is meant here by constitutive goals is the fundamental purposes of the particular system of government. Why is it there? How clearly and formally are its goals set down?

The term 'constitutive goals' is employed for a specific reason. The study of European integration is still approached by political scientists from two different directions. A majority prefer to compare the EU with international organisations, thus using international relations theories as the basis for analysis (see, for example, Carlsnaes and Smith, 1994). A minority explicitly use analytical tools drawn from comparative politics (see the survey in Hix, 1994). Amongst international organisations, the EU is unique in its state-like qualities. However, it is controversial for political scientists – as it is for legal analysts – to regard the EU treaties as amounting to a constitution or the EU itself as representing 'a state'. In consequence, the term 'constitutive goals' is employed to retain neutrality on these questions.

Notwithstanding this point, we need to be aware of the objectives of a system of government if we are to examine its governance capacity. Amongst the salient points here are 'functional scope, areal domain and membership' (Young, 1989, p. 29). A catalogue of basic rights, conferred by treaty or constitution, is also relevant. In short, if we are to judge policy output we need to know what the purposes of governance are in the first place.

2.2 Institutional Structure

The goals of any system of government require a functioning set of institutions in order to ensure that they are met. Here we are concerned with the institutions as a functioning 'system' as well as with the effectiveness of individual institutions in carrying out their tasks. Like any system of government, the EU has a mixture of formal and informal institutions as part of its system. In addition, there are various procedures, codes and norms which contribute to the manner in which the institutional structure works. Thus, analysis of institutional structure must bring together a constitutional–legal component as well as a pragmatic political one. The former sets out institutional roles in terms of treaties, standing orders and the like. The latter brings in the more informal dimension of politics: the role of governmental elites, of less formalised institutions such as the European Council and so on.

Institutions alone are not the A–Z of rule-making, of course. They are essentially conceived as bodies presiding over social choice matters. Hence, they mediate the demands placed upon them by voters, public opinion, political parties or, as is most typically the case in the EU, by the many interest groups organised at the supranational level. Political forces such as these are adept at identifying where the locus of decisional power is and adapt their strategies accordingly. Hence a focus on institutional structure does not centre on institutions (the polity) to the neglect of political forces (politics). Rather, this focus reflects the important role of the institutional structure in presiding over the taking of authoritative political decisions.

2.3 The 'Toolkit' of Governance

Governance capacity is not only dependent upon an efficient institutional structure but also needs appropriate forms of decisions and of putting them into effect. These forms can be examined at various levels of detail: on a general level in terms of regulatory strategies; on a specific level in terms of forms of legislation and enforcement mechanisms. Making correct choices from the toolkit of governance is important in determining the success of policy output. And if this is true in respect of setting and influencing the rules, it is also relevant to the all-important subsequent stage of implementing the rules: the subject of the next chapter.

In abstract terms, therefore, it is these three components – constitutive goals, institutional structure and the toolkit of governance – that shape the output capacity of any system of government. Thus, the pertinent question is: how far did the SEM programme, together with the SEA, create a quantum jump in this governance capacity?

3   TRANSFORMING THE GOVERNANCE OF THE EUROPEAN COMMUNITY: THE SEM AND THE SEA

3.1 Constitutive Goals

Taking the decision to create the SEM by the end-1992 deadline initially had no formal character in constitutional terms. It was in fact a decision taken at, and recorded in the (non-binding) 'conclusions' of, the June 1985 Milan European Council meeting. There, the White Paper on completing the internal market was given political approval as a policy programme but, at that stage, constitutional and institutional change was absent. It was not until ratification of the Single European Act, the product of a set of constitutional negotiations initiated (against British opposition) at the Milan meeting, that formal change in constitutive goals came about. The SEA also included reference to the 1992 deadline, although this was presented in a somewhat ambiguous manner.

Emphasising the initial, political rather than constitutional, nature of the SEM commitment is not simply a matter of splitting hairs. Governance transformations are inevitably the product of complex bargains. Accordingly, the SEM project was part of a wider bargain. This bargain also included the SEA.[3] Fortunately, the ESRC's Single Market research programme did not set its agenda of projects exclusively around the White Paper on completing the internal market. Economic and social cohesion, human resources, environmental regulation and related issues of technology, competition and trade policy were included within the Programme's scope just as they were included in 'the new European

---

[3]   The link with the SEA almost came about by accident. If it had not been for the decision of the Italian presidency, at the June 1985 Milan summit, to force through the convening of an intergovernmental conference, there might have been no SEA, in which the rest of the bargain was enshrined! I am grateful toNiels Thygesen for reminding me of this.

bargain'. The Programme thus avoided the perception – sometimes articulated from within British ministerial circles – that the SEM was a self-contained political agenda and that other parts of the SEM/SEA bargain were a matter of optional interest. And this is not to repeat the oft-articulated point that the British government was once again at odds with its EC partners. In reality, they too found individual developments arising indirectly from the bargain as unanticipated. For example, had the French government anticipated the way in which the SEM dynamic would lead to closer Commission scrutiny of state aids? Thus, the boundaries of the SEM/SEA bargain are difficult to delineate, as are the wider effects on the integration process. Certainly it would make little sense to look only at the adoption of the White Paper to identify changes in the EC's constitutive goals.

The admixture of political (SEM) and constitutional–legal (SEA) methods of re-defining the constitutive goals of European integration is interesting in another respect. Past re-assessments of these goals had always involved either informal or formal approaches but never before both as part of the same package deal. Joseph Weiler drew attention to the two dynamics in the early 1980s. He saw the two dynamics as a constitutional and 'judicial-normative' one, on the one hand, and a 'political-decisional' one, on the other (Weiler, 1982). The former is reflected in formal treaty changes or in developments in EC jurisprudence. The latter is characterised by gentlemen's agreements, 'soft law', declarations of the European Council and by the less formal patterns of work, such as those conducted in the Common Foreign and Security Policy and Justice and Home Affairs pillars of the EU. In the past the constitutive goals had been set either by means of treaties, such as the 1957 Treaties of Rome, or by means of political declarations, such as at the 1969 summit meeting in the Hague. It may be questioned, therefore, whether this admixture of the two dynamics played some role in assuring the successful internalisation by many policy actors of the new EC constitutive goals of the late 1980s. It was certainly important in keeping the UK government engaged in the evolving integration process, given its persistent reservations about a purely constitutional–legal route to change.

So, what were the relevant changes in constitutive goals which enhanced the governance capacity of the EC, thereby facilitating the rule-making process?

Given our central focus on the SEM, and its initial *political* endorsement by government heads, we deal first of all with the changes in constitutive goals that were achieved through Weiler's *political-decisional* dynamic. Arguably the two key parts of the political endorsement were the fleshing out of (largely already existing) treaty goals through a programme of action, namely the White Paper; and the adoption of the 1992 deadline for introducing the necessary legislation. Lord Cockfield, in his account of the creation of the single market, regards four elements of the method of setting out the goals as important to its adoption in Milan and the subsequent dynamism the project achieved (1994, p. 29–75).

The first was the setting out of a clear programme for achieving the internal market. Cockfield argues that the use of a White Paper – something of a novelty within the EC at the time – was itself a device used to give the internal market initiative importance by including the philosophy or principles to be followed and the programme in detail' (Cockfield, 1994, p. 34). The programme thus provided a fresh political strategy for achieving the existing constitutive goals of the EC. The second element was the 1992 deadline with its mobilising effect. A third consideration was giving the programme some kind of 'philosophical framework', to capture the imagination of those affected. Implicitly this was neo-liberal but it was not expressed in such ideological terms by the Commission, for that could have been counter-productive in some member states with less normatively compatible traditions of economic management. Finally, the emphasis placed upon 'removing barriers' was regarded as getting to the root of the incomplete single market. In addition, this emphasis upon obstacles did not discriminate between the four freedoms, thus avoiding possible pressures to put, say, liberalising services as a lower priority than liberalising goods. The subsequent 'costs of non-Europe' study was a useful way of both providing valuable evidence for sustaining the programme's momentum and demonstrating its economic advantages.

All four of these elements were political-decisional in character.[4] Only the 1992 deadline might be regarded as having a constitutional-legal dimension, since it was introduced formally by the SEA in Article 8a (EEC) and is mentioned also in Article 100b. However, there is ambiguity because of the SEA's 'Declaration on Article 8a of the EEC Treaty' which specifies that, 'setting the date of 31 December 1992 does not create an automatic legal effect'. The precise legal status of the end-1992 deadline is, in consequence, ambiguous. However, since the deadline was agreed to by the European Council before the SEA had been negotiated, I include it in the political-decisional category. All four elements entailed a new political strategy for achieving existing treaty goals rather than any fundamental revision of them.

The final political-decisional aspect comprised the inter-connection between the White Paper and the other policy issues which were part of the political bargain. The SEM and the SEA had similar roots in the 1983 declarations at the Stuttgart European Council and the 1984 Fontainebleau summit, where the British budgetary problem had been resolved. The notion that the SEM programme was a free-standing initiative was one confined to the British government. In his account of getting the White Paper agreed to inside the Commission, Cockfield explains that he had to buy support by means of

---

[4] It could be argued that all four of these elements are part of the toolkit of governance, i.e. representing simply changes to the means of achieving the original goals of the EEC Treaty. However, this would over-state the case that the SEM programme was not in fact new, and be out of touch with the way in which it was perceived by policy-makers.

promising other commissioners from the southern member states to back their demands for a doubling of the structural funds (1994, p. 45). If this was necessary inside the Commission, where the deployment of naked national interests is barely compatible with commissioners' oaths of neutrality, then it is difficult to see how the contours of the overall political bargain could be in question in the European Council, where the defence of national interests is of paramount concern. Hence, whether explicit or implicit, there was always a linkage with the other policy areas on which the government heads had been making declarations in 1983–84. These areas included monetary integration (where changes were cosmetic), economic and social cohesion, technology policy, environmental policy, as well as co-operation in foreign policy matters. The new objectives in respect of these policies were then formalised in the SEA. The connection between the SEM and the other policy changes brought about in the SEA was the product of the Milan summit and was contingent upon the actions of the Italian presidency at that meeting.

The political bargain was important because not all member governments had the same zeal concerning the SEM goal. Hence the contour of the political bargain gave those governments the necessary incentives to ensure that they could not jeopardise the SEM without jeopardising their own priorities. Thus, the policy linkages played their own important part in enhancing the governance capacity of the EC in the specific SEM domain. And that is without considering the striking progress achieved in the other policy areas.

As this outline indicates, there were important integrative developments of a political-decisional nature which contributed to the increased governance capacity of the EC on internal market issues. A new political bargain designed to achieve existing goals is the essence of what I have argued. However, that is not to suggest that there were no contributions of a constitutional–judicial nature to the new goals. The jurisprudence of the ECJ was important. In the core issue of standards and legal requirements the *Cassis de Dijon* judgement opened the way for 'the new approach' to regulation. Consequently, this and other jurisprudence was utilised in the development of the White Paper as a political programme.

The other constitutional contributions to defining the goals of integration were provided by the treaty changes incorporated in the SEA. We are concerned here with changes in the goals of integration; institutional changes brought about by the new treaty will be considered below. In essence the SEA's revisions to constitutive goals enshrined the political bargain which had been reached in outline by the time of the Milan summit. Thus, it spelt out that the 'internal market shall comprise an area without internal frontiers in which the free movement of goods, persons, services and capital is ensured'. This formulation, with its emphasis on removing frontiers, amounted to only a marginal adjustment of constitutive goals. The other revisions related to the linked policy areas: the new chapter on economic and monetary integration; the new titles on economic and social cohesion, research and technology policy and the environment; some minor changes on social policy; and the separate intergovernmental provisions on foreign policy co-operation.

The EC's constitutive goals were amended significantly by the SEA. However, in respect of the single market goal, the changes were negligible. Of much greater importance was the enshrinement of other components of the political bargain, outlined above. Interpreting these changes in narrow terms, they made little real contribution to facilitating the governance of the single market. However, in reality it was the overall package deal which made a major contribution to the SEM's success. The new goals of the SEA had an animating effect on the integration process more widely.

3.2 Institutional Structure

The SEA was much more important to the success of operationalizing the SEM project. Here limited changes to the decision-making process were to provide new momentum. The key decision was the introduction of qualified majority voting (QMV) to core areas of the SEM, including legislative harmonisation (Article 100a), capital controls (Article 70) and the freedom to provide services (Article 59). However, other policy areas were also made subject to QMV: from more peripheral parts of the SEM, such as air transport liberalisation, to indirectly linked areas (health and safety – Article 118a) and the wider package (parts of regional policy and research and technology matters). To retain balance, it must be recalled that some areas of the SEM retained unanimous voting. Taxation matters are a case in point, and Stephen Smith sees unanimity as a major reason why rule-making on indirect taxes has been highly problematic and with some significant departures from the Commission's original legislative intentions (Smith, 1993).

Nonetheless, the institutional changes clearly enhanced the decision-making capacity of the EC and particularly in respect of the White Paper programme. Data on the impact of the increased use of QMV have been provided in various forms. The Commission has published its scorecards on achieving the SEM: something that was in part provided for in the SEA, in what became Article 8b EEC. This monitoring of implementation was also an important contributory factor to mobilising decision-making, not only at the rule-making stage but also in respect of transposition into national law of directives. The idea of league tables' on transposition did help to put pressure on those member states neglecting their duties. It also made them vulnerable to pressure from other member governments when advocating further integration. Italy, for example, seemed more conscious of its record on implementation and pushed through 'omnibus' enabling legislation. The Commission continues to make reports on single market rule-making and implementation even after the passing of the end-

1992 deadline.[5] Analyses on the impact of QMV on decision-making have also been published, although studies of the overall situation – as opposed to a case-study approach have been somewhat limited (see, for example Engel and Borrmann, 1991).

The other principal constitutional change in the SEA was the introduction of new procedures concerning the European Parliament (EP). In the context of the SEM it was the new co-operation procedure which was the innovation. The co-operation procedure was not introduced with regard to accelerating decision-making but more as a move towards enhancing governance capability according to the benchmark of democratic rule. However, contrary to initial fears that the deadlines of the co-operation procedure might result in legislative stalemates, there is little evidence of the EP's greater involvement hampering the decisional process. Indeed, engaging the EP in much of the SEM legislation may be judged as having harnessed additional resources in the EC's institutional system.

Again, however, the constitutional–legal system did not amount to the whole story. The Commission's Directorate-General for the internal market, along with the Council of Ministers were vested with new norms: in the former case, almost a new 'culture'. Self-congratulatory it may be but there is surely some truth in Cockfield's noting that Fernand Braun (Cockfield's director-general for the internal market) considered that 'at long last and for the first time in many years … [the staff] knew exactly what was expected of them' (Cockfield, 1994, p. 42). Thus the normative change in the administrative culture of the Commission was also a contributory factor.

There were knock-on effects, too, in respect of ideas on policy. The studies on the costs of non-Europe were largely based on mainstream neo-classical applied economics. This thinking began to assume some kind of ideational hegemony within the Commission and certainly in its directorate-general for the internal market. However, as Weale and Williams (1992) have pointed out, these ideas (and the costs of non-Europe studies) paid scant regard to environmental externalities. In consequence, the increased decisional capacity on internal market matters was not replicated immediately in the environmental policy domain. First, DG XI (environment) had to set up a task-force on environmental policy and the single market in order to seek to integrate the two policy areas to a greater degree. And that did not occur until 1989.

It would be interesting to know what exactly the impact of the single market objective was in respect of the judgements of the ECJ. It has been noted that the Court has tended in the past to err on the side of the supranational institutions when making judgements about matters of competence (supranational versus

---

[5] In its report for the year ending 1993 it reported that 264 of the 282 pieces of legislation proposed by the Commission had been agreed in the Council. 219 measures required transposition into national law by the member states but, of these, only 106 had been adopted by all member states.

national) (for instance, Weiler, 1994). How far was the Court infused by the new norms of completing the internal market? Certainly, a number of legal judgements passed down following agreement on the White Paper helped speed up decision-making in the Council. To take the case of air transport liberalization, the *Nouvelles Frontières* (1986) and *Ahmed Saeed* (1989) judgements declared existing bilateral regulation of air fares, access and capacity to be against the treaties, thus expediting the passage of legislation to fill a regulatory void.

So much for the changes in the EC's institutional structure; but what of the response in the wider political arena? Two areas of developments are particularly interesting concerning, respectively, the response of member governments and that of interest groups. Again, these are political responses rather than ones triggered by constitutional change.

For member governments there were two developments which supported an increase in the governance capacity of the EC. The first was that the single market's programmatic content and time-scale proved to form a convenient instrument in domestic politics. In France '1993' appeared to fulfil the need for 'le grand projet' in domestic industrial policy: a successor to the role played by economic plans in earlier times. In the UK the SEM objective was seen as an extension of the Conservative Government's support for enterprise in the 'Europe – open for business' campaign. More characteristically for Germany, the approach was to hold a series of tripartite European conferences, aimed at building consensus between the social partners to address the challenges of the SEM (Bulmer, 1992, p. 66). In addition, the need for member governments to ensure 'their' economy was well prepared for completion of the SEM reinforced the commitment to the goals and ensured the mobilisation of national institutional resources for their achievement. Indeed, having mobilised these resources, the British government of Mrs Thatcher found itself subject to domestic criticism when it sought to isolate certain policy areas from the new dynamics of integration, most notably the macroeconomic and monetary domains.

It was not just domestic institutions which were mobilised for achieving the SEM. Business and its interest groups were also to the fore. Indeed, a small number of European multinationals had formed an important ally of the Commission before the White Paper was adopted in Milan (see, for instance, Sandholtz and Zysman, 1989). That interest groups were mobilised by the SEM was made clear by the growth in individual companies, transnational interest groups and freelance lobbyists based in Brussels. This boom has been highlighted in the work of Mazey and Richardson. They cite Commission data to the effect that there are more than 500 international and European federations in Brussels; 50 offices representing regional and local authorities; more than 200 firms with direct representation; and about 100 consultants and a further 100 law firms specialising in advising on EC matters (Mazey and Richardson, 1993a, p. 15; more generally, Mazey and Richardson, 1993b).

The growth which this represents demonstrates the way in which non-governmental actors responded to their perceptions of the increased governance capacity of the EC. Mazey and Richardson call this 'shooting where the ducks are': that is to say, following the first rule of lobbying by identifying where power lies (1993a, p. 16). Taking a more abstract view of that development, we may regard it as one manifestation of the way in which non-governmental actors reacted to the change in the organisational configuration of the supranational state. This perception mirrors the way in which a rules-based model of economic activity sees firms as responding to changes in the political environment: in this case the creation of the SEM. In their survey of that literature, Shipman and Mayes see the emergence of firms engaged in similar economic activity becoming a 'rule-following group' (1991, p. 3).

Another manifestation, which is associated more with the growth of research and technology programmes at the supranational level, has been the way in which companies and research institutions have come to orient themselves more towards the EC because of financial incentives. These developments are part of a pattern whereby the governance capacity of the EC/EU brings with it a constituency of supportive elites. The organisational configuration of the state was identified by Lindberg and Campbell (1991) as one of the impulses for lasting change in the governance of the American economy. Whether this proves to be repeated in the European case – as, indeed, was predicted by Lindberg (in different research) and by other neo-functionalists remains to be seen. The European integration process is arguably too brittle to make such an assertion with complete confidence.

One theoretical point which can be made at this point, however, is that such support from non-governmental actors was important to the integration process. Conceptually it is linked to a differentiation which has been made between formal and informal integration.[6] Thus, William Wallace sees informal integration as characterised by 'intense patterns of interaction which develop without the impetus of formal political decisions, following the dynamics of markets, technology, communications networks, and social change' (Wallace, 1990, p. 9). It therefore differs from formal change, which is achieved politically: 'decision by decision, bargain by bargain and treaty by treaty'. But the two processes are inter-connected, for political change influences the pattern of informal change by changing the conditions which influence private actors. The conclusion must be that part of the favourable conditions created by the SEM/SEA bargain derived

---

[6] It should be noted that Wallace's distinction between informal and formal integration does not correspond to the distinction made by Weiler, and used elsewhere in this paper. Weiler's distinctions are particularly attuned to the issue of governance, whereas Wallace is concerned with the broader notion of integration.

from the balance achieved between informal and formal paths to integration. The governance capacity of the EC was enhanced by the strong participation of non-governmental actors, for that is essential for such a small agency as the Commission with its absence of field agencies in the member states. Indeed, lobbying of the Commission became so extensive that efforts have been made to regulate access. Mazey and Richardson report a 'shake-out', whereby an inner group of lobbyists is emerging for each policy issue. They also report that this development may be part of the development of more stable 'policy communities' as part of supranational governance (Mazey and Richardson, 1993a, p. 21).

3.3 The 'Toolkit' of Governance

The European Union possesses a wide range of tools for reaching decisions. Different types of legal device are available, as are so-called 'soft' law and political agreements (Bulmer, 1993). However, as Majone in particular has highlighted, there is a striking, regulatory pattern to supranational governance (Majone, 1991; 1993). This pattern arises from the modest executive resources of the Commission, the modest financial resources of the EU and the absence of supranational ownership of economic enterprises. Lacking the normal array of public finance instruments, and with a reliance upon measures which place their costs upon private economic actors or the administrations of the member states, 'the only way for the Commission to increase its role is to expand the scope of its regulatory activities' (Majone, 1991, p. 96).

Neither the SEM programme nor the SEA brought about any major departure from this regulatory pattern of governance. However, the regulation of standards did bring about a significant change. The 'new approach' emphasised relatively light-touch legislation defining minimum legal requirements and was supported by mutual recognition of national standards. This approach thus reduced significantly the extent of centralised regulation from the EC level. When combined with the changes in voting requirements on harmonisation matters, it greatly facilitated removal of the barriers to trade in goods. Furthermore, the job of creating new European (or international) standards was entrusted to the standard-setting agencies: CEN, CENELEC and ETSI. Hence this aspect was 'contracted out', with EC financial support, to agencies bringing together national standards specialists. The onus was not upon the EC institutions themselves to legislate on these matters.

The combination of these different approaches to the regulation of standards was to ensure that the EC's decisional apparatus could act in a more streamlined fashion, with the focus upon essential legal requirements. Moreover, the use of mutual recognition – relevant also to the regulation of professional qualifications and of economic activities such as leasing – introduced the notion of competition among rules into significant parts of the single market programme. This issue is addressed by Stephen Woolcock in Chapter 4.

These developments were arguably the ones that were most striking in an overview of SEM-induced changes to the toolkit of governance. The setting of minimum legal requirements was employed in other areas of legislation, notably on health and safety matters.

Beyond these observations, changes in the toolkit have varied according to the circumstances of the issue and, in consequence, can be better grasped in a case study context. However, we can draw attention to the different ways in which the rules have been set, following the categories set out by Shipman and Mayes (1991, pp. 22–3):

- supranational rules;
- negotiated, self-regulatory rule changes at the supranational level;
- competition among national rule systems;
- acceptance of global rules also as European rules; and
- the acceptance of one country's rules as European rules.

One further point which must be borne in mind in the context of case studies is the perspective used for analysis. The kind of approach utilised by Kenneth Armstrong and myself in our case studies and followed in those projects which take a policy issue focus can facilitate greater 'process-tracing' in identifying the influence of member states, EC institutions and interest groups.[7] However, the studies that focus upon individual industries can more easily identify corporate activity and corporate response.[8]

4   TRANSFORMING THE GOVERNANCE OF THE EUROPEAN COMMUNITY: THE MAASTRICHT TREATY

It is not possible to give a comprehensive account of the way in which governance capacity was reformed in respect of the SEM without brief reference to the Maastricht Treaty on European Union (TEU). Of course, the TEU was not put into effect until November 1993, so the vast majority of the White Paper

---

[7]   Armstrong and I have examined six case studies: merger control, airline liberalisation, the regulation of standards, the transport of toxic waste, the 'maternity directive' and public procurement in the utilities sectors. All of these case studies have a focus on the legislative process. On the basis of evidence to hand this approach seems to be shared by several other projects within the ESRC programme: e.g. on environmental policy and on public procurement.

[8]   For instance, the industry cases studies in projects based at the NIESR. See, for an example, Matthews and Mayes (1993).

measures had been agreed by that stage.   Nevertheless, new single market legislation is made subject to a new context.

At the level of *constitutive goals* there are no immediate alterations concerning the single market objective, although a route is now signposted to a higher level of economic integration, namely an economic and monetary union. The broadening of the integration enterprise into the European Union also has some contextual significance. These constitutional changes are matched by political-decisional ones. In particular, there is the issue of subsidiarity. I consider this political rather than constitutional because it became a benchmark in policy-making before the TEU was ratified and it has been given greater precision in the declaration made at the 1993 Edinburgh summit than was clear from the brief references in the Maastricht Treaty. Subsidiarity has already come to play a role in policy-making on SEM issues, for example on indirect taxation matters (see Smith, 1993). And as Cox has shown, subsidiarity has also come into play as a potential means of subverting original policy objectives when it comes to putting them into practice (Cox, 1994).   In broader terms, the exploitation of the subsidiarity principle in the implementation of the SEM may undermine the all-important norm of trust amongst the member states. If the governments and economic actors felt that EC legislation was being subverted – whether by loopholes in EC law itself, by faulty transposition into national law, or by a failure to ensure compliance – their trust in the common goals of a single market could be undermined, with potentially serious consequences.[9]

The *institutional structure* has also been altered by the TEU. The number of different policy procedures, depending on the exact legal base of proposals, has become greater. Single Market legislation is not exempt from these changes. Thus, Article 100a is now subject to the co-decision procedure in the EP, which is designed to enhance the democratic character of decision-making but at the potential cost of inter-institutional stalemates. Many other procedural reforms have been introduced affecting issues linked to the SEM, such as environmental policy and, strikingly, social policy. At the normative level, the institutions are taking subsidiarity seriously; the Commission having to try to pre-empt criticism of its proposals in the Council of Ministers. A growing commitment to de-regulation has emerged since the German government espoused this cause in the particular context of its presidency. Some legislation, including on the SEM, has even been put forward for repealing.

At the level of the *toolkit* of governance there have been no striking changes relevant to the SEM. However, the overall impact of these changes, together with the emergence of an elite-mass cleavage on further integration has checked

---

[9] As Sir Arthur Knight noted in his remarks as discussant, trust is an important factor in the adherence to rules; it may be more important to adherence than more formal, policing arrangements. Trust, as William Wallace has shown, is bound up with notions of 'community', common values and common interests (1990, pp. 16–19).

the increased governance capacity brought about by the SEM/SEA bargain. This change does not represent a major reversal but it clearly has implications for the setting and influencing of rules. Moreover, the fact that this changed context has developed towards the end of the SEM programme creates scope for inconsistency over time in the single market rules. For interest groups and governments opposed to supranational legislation, invoking a subsidiarity defence of the status quo is one response to the new rules of the game.

5 RULE-MAKING: SOME HYPOTHESES

It cannot be the role of this chapter to rehearse the empirical data of individual initiative projects. Nor is it possible to make an extensive list of conclusions: apart from the obvious one that the (still imperfectly complete) single market has been facilitated over the decade by the enhancement of the governance capacity of the EC/EU. However, a number of hypotheses that warrant further investigation can be seen as emerging from individual research projects.

5.1 The Role of Ideas in Defining Policy Parameters

The whole single market programme was influenced by the increased influence of neo-liberalism in the 1980s. On the specific expectations of the programme, the estimations of neo-classical applied economists were also influential. It is worth bearing in mind the words of Peter Hall (1989, p. 362):

> It is ideas, in the form of economic theories and the policies developed from them, that enable national leaders to chart a course through turbulent economic times, and ideas about what is efficient, expedient, and just that motivate the movement from one line of policy to another.

The shift in the EC's political agenda towards market integration, and towards a specific form of it, is one which warrants further examination in terms of the role of ideas, how they spread and so on. Some member governments, when agreeing to completion of the SEM, were not giving an endorsement to this set of ideas but rather to the SEM/SEA package. However, it would be interesting to see to what extent those ideas have taken root in those states.

At a more issue-specific level, it would be interesting to see how ideas have shaped individual pieces of legislation. Some examples will illustrate what I have in mind. If we take the case of air transport liberalisation it is striking that a set of ideas advocated by the governments of the United Kingdom and the Netherlands was transformed, with modification, into the rules (if not yet the practice) of the single aviation market. It is interesting that these two states were competing with each other as gateways for transatlantic air travel. It is no coincidence that they were also gateways for the arrival of American ideas on airline de-regulation. The UK's Civil Aviation Authority (the only national regulatory agency on air transport in the EC), with its independent 'think-tank' capacity, seems to have played a major part in sharing ideas with the Commission.

Michael Gold's work on social policy suggests a similar pattern in another under-staffed Commission directorate-general (1993). As he shows, commissioned research, involving as few as one or two academics, may shape the basic policy ideas used in Commission proposals. The presumption of widespread consultation, particularly at the early stages, may not necessarily be the case. Again the role of ideas and their political influence appear important.

5.2 Creative Law-making

The Commission was able to exploit the enhanced governance capacity of the EC afforded by the SEM/SEA. One case was its introduction of a maternity directive (defining minimum maternity leave and pay) using health and safety regulation (Article 118a EEC) as the justification. This measure, when adopted, effectively required the UK to increase worker protection despite its known reservations on this front. Such creative law-making on the part of the Commission places under the spotlight the political role of creative lawyers in the Commission's legal service. In addition, it would be interesting to have research data on how lawyers in the Commission exploit judgements of the ECJ in drafting EC legislation.

5.3 Decision-making in the Council

Although the SEA (and subsequently the TEU) increased provisions for decision-making by QMV, the assumption that all decisions eligible are taken on this basis is incorrect, at least prior to the EFTA-enlargement. There have been strong pressures to decide consensually, even if with abstentions, but rarely with the opposition of a 'significant' state. More systematic analysis of how decisions are taken in the Council would be welcome, not least to see which states are persistently abstaining or being overruled.

Finally, as experience of the co-decision procedure is accumulated, it will be valuable to attempt to get a clearer picture of the influence of the EP on single market legislation since November 1993.

REFERENCES

Bulmer, S. (1992), 'Completing the Internal Market: The Regulatory Implications for the Federal Republic of Germany', in K. Dyson (ed.), *The Politics of German Regulation*, Aldershot: Dartmouth Publishing, pp. 53–77.

Bulmer, S. (1993), 'The Governance of the European Union: A New Institutionalist Approach', *Journal of Public Policy*, **13** (4), 351–80.

Carlsnaes, W. and Smith, S. (eds.) (1994), *European Foreign Policy. The EC and the Changing Foreign Policy Perspectives in Europe*, London: Sage Publications.

Cockfield, Lord Arthur (1994), *The European Union: Creating the Single Market*, Chichester: Chancery Law Publishing.

Cox, A. (1994), 'Derogation, Subsidiarity and the Single Market', *Journal of Common Market Studies*, **32** (2), 127–47.

Engel, C. and Borrmann, C. (1991), *Vom Konsens zur Mehrheitsentscheidung. EG-Entscheidungsverfahren nach der Einheitlichen Europäischen Akte*, Bonn: Europa Union Verlag.

Featherstone, K. (1994), 'Jean Monnet and the "Democratic Deficit" in the European Union', *Journal of Common Market Studies*, **32** (2), 149–70.

Gold, M. (1993), 'The formulation of EC social policy – preparatory stages', in D. Mayes (ed.), *Aspects of European Integration. Environment, Regulation, Competition and the Social Dimension*, London: NIESR, pp. 36–44.

Hall, P. (ed.) (1989), *The Political Power of Economic Ideas: Keynesianism across Nations*, Princeton N.J.: Princeton University Press.

Hix, S. (1994), 'The Study of the European Community: the Challenge to Comparative Politics', *West European Politics*, **17** (1), 1–30.

Lindberg, L. and Campbell, J. (1991), 'The State and Economic Governance', in J. Campbell, J. Hollingsworth and L. Lindberg (eds), *Governance of the American Economy*, Cambridge: Cambridge University Press, pp. 356–95.

Majone, G. (1991), 'Cross-National Sources of Regulatory Policymaking in Europe and the United States', *Journal of Public Policy*, **11** (1), 79–106.

Majone, G. (1993), 'The European Community between Social Policy and Social Regulation', *Journal of Common Market Studies*, **31** (2), 153–69.

Matthews, D. and Mayes, D. (1993), 'The Evolution of Rules for a Single European Market in Leasing', NIESR Discussion Paper no. 35.

Mazey, S. and Richardson, J. (1993a), 'Effective Business Lobbying in Brussels', *European Business Journal*, **5** (4), 14–24.

Mazey, S. and Richardson, J. (1993b), *Lobbying in the European Community*, Oxford: Oxford University Press.

Sandholtz, W. and Zysman, J. (1989), '1992: Recasting the European Bargain', *World Politics* (October), pp. 95–128.

Scharpf, F. (1988), 'The Joint-Decision Trap: Lessons from German Federalism and European Integration', *Public Administration*, **66**, 229–78.

Shipman, A. and Mayes, D. (1991), 'Changing the Rules. A framework for examining government and company responses to "1992" ', NIESR Discussion Paper no. 199.

Smith, S. (1993), '"Subsidiarity" and the Co-ordination of Indirect Taxes in the European Community', *Oxford Review of Economic Policy*, **9** (1), 67–94.

Wallace, H. (1994), 'European Governance in Turbulent Times', in S. Bulmer and A. Scott (eds), *Economic and Political Integration in Europe: Internal Dynamics and Global Context*, Oxford: Blackwell Publishers, pp. 87–96.

Wallace, W. (1990), 'Introduction: the Dynamics of European Integration', in W. Wallace (ed.), *The Dynamics of European Integration*, London: Pinter/RIIA, pp. 1–24.

Weale, A. and Williams, A. (1992), 'Between Economy and Ecology? The Single Market and the Integration of Environmental Policy', *Environmental Politics*, 1 (4), 45–64.

Weaver, R. Kent and Bert A. Rockman (1993a), 'Assessing the Effects of Institutions', in Weaver and Rockman (1993b), pp. 1–41.

Weaver, R. Kent and Bert A. Rockman (eds.) (1993b), *Do Institutions Matter? Government Capabilities in the United States and Abroad*, Washington DC: Brookings Institution.

Weiler, J. (1982), 'Community, Member States and European Integration: Is the Law Relevant?', *Journal of Common Market Studies*, 21 (1/2), 39–56.

Weiler, J. (1994), 'Journey to an Unknown Destination: A Retrospective and Prospective of the European Court of Justice in the Arena of Political Integration', in S. Bulmer and A. Scott (eds), *Economic and Political Integration in Europe: Internal Dynamics and Global Context*, Oxford: Blackwell Publishers, pp. 131–60.

Young, O. (1989), *International Co-operation. Building Regimes for Natural Resources and the Environment*, Ithaca, NY: Cornell University Press.

3. Implementing the Rules

John A. Usher

This chapter takes a broad view of the concept of implementation, using illustrations from both the projects with which its author is involved, respectively concerned with legal issues in general and competition policy in particular. It deals first with the question of administration of EC rules which themselves directly govern market conduct, taking the example of competition law, and then considers the formal machinery for the national implementation of such EC rules as require national implementation. Turning from institutional and State implementation, the chapter next deals with the mechanisms by which traders may avail themselves of the single market legislation, and concludes with a brief consideration of the extent to which traders are informed about such legislation.

1 ADMINISTRATION OF COMMUNITY RULES – THE EXAMPLE OF COMPETITION

Background

While the elimination of distortions of competition is mentioned among the attributes of the internal market defined in art.7a, it may be submitted that it is an inherent element of it, just as it was of the original definition of the common market. Indeed, in the broader sense of competition, art.100a, which enables legislation to be enacted to achieve this internal market, has been used to eliminate alleged distortions of competition, and its use for that purpose has been approved by the European Court. However, in the narrow sense of competition rules, that is the rules relating to anti-competitive conduct by undertakings, the question arises as to the division of responsibility for enforcement between national and Community authorities.

Substantive Competence

The question of the exclusivity of Community competence is most evident in the ECSC Treaty: The competition rules of that Treaty are triggered by the involvement of coal and steel undertakings and associations thereof, and there is no reference to trade between Member States being affected. Under art.65(1) agreements between such undertakings, decisions by associations of such undertakings and concerted practices tending directly or indirectly to prevent, restrict or distort normal competition within the coal and steel common market are prohibited, and art.65(4) confers sole jurisdiction on the EC Commission to determine whether any such agreement or decision is compatible with that provision, subject to judicial review. The view that such matters are of exclusive Community competence was upheld by the European Court in 1994 in the *Banks* judgement[1] and is reflected in ss.9(1) and (2) of the Restrictive Trade Practices Act 1976, which states that restrictions in agreements between coal and steel undertakings which relate to coal and steel are not to be taken into account in determining whether an agreement is registrable, and in s.34, which provides that an agreement which has been authorized under the ECSC Treaty is exempt from registration.

Art.66 of the ECSC Treaty requires any 'concentration' (including mergers) between undertakings at least one of which is a coal or steel undertaking to be authorized by the Commission – a bid by one UK company to take over another UK company may therefore fall under Community jurisdiction[2] if one of them is such an undertaking.

On the other hand, the competition rules of the EC Treaty, whether it be those applying to private undertakings, public undertakings, or state aids, are only concerned with conduct which "may affect trade between Member States". However, conduct which appears to be limited to one Member State, or even a small part of one Member State may be regarded as affecting trade between Member States if, for example, it takes place in a context of similar practices which may be regarded as cumulatively affecting trade between Member States.[3]

The consequence, as was accepted by the European Court in Case 14/68 *Wilhelm v. Bundeskartellamt,*[4] is that the same conduct may be subject both to national competition rules and to EC competition rules, although any conflicts must be resolved in favour of the EC rules. In the United Kingdom, it would appear from the Restrictive Trade Practices Act 1976 s.5 that the Restrictive Trade Practices Court has a discretion to decline or postpone the exercise of its jurisdiction where an agreement may be void under art.85(1) or authorized under art.85(3) of the EC Treaty; furthermore, that court may review its decision in the

---

[1]   Case C-128/92 *Banks v. British Coal* (13 April 1994).

[2]   For an early example see Joined Cases 160/73R and 161/73R *Miles Druce v. Commission* [1973] ECR 1049.

[3]   As in the first *Brasserie de Haecht* case [1967] ECR 407, although if it concerns exclusive sales or purchase agreements it may well fall within the relevant block exemptions, *Brouwerij Concordia*. It would appear from the recent *Delimitis* decision that what matters is not so much the restriction of supply to that particular purchaser as whether the agreement in its context has the effect of denying access to the market for new competitors.

[4]   [1969] ECR 1.

light of the operation of a Community provision. Similarly, by virtue of s21(1)(a) of the Act, the Director General of Fair Trading may refrain from taking proceedings before that court in the light of any authorisation or exemption granted under Community law.

However, in the area of mergers, it may be suggested that an exclusive competence has been created by secondary legislation, albeit in the guise of an exclusive jurisdiction to administer the system. The EC Treaty was silent on mergers, although certain types of takeover were eventually held to constitute an abuse of a dominant position.[5]   More generally, in 1990 a system of merger control under the EC Treaty came into operation by virtue of Council Regulation 4064/89.[6]   Under this legislation, notably arts.1 and 21, the EC Commission has exclusive competence with regard to mergers with a 'Community dimension' and Member States are in principle prohibited from applying their national legislation. 'Concentrations with a Community dimension' are defined as those where the aggregate worldwide turnover of all the undertakings concerned is more than 5000 million ECU and the aggregate Community-wide turnover of at least two of the undertakings involved is more than 250 million ECU, unless each of the undertakings concerned achieves more than two-thirds of its aggregate Community-wide turnover in one and the same Member State. In the present context it may be observed that art.21(2) of the Regulation prohibits Member States from applying their national legislation to such 'concentrations'. Member States are, however, entitled under art.21(3) to protect legitimate interests, defined as including 'plurality of the media', by measures compatible with the general principles and other provisions of Community law; this may be of particular importance in the context of the United Kingdom rules on newspaper mergers. Furthermore, by virtue of art.9 of the Regulation, the Commission may refer a notified concentration to the national authorities with a view to the application of national competition law where it considers that a concentration threatens to create or strengthen a dominant position as a result of which effective competition would be significantly impeded on a market within that Member State which presents all the characteristics of a distinct market, whether or not it constitutes a substantial part of the common market. The reason for this convoluted terminology is that in the context of the single internal market of the EC, the area of a particular State as such is not necessarily a relevant criterion in determining whether competition is adversely affected.

Conversely, however, under art.22(3) of the Regulation, a Member State may request the Commission to take a decision with regard to a concentration which has no Community dimension where it creates or strengthens a dominant position as a result of which effective competition would be significantly impeded

---

[5]   Case 6/72 *Continental Can v. Commission* [1973] ECR 215.

[6]   OJ 1989 L395/1.

in the Member State concerned, to the extent that the concentration affects trade between Member States. It would appear that Belgium referred the takeover of Dan-Air by British Airways to the Commission on the basis of this provision.[7]

The effect, to put it bluntly, is that for mergers falling within the scope of the Regulation, national law cannot be applied unless the Commission so determines, which would appear to be a clear example of exclusive competence rather than exclusive administration.

Administration and Enforcement

Unlike arts.65 and 66 of the ECSC Treaty, which clearly give the Commission sole jurisdiction to apply their rules, the EC Treaty does not confer on the Commission exclusive powers with regard to the competition rules it contains. Rather, art.87 of the Treaty provides for the Council to take measures to give effect to the substantive rules contained in arts.85 and 86 with a view, *inter alia*, to defining the functions of the Commission. Until such measures were adopted, the EC competition rules were to be enforced either by the national authorities, under art.88, or by the Commission 'in co-operation with the competent authorities of the Member States' under art.89. The Commission's powers to enforce the competition rules alone were conferred on it by Council Regulation No. 17,[8] and although this Regulation confers exclusive power on the Commission to grant exemptions under art.85(3), it otherwise maintains the competence of the national authorities to apply the prohibitions in arts.85(1) and art.86 unless proceeding have been initiated before the Commission itself.[9]

Furthermore, it was not universal in its application: Council Regulation 141/62[10] excluded transport from its scope, and although specific rules for road, rail and inland waterway transport were enacted in 1968,[11] air and sea transport remained excluded until power to enforce the competition rules in the context of sea transport was eventually conferred on the Commission by Regulation 4056/86, and this was initially done with regard to air transport by Regulations 3975 and 3976/87. Thus in its 1980 Report on Competition policy, the Commission noted that when it was faced with a complaint from a Danish airline, Sterling Airways, alleging abuse of a dominant position by Scandinavian Airlines System (SAS), it had to fall back on the system envisaged on art.89 of

---

[7]   Agence Europe No. 5880, 16 December 1992.

[8]   OJ Sp.Ed. 1959-62 p.87.

[9]   Art.9(3).

[10]   OJ Sp.Ed. 1959-62 p.291.

[11]   OJ Sp.Ed. 1968 p.302.

the EC Treaty and seek the co-operation of the competent national authorities in order to be able to investigate the complaint.[12]

Of greater practical importance is the fact that it has been clearly established by the European Court that the prohibitions contained in arts.85(1) and 86 of the EC Treaty produce direct effects, and hence may be invoked by parties to litigation before national courts irrespective of the terms of Regulation 17/62 (or indeed the Merger Regulation)[13] – a matter which will be considered further in the context of the enforcement of single market rules by individuals. Indeed much of the case-law on the competition rules has evolved in the context of questions referred for preliminary rulings by national courts rather than in direct actions seeking the annulment of Commission competition decisions.

Nevertheless, the role of the Commission remains of fundamental importance for those subject to the general EC competition rules. The Commission is the only body which directly enforces those rules at the Community level in the interests of Community policy, rather than national policy or private interest, it is the only body which may grant exemptions under art.85(3), and, on the other hand, it may, under art.15 of Regulation 17/62, impose fines of up to one million ECU, or 10 per cent of turnover where that is greater.

Be that as it may, in 1992 the Commission indicated both in 'soft' legislation and in its formal decisions, a desire for a greater role to be played by national courts and authorities in the application of Community competition rules. In December 1992, the Commission adopted Guidelines on the enforcement of competition rules by national courts, though it should be observed that these Guidelines do not apply to the transport sector or under the ECSC Treaty. For the most part the Guidelines appear simply to codify the case-law of the European Court on the matter, while extolling the remedies available at the national level (for example, damages) which the Commission itself cannot give. The underlying aim is that the Commission should be able to concentrate on those cases of Community interest. In the context of decisions given in individual competition cases, in November 1992, in the *SACEM* case, which involved complaints about fees charged by a French copyright agency, the Commission made public[14] the fact that it had referred the matter to the French competition authorities to deal with, on the basis that the effects of any abuse of a dominant position in that case would mainly be felt on French territory.

---

[12] 10th report 1980 pp.94–96.

[13] Case 127/73 *BRT v. SABAM* [1974] E.C.R. 51 and the second *Brasserie de Haecht* case [1973] E.C.R. 77.

[14] Agence Europe No.5868, 30 Nov.–1 Dec. 1992.

2   FORMAL IMPLEMENTATION OF EC LAW IN THE UK

Legislative Machinery

Any study of the implementation of European Community law within the United Kingdom must start with the European Communities Act 1972, by virtue of which provisions of European Community law become, or are enabled to become, law within the legal systems of the United Kingdom. By the time of the United Kingdom's accession in January 1973, the concepts of direct application and direct effect were well-known in Community circles.   The European Communities Act, therefore, distinguishes between that Community law which is automatically to be law within the United Kingdom, and that Community law which requires further enactment at the national level in order to be effective.

With regard to that European Community law that does require national enactment in order to be available as law in the United Kingdom, s2(2) enables orders in Council to be made, and enables designated ministers or departments to make regulations: (a) for the purpose of implementing any Community obligation of the United Kingdom, or enabling any such obligation to be implemented, or of enabling any rights enjoyed or to be enjoyed by the United Kingdom under or by virtue of the Treaties to be exercised; or (b) for the purpose of dealing with matters arising out of or related to any such obligation or rights or the coming into force, or the operation from time to time, of sub-section 1.

Furthermore, sub-section 2 expressly provides that in the exercise of *any* statutory power or duty, including any power to give directions or to legislate by means of orders, rules, regulations or other subordinate instrument, the person entrusted with the power or duty may have regard to the object of the Communities under any such obligation or rights as aforesaid.

Finally, s2(4) expressly provides that any secondary legislation made under s2(2) may include any provision which might be made by Act of Parliament. In other words, ministers issuing secondary legislation to give effect to Community obligations under sub-section 2 may amend or repeal earlier Acts of Parliament, and may introduce new legislation which would normally be contained in an Act of Parliament. It is perhaps, therefore, hardly surprising that no formal change was made to this mechanism to give effect to the legislation adopted by the Community institutions with a view to completing the internal market by the end of 1992.

Whilst there are express limitations on the powers contained in the European Communities Act, and it is obviously necessary to use other powers to deal with matters falling within those limitations, it may nevertheless be observed that for many years certain matters were dealt with by Act of Parliament even though they clearly fell within the scope of s2(2) of the European Communities Act. Thus, in the area of company law, the First Directive was implemented in s9 of the European Communities Act itself, and the Second Directive on the protection of share capital was implemented by the Companies Act 1980, and the Fourth Directive on company accounts was implemented in the Companies Act 1981. However, more recently, the Third and Sixth Directives on mergers and divisions were implemented by the Companies (Mergers and Divisions) Regulations 1987 and made under s2(2) and, despite the fact that it relates to an entirely new form of commercial entity, the United Kingdom legislation to enable European economic interest groupings to operate in this country was adopted by a statutory instrument, the European Economic Interest Grouping Regulations 1989 made under s2(2).

Precisely because of the wide scope of s2(2), ministerial undertakings were given at the time of accession that a specific power under other legislation would be used to implement a Community obligation rather than the general power of implementation in s2(2), if such a specific power was available. The European Communities Act itself created a number of specific enabling provisions, in the context of legislation relating to food, seeds and other propagating material, fertilisers and feeding stuffs, animal health, plant health and certain aspects of road transport. Use of these specific powers may, for example, enable heavier penalties to be imposed than may be imposed under s2(2). It is also the case, that, as in the Community itself, serious questions of legal basis may arise, so that it is not unknown for secondary legislation giving effect to Community obligations to be made both under the general power of s2(2) and a more specific power in other legislation.

Community Rights and Obligations

Whether use can be made of s2(2) depends essentially on the existence either of a Community obligation of the United Kingdom, or of a right enjoyed or to be enjoyed by the United Kingdom under or by virtue of the Treaties. With regard to Community obligations, it is trite law that a directly applicable regulation, such as the Mergers Regulation discussed above, does not need and must not receive substantive re-enactment into national law. Nevertheless, many regulations by their terms do actually require Member States to take implementing measures, such as the EC Regulation introducing the European Economic Interest Grouping. Indeed, the specific enabling powers created by the European Communities Act with regard to food, the grading of horticultural produce, and road transport, do confer specific powers to issue subordinate legislation relating to the administration, execution and enforcement of directly applicable Community provisions. It is, however, clear that the role of a statutory instrument here is to provide machinery to help the application of the Community law, and not to replicate or to disguise the directly applicable provisions. Furthermore, although a directly applicable provision of Community law may, as a matter of Community law, render automatically inapplicable any conflicting provision of national legislation, there may still be a Community obligation formally to repeal such national provisions, since their apparent maintenance in force may give rise to a state of uncertainty as to the possibility of relying on Community law. On the other hand, the Community obligation to enact into domestic law directives (the legal instruments archetypically used in the internal market programme) which are not directly applicable in terms of the EC Treaty is not affected by the fact that provisions in a directive may be capable of direct effect. This is explained partly by the wording of the Treaty, which expressly envisages national implementation of directives, and partly by the fact that the direct effect of a directive is a residual concept, which may in general only be invoked against the defaulting Member State whereas the directive itself may well require obligations to be imposed by that Member State on other subjects of the law.

The obligations in question are not necessarily limited to those imposed by EC legislation. When the President of the European Court ordered the United Kingdom, as an interim measure, to suspend the application of certain provisions of the Merchant Shipping Act 1988 in Case 246/89R *Commission v. UK*,[15] the necessary amendments to the Act were made by a statutory instrument issued under s2(2).

The 'rights' enjoyed by the United Kingdom to which effect may be given under s2(2) would appear to extend to certain express powers, such as the power in the Lawyers' Services Directive to reserve certain defined activities to prescribed categories of lawyers, and to require lawyers from other Member States to work in conjunction with the local lawyers, and to require lawyers from other Member States to work in conjunction with the local lawyer when representing a client in legal proceedings. However, the view seems to be taken that a bare permission or mere toleration in Community law would not justify the use of s2(2), such as legislation declaring payments that would normally be unlawful state aid to be compatible with the Common Market.

The European Court has for many years held that Community obligations may not be implemented by simple administrative practice since by their nature administrative practices may be altered at the whim of the authorities. Despite the espousal of the cause of deregulation by the present British government, it would in fact appear to have been general practice of successive British governments to give effect to the Community obligations through formal legislation. There do nevertheless appear to be examples of non-legislative action. In a rather technical area, the open systems interconnection information aspects of the public procurement provisions in Council Decision 87/95 on standardisation in the file of information technology and telecommunications

---

[15] [1989] ECR 3125.

appear to have given rise in this country to circulars from the Department of Trade and Industry and more detailed documentation produced by the Central Communications and Telecommunications Agency. On the other hand, it may be suggested that there is no legal need to use formal legislation to implement a mere permission accorded to a Member State by Community law provided any correlative obligations may be enforced by other means. So, for example, the power under Council Regulation 857/84 art.4(1) for a Member State to grant compensation to producers undertaking to discontinue milk production definitively was at first implemented in the United Kingdom by contracts with individual producers on a non-statutory basis.

Anticipated Implementation

There have been examples of UK law being changed to give effect to anticipated Community obligations. Perhaps the best known example is the Finance Act 1972, which introduced value added tax, and conveniently enabled the government of the day to keep a manifesto promise to abolish selective employment tax, even though the Act of Accession did not require the UK to implement the VAT Directives until six months after Accession. More recently, the government anticipated Council Directive 89/48 on the mutual recognition of higher education qualifications in order to enable teachers to be recruited from other Member States for the 1989–90 school year even though the Directive did not require implementation until 1990.

What has caused serious problems is UK legislation which appears to reflect proposals being discussed in the Community institutions but which enters into force before the Community legislation has been adopted. In *Duke v. GEC Reliance*,[16] the view was expressed in the House of Lords that the Sex Discrimination Act 1975 could not be regarded a being intended to give effect to the 1976 Equal Treatment Directive (which had been under discussion when the Act was passed) so that, as it was put, a court was not obliged to distort the meaning of the statute so as to make it accord with the terms of the Directive as interpreted by the European Court in Case 152/84 *Marshall v. Southampton A.H.A.*,[17] where it was held to prohibit the imposition by employers of discriminatory retirement ages. If the UK Act as such could not be so interpreted, the Directive could not by itself impose obligations on a private sector employer, then there was nothing to prevent a private employer from requiring women to retire earlier than men, at the relevant time.

---

[16] [1988] 1 All ER 577.

[17] [1986] ECR 723.

However, in Case C-106/89 *Marleasing v. Comercial Internacional de Alimentacion,*[18] it was made clear that the duty of a national court to interpret national law in accordance with the terms of a Directive extended to all relevant national legislation, irrespective of whether it was adopted after the Directive so as to give effect to it. The case involved a dispute between two Spanish companies as to whether one of them was in law a nullity. The possible causes of nullity of companies are defined restrictively in Council Directive 68/151, the first company law harmonisation Directive, which had not at the time been implemented in Spain. The Court repeated that the provisions of the Directive could not be enforced by one company against another, but emphasised the duty of the national court to interpret Spanish legislation, whether enacted before or after the Directive, in the light of the text and objectives of the Directive, to the extent that such an interpretation was possible. The consequence, therefore, appears to be that if there is a provision of national law which may conceivably be interpreted so as to accord with the terms of the Directive, then the Directive may be enforced against any subject of the law, even if no formal national implementation has taken place.

Consequences for Compliance

To the extent that provisions of Community law require the adoption of formal national legislation, s2(2) of the European Communities Act enables designated Ministers to issue regulations which may do anything which could be done by Act of Parliament, with the result that United Kingdom governments have not usually encountered problems with the legislative process in giving effect to their Community obligations.

The United Kingdom has therefore usually appeared in a good light in successive general Commission Reports on the enforcement of Community law and in the special Reports on the implementation of the 1992 programme. In the latter context, the UK has usually appeared in the top three of the league table with Denmark and France. However, it would appear from a Commission Report in December 1992[19] that the position changed in the second half of 1992. According to this, the United Kingdom had fallen to third from the bottom of the league, having failed to implement 46 of the 215 single market instruments which should by then have been implemented. Only Italy and Spain had (marginally) worse records. There would appear to have been delays even in areas where the UK hàd a particular interest, such as financial services.

Whether there were political reasons – possibly connected with domestic problems over the internal implementation of the Maastricht Treaty – is not for

---

[18] 13 November 1990.

[19] Agence Europe No.5870, 3 December 1992.

this lawyer to say. However, during the course of 1993, the UK would appear to have regained its usual position.

3 PRIVATE IMPLEMENTATION OF INTERNAL MARKET LEGISLATION

Enforcement by Traders

It may be suggested that it is no exaggeration to describe the use of the concepts of direct application and direct effect of EC law by traders to enforce internal market legislation as private implementation of that law.

By the time of the United Kingdom's accession in January 1973, the concepts of direct application and direct effect were well-known in Community circles. The European Communities Act therefore distinguishes, as has been mentioned, between that Community law which is automatically to be law within the United Kingdom, and that Community law which requires further enactment at the national level in order to be effective.

Under s2(1) of the European Communities Act, all such rights, powers, liabilities, obligations and restrictions from time to time created or arising by or under the Treaties, and all such remedies and procedures from time to time provided for by or under the Treaties, as in accordance with the Treaties, are without further enactment to be given legal effect or used in the United Kingdom, shall be recognised and available in law, and be enforced, allowed and followed accordingly; and the expression 'enforceable Community right' and similar expressions are to be read as referring to rights etc. to which sub-section 1 applies. In other words, making due allowance for the tautology so beloved of United Kingdom draftsmen, this sub-section means in practice that if by virtue of Community law a right or duty arising under Community law is to be available as law in the United Kingdom, it shall, as a matter of United Kingdom law, be available as law in the United Kingdom. Furthermore, section 3(1) of the European Communities Act effectively requires courts in the United Kingdom to follow the case law of the European Court of Justice, and, of course, the concept of direct effect is one of the most important creations of that case law.

Examples can therefore be found of Community law being invoked by individual litigants before United Kingdom courts as early as January 1973. It should, however, be said that many of the early examples involved litigants invoking the competition rules of the EC Treaty in order to escape the normal consequences of having breached a contract.

The attitude of courts in the United Kingdom to the direct effect of Directives is, however, of particular interest given the emphasis on this form of legal instrument as the mechanism for achieving the approximation or harmonization of laws in order to complete the internal market even under Article 100a. It is therefore worth remembering that the question of whether a provision in a Directive could give rise to rights enforceable by individuals before their national courts was raised for the first time before the European Court of Justice in the very first reference to be made by an English court. This appeared in the context of public policy restrictions on the free movement of workers in the *Van Duyn* case.[20]   Subsequent references from English courts endeavoured to cajole the court into holding that provisions of Directives could be directly enforced against private sector employers. It was in a further English reference in the *Marshall* case where the European Court finally held that the provisions of a Directive may only be invoked against the State (now reaffirmed in *Faccini Dori*),[21] but that so as to ensure that the State should not profit by its failure to implement a Directive on time, that definition should cover the State not just in its rule-making capacity but also as an employer.[22]   It was in a further English reference in *Foster v. British Gas*, that the European Court went on to hold that the clear provisions of a Directive which had not been implemented on time could be relied upon in a claim against any body (whatever its legal form) which had been made responsible, pursuant to a measure adopted by the State, for providing a public service under the control of the State and had for that purpose special powers beyond those which resulted from the normal rules applicable in relations between individuals.[23]

It has now also been made clear in relation to a Member State's failure to give proper effect to a Directive that limitation periods cannot be invoked to prevent an individual claiming rights under a Directive against a defaulting Member State.[24] In the view of the European Court, private citizens cannot be taken to know their rights under a Directive until it has been correctly implemented, and therefore time does not begin to run until it has been correctly implemented. Similarly, as was held in the second *Marshall* case[25] limits on the jurisdiction of tribunals with limited jurisdiction may have to be ignored, in order to ensure that there is an effective remedy for a breach of EC law, at least where it takes the form of failure to implement a Directive giving rise to enforceable individual rights.

---

[20] Case 41/74, [1974] ECR 1337.

[21] Case C-91/92 *Faccini Dori v. Recreb* (14 July 1994).

[22] Case 152/84, [1986] ECR 723.

[23] Case C-188/89, July 12, 1990.

[24] Case C-208/90 *Emmott* [1991] ECR I-4269.

[25] Case C-271/91 *Marshall v. Southampton AHA (No. 2)* (2 August 1993).

Remedies

The remedy which has been most frequently used when seeking to enforce Community law against the public authorities in England has been an application for a declaration. So, for example, Miss Van Duyn in the case mentioned above sought a declaration that she was entitled to enter and stay in the United Kingdom. Other forms of judicial review may also be invoked, but it had been thought that a court could not grant interim relief pending trial against a minister in the form of an injunction. In the *Factortame* case,[26] therefore, the House of Lords held that it could not order the minister to suspend the entry into force of provisions of an Act of Parliament which were alleged to breach directly effective Community law rights; it nevertheless asked the European Court whether, as a matter of Community law, it should be able to grant such interim relief. The answer given by the European Court was that the full effectiveness of Community law would be impaired if a rule of national law could prevent a court seized of a dispute governed by Community law from granting interim relief in order to ensure the full effectiveness of the judgement to be given on the existence of the rights claimed under Community law. It therefore followed that a court which in those circumstances would grant interim relief, if it were not for a rule of national law, was obliged to set aside that rule. In the result the House of Lords granted the injunction – and has subsequently held such a remedy to be available as a matter of national law.

The fact that directly effective Community law rights are converted into enforceable Community rights in the legal systems of the United Kingdom by section 2(1) of the European Communities Act has an important consequence with regard to the availability of damages. Breach of statutory duty is an established head of tortious liability in English law, and in the *Garden Cottage Foods* case in 1983 the House of Lords held that a breach of a provision of Community law creating enforceable rights in favour of an individual constituted a breach of a statutory duty under English law for which damages could be awarded.[27] This concept gave rise to little difficulty where damages were sought against a trader; greater difficulties arose, however, where damages were sought from a minister. The majority in the *Bourguoin* case[28] which arose out of the United Kingdom's unlawful prohibition of imports of poultry meat, suggested that the proper remedy against the minister was judicial review, and that an action for damages would only exist if either there was an abuse of power, or where the minister had committed misfeasance in public office, in other words if it could be shown that he knew he was breaching Community law and that his

---

[26] [1989] 2 All ER 692.

[27] [1983] 2 All ER 770.

[28] [1985] 3 All ER 586.

act would injure the plaintiff. In other words, the majority in the Court of Appeal was unwilling to accept that a simple breach of enforceable Community rights, by itself, committed by a minister should give rise to a liability in damages. It may be observed, however, that the case was settled before it reached the House of Lords on the payment of £3,500,000 by the United Kingdom Minister of Agriculture to the French poultry producers whose products had unlawfully been excluded from the United Kingdom market.

The matter has now been taken a stage further: it would appear from Cases C-6 and 9/90 *Francovich v. Italy*[29] that there are circumstances under which a Member State may be liable in damages for harm caused by its failure to implement a Directive even where the provisions of the Directive do not give rise to directly effective rights against the State. Italy had failed to give effect to Council Directive 80/987 on the protection of employees in the event of the insolvency of their employer, and the Italian government was therefore sued for damages by a number of people who had been employed by firms which had become insolvent and who had not received the payments guaranteed to them under the Directive. On the question of direct effect, the Court held that while it was clear that the Directive imposed a guarantee of payment and how much was to be paid, it was not clear that the State itself was the debtor against which the guarantee could be enforced. Nevertheless, the Court went on to hold that the full effect of Community law rules could be undermined if individuals whose rights were harmed by a Member State breaching Community law could not obtain damages, and reparation was indispensable where the full effect of Community law depended on the action of Member States, as is the case with Directives. As in the case-law on interpretation, the Court invoked the principle of Community solidarity in Article 5 of the EC Treaty, stating that it imposed an obligation on the Member States to wipe out the illegal consequences of a breach of Community law. It concluded that there was a liability to pay damages to compensate for the harm caused by failure to implement a Directive subject to three conditions: the Directive should require rights to be conferred on individuals, the content of these rights should be identifiable from the provisions of the Directive, and there should be a causal link between the obligation imposed on the Member State and the harm suffered by the applicant. While the procedural rules for such an action for damages are left to national law, and should not be less favourable than those relating to parallel national remedies or make the action virtually impossible,[30] there could hardly be a starker illustration of the relationship between Community law and national law.

---

[29] 19 November 1991.

[30] Repeating Case 199/82 *San Giorgio* [1983] ECR 3595.

It was recognised by the House of Lords in *Kirklees B.C. v. Wickes*[31] that the earlier English authorities would need reconsideration in the light of this development.

4 PERCEPTIONS AND BEHAVIOUR OF TRADERS

For all that a lawyer is tempted to look at legal machinery and legal acts, it may be suggested that the real test of national implementation of the single market programme lies in the extent to which it influences market conduct. To some extent, there may well be a link between a trader's awareness of the Community Single Market Programme and the use of legal remedies. Indeed, an analysis of the growth of litigation involving points of EC law, and the frequency with which EC points are taken in litigation in general may provide one barometer of the extent to which there is a general awareness of the opportunities offered by the single market. However, such an investigation may not be wholly reliable statistically in the United Kingdom, since the publication of law reports depends to a considerable extent on the choices made by the editors, there being no obligation to publish a general series of such reports. It might, however, be wondered for example how far the publicity given to the recent Sunday trading cases[32] has inculcated a greater awareness of the possibilities of invoking Community law.

Whilst there may have been no formal change to the legislative or administrative machinery designed to give effect to Community law in the United Kingdom as a result of the Single European Act and the challenge of 1992, there was a change in the public face of government, as exemplified in the Department of Trade and Industry, with regard to the information it supplied to business. The Department of Trade and Industry mounted a high-profile publicity campaign designed to promote an awareness in the business community of the implications of 1992. It may perhaps be suggested that it sometimes gave the impression that something very specific was going to happen in 1992, rather than making traders aware that much of the Community was already, to use the jargon, 'open for business'. The campaign made use of telephone numbers and post office box numbers which included the figures 1 9 9 2, and it comprised in particular an action checklist for business, a series of fact sheets for business, the creation of a database called Spearhead which contained more detailed information, a telephone hotline to answer questions on individual measures, and a series of videos aimed to raise awareness of the problems and possibilities of the Community. The action checklist emphasised the need to ask fundamental

---

[31] [1992] 3 All ER 717.

[32] Beginning with Case 145/88 *Torfaen B.C. v. B.+ Q. plc* [1990] 1 All ER 129.

questions about the future of a business, whether it wished to take advantage of the single market or to defend its existing customer base. It then listed questions and tasks in the areas of marketing, sales, distribution, production, product development, purchasing, finance, training, languages and recruitment and information technology. It concluded with a short list of possible sources of relevant information.

What is, however, of general interest is the fact that, although the Spearhead database was ostensibly concerned with single market information, it contained details of more than six hundred measures awaiting implementation or under discussion, a figure approximately twice that of the number of measures specifically envisaged in the Commission's White Paper. Dare it be suggested that this is useful evidence that the Commission's White Paper is not in fact necessarily the be-all and end-all of the internal market.

In assessing the reactions of business to the specific trading opportunities that appeared to be created by the internal market, the Confederation of British Industry (CBI) did carry out its own sample survey at the end of 1988, in preparation for its own publicity campaign in the form of a nationwide 1992 roadshow. The result of this survey was published in *The Times* on 9 January 1989, and indicated that of all of those responding, 80 per cent were not reviewing their strategy in the light of 1992, 90 per cent were not undertaking market research on the continent, 93 per cent were not taking initiatives to train employees in continental languages, and 95 per cent did not have sales agents in the rest of the EC. Conversely, only 1 per cent were contemplating opening new manufacturing plants on the continent. This caused the then Deputy Director General of the CBI, Mr John Owens, to comment 'nearly 10,000 British companies are sleep-walking towards 1992'.

In fairness, it should nevertheless be said that there were certain sectors of United Kingdom industry which did make a serious effort to arouse the awareness of their members to the possibilities and challenges of 1992. So, for example, the British Paper and Board Industry Federation set up a 1992 Working Group which issued a series of papers under the title '1992 Action Now'. Amongst other things, they suggested that every company should have a copy of the Commission's White Paper and a copy of the Cecchini Report. They also sent a copy of the Commission's booklet on 'Europe: Developing an Active Company Approach to the European Market 1992' to every chief executive of their member companies. Furthermore, they dealt in their papers with matters going beyond a simple reproduction of well-known materials, such as discussion in their Paper No. 5 of the energy market and the possibilities, for example, of using French electricity and the possibility of buying gas from other Member States.

5 CONCLUSION

It will have been seen that discussion of the implementation of Community rules raises questions of the day-to-day administration of those rules, of their formal incorporation into national law, and of their enforcement and protection at the national level. It also however raises the question whether there is a dichotomy between the legal framework and market performance: is it only the tourists who fill their cars with French wine, spirits and beer who have perceived the reality of the single market?

4. Competition Among Rules in the European Union

Stephen Woolcock

1 THE ISSUES

Competition among rules in the European Union is important for a number of reasons. First, the nature of European regulation, and thus the political economy of the Union, will be shaped by the balance between central regulation and competition among national policies. Broadly speaking, the greater the scope for effective competition among rules within the European Union, the less the need for central regulation. Effective competition among rules can be said to exist when different national policies can be accommodated without the differences resulting in barriers to market access and without regulatory failure.

The scope for competition among rules is therefore related to the debate about 'subsidiarity' or the question of criteria for deciding when regulation should be at a European, when at a national and when at a sub-national level. A test for when effective competition among rules applies, could offer an objective test for decisions on subsidiarity. The successful application of competition among national rules in the European Union also has the advantage of obviating the need to resolve the difficult issues, of efficacy with accountability, involved in establishing European level regulatory agencies. There is a view that European integration has resulted in a 'regulatory gap', whereby EC legislation has restricted national regulatory competence without replacing it with a European regulatory competence (Dehouse, 1992). This gap has come about because national governments have been willing to support legislation establishing an Internal European Market which constrains national regulatory powers, but unwilling to cede regulatory powers to European level agencies. In the longer term the regulatory gap will have to be filled unless some alternative approach can be found. Competition among rules offers such an alternative approach. If there is extensive scope for competition among national rules, it would allow national governments to resist centralisation while retaining some national sovereignty. To put it somewhat differently, extensive scope for competition among rules offer a kind of 'middle way' between continued policy integration and, ultimately, the establishment of more powerful European regulatory agencies and disintegration with its associated economic costs in terms of market fragmentation.

A second, related issue is whether competition among rules will be effective. The 'new approach' to market integration developed in the European Union during the 1980s, depends to an important degree, on the credibility of the competition among rules approach. The new approach is based on mutual recognition, home country and the idea that there will be competition between different national standards or regulatory policies over and above a floor set by common minimum essential requirements. Thus, in so far as the Internal Market programme relies on competition among national policies, its credibility relies on competition among rules being credible and effective. As the Internal Market Programme is a central element of the European Union, the credibility of the Union is also dependent on the efficacy of competition among rules as a means of accommodating nationally diverse policies. If competition among rules becomes a competition in laxity of implementation and enforcement, rather than credible policy, the credibility of the Internal Market, and thus of the Union itself, will have been undermined.

A third issue is whether competition among rules will result in sub-optimal or zero regulation. This is the 'race to the bottom' issue. Competition among national policies within a single market for goods and services is sometimes seen as threatening to bring about progressive deregulation. Progressive deregulation would come from efforts by national regulators to avoid capital flight or relocation of economic activity to locations where the costs of regulation are lower (McGee and Weatherill, 1990). This concern is often expressed by organised labour concerned about regulatory competition resulting in lower wages and working conditions, by environmental groups concerned that it will result in a lowering of environmental standards and by consumers concerned about it resulting in downward pressure on product and safety standards. More broadly speaking, competition among national rules and taxes may result in a progressive lowering of the ability to tax and thus a weakening of the welfare state (Begg *et al.*, 1993).

As will be discussed below, there are limits to the effective scope of competition among national rules, for example, as a result of negative externalities, such as cross border environmental pollution. Within the limits set by such externalities, there is still a fourth issue concerning whether competition among national policies will result in convergence or divergence of national regulatory policies. The presumption on the part of proponents of European integration is that regulatory competition will bring about convergence and thus, ultimately, a common European policy. But it could also result in divergence as differences in national policies are consolidated. A third alternative, preferred by many economists, would be a steady state condition in which there was neither convergence nor divergence but a form of open-ended competition among national policies.

Finally, there is the issue of what impact experience with competition among rules has on third countries. Will competition among rules be seen as a model – for other countries, regional groupings or multilateral agreements – for how to accommodate national policy differences without protection? Experience within the European Union may heighten or dispel fears about the 'race to the bottom' in other regional or multilateral agreements. Lastly, the nature of regulation within the EU will also determine the kind of entity Europe's trading partners will have to deal with. If there is considerable scope for competition among rules, they will continue to be faced by a Europe characterised by diversity. If there is limited scope for competition, Europe's trading partners will face central regulation in more and more areas of policy.

2   COMPETITION AMONG RULES IN THEORY AND PRACTICE

2.1 Definitions

Before going much further it is necessary to attempt to define competition among rules. Competition among rules occurs when regulators, market participants, consumers and interest groups respond to different rules operating in other locations. The term competition among rules is broad and encompasses both regulatory emulation and regulatory competition. Regulatory competition can occur when regulators concerned with discrete pieces of regulation compete in an effort to attract factors of production or to promote the competitiveness of local companies, or act to match such action taken by regulators in other locations. For example, the German tax authorities may respond to reductions in corporation tax elsewhere in Europe by reducing German corporation tax in order to prevent German investment moving to lower taxed locations. Efforts to promote the competitiveness of the local economy need not, of course, result in 'deregulation'. Regulatory decisions to enhance social or environmental policies may also be seen as a means of promoting competitiveness.

Competition can also occur between regulatory systems as opposed to discrete pieces of regulation or legislation. Differences in regulatory systems may result from divergent national regulatory approaches or from different philosophies. For example, the laissez-faire approach to regulatory policy of Britain, with its emphasis of lower levels of regulation, might be seen as competing with various forms of social market economy in continental Europe, in which social consensus and cohesion plays a greater role in regulatory decisions. Competition among rules may, therefore, sometimes mean competition between national systems. Efforts to define competition among rules are also complicated by different understandings of what constitutes regulation. For example, in the United States, regulation is understood as being, primarily, what independent regulatory agencies do to pursue objectives set down in statutes (Majone, 1990). In Europe regulation tends to be understood as every form of intervention in the market, including legislative actions, actions by executive bodies and actions by independent regulatory agencies.   This results in legislation, such as EC Directives, as well as the decisions of implementing agencies such as the Bundeskartelamt, both being referred to as 'regulation'.

Regulatory arbitrage is the process by which market players respond to changes in regulation or differences between regulations or regulatory systems. Regulatory arbitrage consists of judgments about the relative merits of different locations for investment or employment.

Finally, regulatory emulation may be defined as adopting the policy pursued by another country or state on the basis that policy has been seen to be effective. The main difference from regulatory competition is that there need be no direct interaction between the two markets. Regulatory emulation may result simply from the responsible agencies in one country observing the effectiveness of a policy in another country and then introducing the same, or a slightly modified policy. For example, many European governments and interest groups observed that the German system of an independent central bank helped provide monetary stability.   There has, therefore, been a degree of regulatory emulation of the German policy in other European countries.   In practice it may be difficult to distinguish between regulatory emulation and regulatory competition.

2.2 Competition Among Rules in Theory

The theoretical basis for the concept of competition among rules is often traced back to the seminal work on models for markets in public goods proposed by Tiebout (Tiebout, 1956). The Tiebout model was based on the assumption that voters/consumers would express their preferences for a given mix of public goods by 'voting (or threatening to vote) with their feet'. This competition ensured that local authorities provided the public goods demanded by the voters/consumers as efficiently as possible. The Tiebout model was developed with US county administrations in mind and was based on the assumption of free movement of people and goods and services. The Tiebout model does not apply more generally in the United States (that is between states) and certainly not in Europe where there is only very limited labour mobility and the added dimension of national versus European Union competence when it comes to the question of policy integration. But no one claims that the Tiebout model is applicable. Its main contribution was to provide the basic theoretical framework on which subsequent work, especially in the field of fiscal federalism, then built.

The theoretical literature was considerably strengthened by the ideas of Hayek. If competition could be a continuous process of exploration in markets for goods, why should it not be applied to 'markets for policies' or by extension for regulation? Competition among rules or regulation could, therefore, be seen as a means of ensuring dynamism in policy making in order to match the dynamic change in markets by ensuring a never ending search for better rules or regulation. Thus, in some economic writings on the topic competition among diverse rules came to be seen as preferable to a single set of rules (Hosli, 1992). Competition among rules could be said to have a number of advantages over common or harmonized policies. Competition offered choice and diversity in policy, as opposed to the rigidity of a single centralized system of rules. Following Hayek, competition among regulatory authorities offered the advantage of continuous experimentation, without which improvements and modernisation of policy would be more difficult. Competition among regulatory authorities also offered a means a minimizing the costs of regulatory failure. Regulatory failure by one authority would be more easily identified and the risks of regulatory failure at a lower level was less costly than regulatory failure at the centre.

The limitations of competition among rules were also recognised. These mainly took the form of negative externalities. Economic writing on the topic, therefore, tends to focus on how to maximize the application of competition by internalising these externalities.

The more general theoretical work has also been applied to the case of the European integration. For example, Siebert and Koop argue for 'institutional competition' within the European Union rather than *ex ante* harmonisation (Siebert and Koop, 1990). The concept of competition between policies rather than centralization has been one of the central tenants of German Ordoliberalism (Sally, 1994). The Ordoliberalism of the Freiburg School argued against centralization of regulatory authority. Although its influence in German federalism may have waned in recent years, the preference for decentralization may still have some influence on German views on the transfer of power to European authorities. In addition to the benefits of competition among rules listed above, the benefits in terms of European integration would also include the elimination of any need for common policies at the European level (Siebert and Koop, 1990).

2.3 Competition Among Rules in Practice

In addition to the theoretical understanding of competition among rules, a highly pragmatic understanding of the concept has emerged from efforts to address the problems of divergent technical regulations within the European Union. Experience during the 1970s showed that barriers to trade resulting from different national technical regulations could not be effectively removed by harmonisation. If it took 11 years to agree on the technical regulations for mineral water, it was clear that a genuine internal market would never be achieved. National technical regulation and legislation was, in any case, outpacing European efforts at harmonisation (Sun and Pelkmans, 1993).

Beginning in the 1970s the EU, therefore, progressively developed its new approach to technical regulation. This consisted of establishing harmonised, minimum essential requirements and then providing for mutual recognition of different national regulations that exceeded these common standards. This approach emerged, in part, as the product of discussions on how to reconcile different approaches to technical regulation in Germany and France and, in part, from rulings of the European Court of Justice, most notably in the Cassis de Dijon case, which employed the principle of mutual recognition. The new approach means that, provided minimum health and safety regulations were satisfied, any product sold in one member state can be legally sold in other member states. European harmonisation may determine a common set of minimum requirements, but even when there are no such harmonized rules, the ECJ may decide that 'equivalent' protection for consumers exists. Voluntary technical standards may help in this determination but they are only one means of proving compliance. The development of such voluntary technical standards is delegated to the non-governmental standards bodies. Finally, conformity assessment is carried out in each member state, by certified bodies and their test results recognised by the regulatory authorities in other countries. When initially developed the new approach represented a compromise between the French (and Italian) practice of including technical norms in its legislation, and the German practice of delegating standards making to the standards bodies and using compliance with DIN standards as convenient means of proving compliance with statutory requirements. The need for a compromise was, in part, driven by a heated trade dispute between France and Germany in the early 1980s over the impact of the respective national practices on market access.

Once developed for technical regulations, the approach was adapted to other areas of economic integration in Europe. In services mutual recognition took the form of home country control, in other words recognition of the regulatory jurisdiction of other member states' authorities in most aspects of service provision (excluding market conduct). Minimum essential health and safety standards found their parallel in minimum prudential requirements for financial services. Competition among national regulators was seen as the best means of achieving the ultimate objective of creating a single market and, following a period in which national regulations compete, a common EU regulatory policy based on a synthesis of best practice. The expectation, therefore, was that competition among the national rules would bring about convergence (Majone, 1990: p 40). This elaboration of the 'new approach' to cover services was motivated by the practical objective of injecting momentum into European market integration. The practical application of competition among rules in the

ean Union was, therefore, motivated by pragmatism. It saw competition
g rules as *complementary* to harmonisation, not as an *alternative* (Sun and
Pelkmans, 1993).

Consideration of competition among rules in practice also requires some
consideration of the disadvantages. First and foremost, negative externalities
limit the scope for competition among rules. For example, competition among
environmental regulation is generally accepted as being inappropriate when
pollution created by low standards in one country affects another country, such as
in the case of acid rain or river borne water pollution. There are also transactions
costs associated with continuously changing national regulations. Transactions
costs concern the administration of regulation, but most importantly those
affected by changes in regulation. Business interests are just as likely to stress the
costs of frequent policy changes and regulatory drift (progressive change in
regulatory policy) as they are to call for regulatory competition. This has not
prevented business interests using regulatory competition as a rationale for policy
ranges generally sought by them, such as tax reductions and lower non-wage
labour costs. Business interests may also stress the benefits in clear and
predictable regulation, even when this may be less liberal.

3   THE CONDITIONS FOR EFFECTIVE COMPETITION AMONG RULES?

The kind of conditions that have to be satisfied for effective competition among
rules will vary depending upon the form competition among rules takes. In the
case of regulatory emulation, all that is needed is sufficient transparency for the
observer to be in a position to assess the effectiveness of the policy in its national
application.

The preconditions for regulatory competition are, however, more demanding,
especially when it comes to regulatory competition between discrete regulatory
policies. In the case of regulatory competition, the fundamental precondition is
that regulatory jurisdictions market interact (Nicolaides, 1991). This means, in
effect, that actions taken by a regulator in one jurisdiction must have effects on
factors of production or market participants in other jurisdictions. In practice this
means the four freedoms, that is freedom of movement for goods, services, capital
and labour (Siebert and Koop, 1990). If the factors of production are not mobile,
there will be little competition. For example, differences in the regulation of
commercial airlines will have little effect on investment if foreign ownership or
control of national flag carriers is prohibited. There is a need for open markets in
goods and services because without it companies located in a country which
introduces regulation with adverse effects of competitiveness would not be

penalized through lost market share, at least in the short run. Thus there would be little incentive for regulators to modify their policies.

In the European Union the free movement of capital has been achieved since the implementation of the 1988 Directive on capital liberalisation in 1990. Foreign investment is still *de facto* blocked or partially restricted in a few sectors, such as airlines, nuclear energy and the utilities, etc. as a result of national monopolies (OECD, 1992). This, together with the possibility of private restrictive agreements and monopolies, means an effective European level competition policy may be a precondition for competition among rules. The EU has developed reasonably effective competition policies, especially under Art 85 and 86 (EEC) against private restrictive practices, but is still in the early stages of using Art 90 (EEC) against public enterprises and monopolies.

Although there is capital mobility in the EU there is little labour mobility despite legislation introducing mutual recognition of the professions (Brazier, Lovecy and Moran, 1993). This is due to continuing regulatory issues, such as in the field of pensions and social security rights, but, more importantly, due to language and cultural factors. The lack of labour mobility has led proponents of regulatory competition to accept that regulatory competition is essentially competition among locations for mobile capital (Siebert and Koop, 1990).

The continuing efforts to complete the internal market mean that there are fewer and fewer barriers to markets for services and especially goods. But local preferences, and the need for a local presence in order to gain effective access to certain markets, still mean that the effects of regulatory competition could be dampened even in such markets (Woolcock, Hodges and Schreiber, 1991). Outside Europe, developments during the 1980s have also resulted in a significant liberalisation of capital. This, combined with technological developments, means that capital mobility is high among OECD countries and a growing number of middle income and developing countries. Goods markets are relatively open and services markets are beginning to open. Consequently, the conditions for regulatory competition exist on a global scale.

The second condition for effective regulatory competition is transparency, both with regard to the nature of regulatory differences but also the effects of such differences. If companies are to opt for preferred locations based on differences in regulatory policy or practice, they must be fully aware of these differences. Equally, regulators must be clear of the distinctions between their policies and those of other countries or regions, if they are to 'compete' or adapt their regulatory policies to move closer to other countries. In general this requires clear and probably codified regulation. The absence of a clear and predictable regulatory environment may, in itself, be a deterrent to investors, who may opt for a more regulated location if it offers predictability.

Consumers and interest groups, such as environmental lobbies, must also be aware of the differences in products, levels of environmental or safety protection if they are to exercise their preferences both directly through purchasing decisions, or indirectly through pressing for higher standards. [i]In the European Union transparency has, in general, been the first objective of any EC legislation aimed at liberalisation or harmonisation. But transparency is still a real issue. Simply, the national provisions implementing the Internal Market Directives can be numbered in thousands, assume different legal forms, incorporating different national practices and in different languages. Specialists in regulatory bodies and companies with a direct interest in a fairly narrow sector may be able to retain an overview, but it is questionable that consumers really have good comparative information. In other words, there is still a real issue of asymmetrical information among regulators, the regulated sectors and consumers.

In some cases there may be no opportunity for consumers to express their preference effectively. For example, the German system of recycling packaging created waves in the EU and nearly bankrupted the system provided because consumers used the opportunity of recycling in such large numbers. In other countries the absence of credible recycling systems means that consumers have not had the opportunity of exercising a preference for recycling even at higher cost.

While there are problems with transparency in the nature of regulatory differences, these are less important than a general lack of transparency in the effects of different national regulatory policies. For regulatory competition to be effective regulators must know the effects of any change of policy or difference created between national regulations. If the effects of a change in a discrete policy area, say corporation tax, on a key parameter, such as inward investment, is unclear because numerous factors affect investment decisions, the regulatory authority is less likely to act than when the effect of a policy change is immediate and obvious. An example of transparency in the effects of a regulatory change is the introduction of a withholding tax on investment in Germany which resulted in a significant shift of portfolio investment to Luxembourg (see below). In this case the high mobility of portfolio investment and transparency with regards to the effect of a policy change resulted in intense regulatory competition and forced the German regulators to change policy.

In many cases there will be limited transparency with regards to the effects of a change in regulatory policy because of linkages between policies. Regulatory policies are seldom discrete but generally embedded in a network of policies and practices. For example, in the case of competition between different forms of corporate governance, a change in takeover rules in one country is unlikely to result in regulatory competition, because of the network of regulation (capital markets, disclosure, bankruptcy legislation, company law, and so on) and market practice, which go to make up the system of corporate governance in a country. Thus, when Britain introduces or maintains regulation of takeovers favouring a market for corporate control, the pressure on other European countries to follow suit is limited (Woolcock, 1994a).

Another essential precondition for effective competition among rules is effective implementation and enforcement. A lack of implementation or enforcement of either national or European legislation means a general uncertainty about which 'rules' apply in any given location. This will limit regulatory competition. Lax implementation could result in competition in laxity and an undermining of the credibility of the Internal Market. If national authorities have no confidence in the measures taken in other countries, for example to ensure standards in food production, they would take action at the border in order to protect national consumer. In other words, competition in laxity would mean costs in terms of a renewed fragmentation of the European market. The importance of effective enforcement was recognised at least in 1992, with the establishment of the Sutherland Committee. The Sutherland Report and the subsequent European Commission proposals focused on strengthening mutual trust among regulators as a means of ensuring effective enforcement (Sutherland, 1992, Commission of the European Communities, 1993).

This brings us to the question of mutual recognition. It is possible to argue that mutual recognition is a precondition for effective regulatory competition. This may or may not be the case, the existence of global capital mobility certainly creates a form of regulatory competition. But there seems little doubt that mutual recognition intensifies regulatory competition. If the regulatory authority in a country is obliged to accept goods produced to a foreign standard or services provided according to the regulatory jurisdiction of a foreign regulator, there is a high degree of interaction between regulatory agencies. Within the European Union the 'new approach' introduced mutual recognition, so that conditions for regulatory competition are better than elsewhere.

This raises the question of what conditions have to be satisfied for mutual recognition to be effective. As a number of observers of European integration have pointed out, regulatory rapprochment is an important precondition for the credible exercise of mutual recognition. Mutual recognition is not really recognition of the other country's regulation, but that the other country's regulation is broadly equivalent in its objectives and effects (Majone, 1993 and Sun and Pelkmans, 1993).

4   THE IMPACT OF COMPETITION AMONG RULES

Before seeking to address the issues raised at the beginning of the paper in the conclusions, this section summarises a number of case studies. In so doing it draws on work carried out by other participants in the ESRC research programme.[1]

One can distinguish between different levels of competition among rules. At the national level, competition occurs between different national regulatory styles. At the horizontal and sectoral level it occurs between different statutes or regulation. This section considers the last two forms of competition among rules. Competition between national regulatory styles is not covered.[2]

4.1 Horizontal Policy Issues

The horizontal policy level covers issues such as social and environmental policies or national policies on technical regulations. The case studies considered in research by the author and other participants in the initiative tend to suggest that competition among rules at this level is generally between different national regulatory structures or philosophies, rather than between discrete pieces of regulation.

Perhaps the best example of competition between different regulatory structures can be found in clash between German and French approaches to *technical barriers to trade* in the early 1980s. The regulatory structure favoured by Germany was one based on the use of performance or output requirements combined with reference to voluntary technical standards. The structure favoured by France (and Italy) was one based on the inclusion of detailed specifications in statutory provisions. As illustrated by the adoption of the new approach, the German approach (minus any obligation to use a specific standard) proved more suitable for the EC level, mainly because it obviated the need to agree on what common regulatory requirements would be included in any EC legislation.

There are also differences in *tax structures* where some countries have relied on greater direct taxation and others on indirect taxation. Arguably the effects of competition among the tax regimes has brought about a convergence of structures, accompanied by some harmonisation, such as the provision of a floor for the levels of indirect taxation. Levels of corporation tax have, for example, converged over the last decade from around 50 per cent to an average of about 35 per cent in the EC. This suggests there has also some pressure for reductions in tax levels (Begg *et al.*, 1993). This reduction more or less coincides with the

---

[1] The author is grateful to all those who contributed to the discussion of case studies in competition among rules during a series of study group meetings organized at the Royal Institute of International Affairs during the autumn of 1993. He is particularly grateful to those who took the trouble to present papers. These were Stephen Smith (on taxation), Paul Cheshire (competition between locations), Albert Weale (environment), Michael Gold (social policy), George McKenzie (capital markets) and Francis McGowan (air transport).

[2] For a discussion of competition among rules at the national level see Woolcock, 1994b.

removal of capital controls and the concomitant increase in capital mobility towards the end of the 1980s.

National philosophies differ in *social policy*. The current British government and business view of social policy assumes that enhanced social provision means a reduction in efficiency. The predominant view in most continental European countries is that enhanced social provision contributes to social consensus and cohesion and thus to efficiency and prosperity (Gold, 1993). There is as yet little evidence of convergence between these different philosophies, despite competition in social policies in the EU. This does not mean that there has not been progress in adopting European policies on 'social regulation' such as on health and safety at work (Majone, 1992).

Another example of different national philosophies can be found in *environmental policies*. National policies have also achieved different stages of development in this field. In Germany, the Netherlands and Denmark environmental economics and the integration of environmental objectives in economic policy making has reached a developed stage. As a result these countries have developed clear national targets for the environment, which other policies are then geared to help achieve. This is not (yet) the case in countries such as Britain and France or in some of the 'southern' member states of the European Union where economic policy objectives have not yet been as affected by environmental policy objectives. In environmental policy one can see some convergence between policies. The Treaty on European Union included, for example, a requirement to consider environmental policy objectives in all EC policies. But this is still to be translated into detailed policy as it has been at a national level in the Netherlands and Germany.

There are some signs that competition among rules tends to work on horizontal levels through the pressure for convergence from below, that is from technical negotiations between experts rather than from open regulatory competition between countries. This was the case in the convergence between national approaches to technical regulation. It also appears to be the case in the environmental sector. This may be because national regulatory structures or styles are so entrenched that no government or national regulatory agency is prepared to accept, explicitly, that it has been forced to change to fall into line with what other countries do. As the technical regulations (paradigm) case showed, however, experts working on practical issues may soon find ways of getting around differences in structure or style.

Regulatory emulation seems to have been important in some cases. For example, the general move towards independent central banks is, in part, due to the observation, over many years, of the effectiveness of the German model in maintaining price stability and sustained economic growth. But the political weight of a country, or countries, has also clearly affected discussions. In the case of monetary policy, Germany's economic strength meant that it was able to hape the agenda. In environmental policy the importance of Germany has also played a role. But consider, by way of contrast, the Danish unilateral move to raise the level of environmental regulation in the case of bottles.

4.2 Sectoral Level Competition Among Rules

At a sectoral level the degree to which individual regulations are embedded with others is less, so that one would expect a higher degree of competition among rules. But even here there are factors which limit the impact of competition among rules.

The adoption of the EC Directive on Free Movement of Capital in 1988 required the removal of all *capital controls* by 1990 (or slightly later for Greece and Portugal). Even in core areas of the Internal Market, however, this did not mean total free capital movement. For example, regulation of financial markets, designed to limit investor and systemic risk, still differed from country to country. It was therefore necessary for the EC to adopt legislation to open financial markets. As noted above, the existence of national public or private monopolies, such as in the energy, transport or telecommunications sectors can limit investment.

In the EC the efforts to establish a single financial market have included provisions on banking, investment services and the creation of a single currency. The banking provisions were implemented at the beginning of 1993. While these provided for a single passport and home country control for banking, the need for local market presence in order to gain effective access, at least in retail banking, has meant that the degree of competition between the major national banks has been fairly muted to date (Woolcock, Hodges and Schreiber, 1991). In the field of securities, transactions concern a smaller number of market operators. Consequently, one would expect that the free movement of capital would result in more intense competition among rules. But even here the evidence to date suggests that regulatory competition is limited.

The growth in trading in securities in the London market is a reflection of the size of the London capital market, which is itself a result of past regulatory policies. London now accounts for no less than 95 per cent of all the foreign equity traded within the EC. This business is important for London, accounting for some 44 per cent of its turnover, and has, therefore, resulted in efforts to consolidate London's leading position. The development of trading systems, such as the SEAQ, were designed to attract foreign equity trade. This competition for equities trade has had a significant impact on some continental markets. Amsterdam has, for example, lost an important share of equities trading to the London. Even 30 per cent of German shares are traded in London but, as this mainly affects the larger companies, it is less of a threat to the German stock exchanges. But the competitive pressure has led to regulatory changes in Germany in an effort to retain market share (Steil, 1993).

In the area of securities there have been efforts to limit competition by national legislation, such as the Italian law introduced in January 1992 which requires securities firms to be separately capitalised if they are to conduct business in the Italian market. This makes it more expensive for non-Italian firms to participate. The so-called Club-Med-Group of countries including France, Italy and Belgium have also sought to prevent their nationals trading on 'un-regulated' markets. The British have seen this as an attempt to prevent the growth of trading on the SEAQ system. The Club-Med-Group of countries have also succeeded in getting a transitional period until 1996 during which they will be able to retain their dualist structures. In other words, banks will not be able to operate on securities markets in these countries until 1996 (Steil, 1993).

In investment services, as in other areas, EC level legislation has set out to establish common minimum regulatory requirements, such as the inclusion of securities firms in the capital adequacy provisions. Such legislation will, therefore, limit the degree of regulatory competition and regulatory arbitrage in a sector in which one would expect competition to be at it most intense. There is also some doubt that there will be a 'competition in laxity', and there is a broad expectation among analysts that regulators will want to provide investors with a security for their investment. This means providing a well regulated and secure market rather than participating in a 'race to the bottom' (Steil, 1993).

As noted above, one example of how regulatory competition is more intense in a discrete case is that of the withholding tax on investment income. In 1989 Germany introduced a 10 per cent withholding tax on investment income, but within about six months some DM 100 bn in capital flowed out of Germany into other countries (Begg *et al.*, 1993). The German tax authorities tried to persuade their EC partners to introduce a similar tax, but when this attempt failed, the German authorities were obliged to drop the tax. Such intense competition between tax levels is what might be expected in an area so immediately affected by the free flow of capital, but it appears to be the exception more than the rule.

The *pharmaceuticals sector* in Europe illustrates how the absence of mutual trust in regulation, in this case in the certification and registration of new drugs, prevents the operation of mutual recognition. In the late 1970s efforts were made to introduce a form of mutual recognition, the so-called multi-state procedure, in order to reduce the costs of duplication of national registration procedures for new drugs. Under this system, when a new drug was approved by one national registration authority, the applicant company could apply to another four national registration authorities with the expectation that these would also approve the drug. But national drug registration authorities were not prepared to recognise drugs registered in other countries. The procedure was seldom used, and when it was the national regulators reverted to safeguard actions in order to block mutual recognition.

Efforts to strengthen the multi-state procedure in the early 1980s failed for similar reasons. In 1990 the European Commission proposed the introduction of a two level approach. Under the new proposals, finally adopted in 1992, new sophisticated products will be registered by a new centralised European Medicines Agency and more straightforward drugs based on established active elements will be subject to mutual recognition. The central medical agency will draw on national expertise, but will in effect be one of the first quasi-independent regulatory bodies to be established in the EC, although its scope for discretionary decision making is constrained. In order to limit the risks of regulatory capture, the legislation setting up the agency seeks to ensure that decisions are based on scientific judgments. Ultimately, decisions will be taken by the European Commission, following the expert opinion of the scientists. The Commission will have some flexibility to take account of Community interests, but in order to safeguard against the abuse of such powers, decisions to approve or disapprove registration will be subject to review by the European Court of Justice.

There has been some convergence of regulatory policy in pharmaceuticals, on the length of the patent life of new drugs. The effective patent life, in other words the number of years a patented drug can be sold on the market before it faces competition from generic drugs offering the same effects, is of central importance to the pharmaceutical industry. The longer the effective patent life the more funds companies can recoup from their investment and thus the more they can invest in the development of new products. In an example of international regulatory competition, the pressure came from the United States and Japan, where legislation was introduced to extend the effective patent life. European industry pressed for similar action in Europe, which was, after some resistance from a number of countries, finally adopted.

The pharmaceutical sector, therefore, illustrates that mutual trust is essential for mutual recognition to work. It shows how the linking of a regulatory policy, price controls on drugs, to other policy areas, can help ensure that divergent national regulations continue to exist within the European market. In fact the divergent pricing policies created divergent industrial structures, which in turn helped to perpetuate the national policies. Finally, the sector shows that regulatory competition is not restricted to Europe, it can also operate globally.

4.3 A Race to the Bottom?

Much of the concern expressed about competition among rules is based on the fear that there will be a process of competitive deregulation which leads to a race to the bottom or sub-optimal regulation. This fear does not seem to be justified by the empirical work that has been carried out. The case studies considered by the RIIA study group, as well as earlier work by other authors, has, on the contrary, shown that the 'race to the bottom' scenario is unlikely.

In the European Union the risk of 'a race to the bottom' starting is limited by the efforts to establish common, minimum standards. In some cases there is a desire to establish harmonised regulation. This desire to limit the effects of competition is shared by governments, as illustrated in the case of taxation, where *harmonisation* set an effective floor of 15 per cent on any competition in value-added tax. There is also pressure from labour, consumer and environmental interest groups for minimum standards in labour market regulation, product safety and environmental protection. In labour market regulation there has been a broad consensus favouring harmonisation of health and safety provisions (Majone, 1992). Even in areas where there has been no agreement among all member states, such as employee consultation, the British opt out will not prevent the eleven agreeing on common rules.

There is also clear evidence of the ability of national regulators to maintain standards above those of the common EC floor. This is possible when, for example, there exists a broad national consensus on the need for such higher standards. This would suggest that the kind of pressure that would otherwise be forthcoming from companies that face higher costs, either does not materialise, because the companies themselves are a part of the consensus, or is neutralised by the political desire on the part of governments not to risk undermining the national consensus between parties or with interest groups. This kind of a consensus has been important in the social policy field in Germany and in the environmental policy field in Germany, the Netherlands and Denmark. The case of the German Packaging Ordinance shows how the consumer preference for recycling was more than strong enough to overcome domestic opposition from industry. It also shows how competition can result in higher standards within the EU, not just lower standards (Paul, 1994).

The existence of a broad national consensus means that governments are reluctant to change policy and thus undermine the consensus. With qualified majority voting on important Internal Market issues it only takes three member states to block any liberalising measure. Thus, if a number of countries are determined to retain higher environmental standards, they are able to do so. Provisions in the Treaty on European Union also make efforts to achieve high environmental standards an EU objective.

As noted above regulatory policies are often embedded in national regulatory regimes or practices. This limits the transparency of the effects of regulatory competition and makes it less likely that national regulators will seek to 'compete' by reducing the level of regulation.

Apart from these more political checks on any race to the bottom, there is also an economic rationale for maintaining levels of regulation. First, there is the case that market imperfections or externalities exist which require regulation.

Second, the case can and is made that higher levels of regulation bring benefits in terms of enhanced competitiveness. In environmental policy, for example, the case has been made that industry will benefit from higher national standards in that it will develop more sophisticated environmental technologies, which will enable it to compete more easily. This case has been made in Germany and has, by and large, been accepted by German industry.

A similar case for 'trading up' is made in the field of social policy. This case argues that if European industry is to compete with low cost countries in the developing world or with middle income countries that have considerably lower wages, it must trade up and produce higher value-added products. The case is made that European industries will never be able to compete head-to-head with the NICs on wage costs, so that attempts to trade down and produce goods more cheaply through lower wages will weaken rather than strengthen the competitive position of European industry. A sectoral level example of the case for trading up can be found in the regulation of financial markets. While a case might be made for deregulation as a means of attracting more international investment and business, the experience of the early deregulation initiatives in the 1980s was that investors are also concerned about the protection of their investment and are reluctant to place funds in a capital market which cannot provide sufficient protection for the investment. Therefore regulation to ensure the prudential security of financial institutions becomes a means of attracting investment.

In any given case a number of such factors may be brought to bear and thus limit the downward pressure that might otherwise result in a race to the bottom. The evidence so far, therefore, suggests that a race to the bottom is an unlikely scenario, although it cannot be excluded in all cases. In many cases the new directives have only just been introduced and it may be some time before it is possible to conclude, with any certainty, what the long term effects may be. While arguing that there is no major risk of a 'race to the bottom', Begg and others have suggested that possible future trends in taxation may result in continuous pressure on the ability to fund the welfare state. Corporation tax rates, as noted above, have already converged towards a lower level. It is not clear whether there will be further downward pressure on corporation taxation. On the one hand, it is possible to argue that most of the impact will have come with the introduction of full freedom of capital in 1990 (or 1992 for some member states). But capital mobility could further increase if there is an erosion of some of the still quite important local market characteristics which at present limit mobility.

At present labour mobility is also low and the indications are that it will remain relatively low. Marginal increases in labour mobility among high wage earning groups could, however, create downward pressure on higher levels of income tax and thus exacerbate the problem (Begg *et al.*, 1993).

5 CONCLUSIONS

This chapter posed a number of questions in the introduction. The first of these was what would be the balance between centralisation and decentralisation, between harmonisation and competition among rules? The preliminary finding that emerges from the case studies considered in this paper is that the scope for competition among rules is fairly limited. The main reason for this is that the conditions for effective competition among rules are not fully satisfied. There are still asymmetries of information and areas in which there is no transparency as to the nature of regulatory differences. The main limiting factor, however, appears to be in the absence of much transparency in the effects of different regulatory policies. If regulators are not convinced that changing policy in order to 'compete' will have much effect, they are unlikely to wish to sacrifice other policy objectives. This finding must be seen as preliminary, because there is still much work needed before it is possible to say we have a real understanding of what is going on. The finding is, however, broadly in line with other work.

If it is correct that the scope for competition among rules is important but limited, it is unlikely to offer an easy option for a middle way between integration, and the ultimate establishment of European regulatory agencies and disintegration. In other words, competition among rules will not spare national governments and regulators the difficult question of how to establish European level regulatory bodies, which are both effective and accountable.

Fears about regulatory competition resulting in a 'race to the bottom', 'zero regulation' or sub-optimal regulation seem to be uncalled for. There are a number of factors that will, in practice, limit any downward competition. Indeed, as the case of packaging has shown, competition among rules can also result in higher standards. This does not mean that there will be no cases of downward competition. When the conditions for regulatory competition are satisfied there will be pressure. This was shown in the case of the German withholding tax, where capital mobility was important and the effects of the proposed increase in German taxes were transparent.

As many authors have pointed out competition among rules is not static. Indeed, one of the major benefits is seen to be that it provides for dynamism and continuous experimentation. Where competition among rules is effective, that is in the area above the common regulatory floors, there will be pressures for convergence and thus greater integration. As has been shown above, these could well come from below, in the sense of convergence in detailed technical fields leading to convergence in national styles or approaches. But there will also be pressure for divergence. The linking of policies in clusters could tend to consolidate national policy differences by weakening the effects of competition among rules. Competition would then revert or continue between national systems rather than between different approaches to regulation. This could then result in divergence.

In other words, the open-ended model of competition between different regulatory policies, in which there is a constant search for the best regulation, does not seem likely to be stable in reality. This is because the conditions for competition among rules are unlikely to be fully satisfied. Ultimately, it may still be a question of a choice between convergence, in which there are positive spill-over effects, or divergence in which the embedded nature of regulatory policy in national policy styles or philosophies results in spill backs.

On the other hand, regulatory rapproachment will tend to diminish the potential for competition between the poles of the lowest and highest standards within the EC and thus the pressure for convergence. As a result the impact of competition among rules will diminish with convergence, with the result that some residual national differences will remain. All this suggests that competition among rules will fulfill an important but limited role in European regulation. For reasons of externalities as well as the failure, in many cases, to meet the conditions needed to ensure that competition among rules operates, there will be a need for European level regulation. Competition among rules will, therefore, not spare the EU the difficult task of devising means of regulating European markets.

Will the EU's application of competition among rules be emulated by others? Regulatory competition within the EU is probably more intense than in other regional agreements, such as NAFTA, because of mutual recognition. The fact that there is no unrestrained 'race to the bottom' may, therefore, provide an important lesson for other regional agreements or multilateral agreements. The limits on downward pressure are, however, in part, a result of policy integration which does not exist to the same degree in other regions. The mutual recognition approach does already provide a model for third countries (Braithwaite, 1993), although it has only been applied to a very limited extent so far in NAFTA (compliance assessment) and GATT (non-binding call for it use in technical regulations).

Developments in European regulatory policy will have an important impact on third countries, because of the growing importance of regulatory policy in market access. At the moment it is simply too early to say what these developments will be. The EU will continue to incorporate competition among national regulations in a number of areas, and thus retain its diverse character *vis-à-vis* third countries, but the pressure for regulatory rapproachment, and possibly more central regulatory decision making, seems likely to continue. This means that third countries may have to come to terms with European level regulatory agencies.

REFERENCES

Begg, D. *et al.* (1993), *Making Sense of Subsidiarity: how much centralization for Europe?*, Centre for Economic Policy Research, London.

Braithwaite, J. (1993), *Prospects for win-win international rapproachment of regulation*, paper for OECD Symposium on managing regulatory relations between different levels of government, Paris, October.

Brazier, M., Lovecy, J. and Moran, M. (1993), *'Professional Regulation and the Single European Market: a study of the regulation of doctors and lawyers in England and France'*, January, mimeo.

Commission of the European Communities (1993), *Reinforcing the effectiveness of the internal market*, COM(93) 256, 2 June.

Dehouse, R. (1992), *Integration v. Regulation? Social regulation in the European Community*, European University Institute, Law 92/93.

Gold, M. (1993), *Social rights: continuity or convergence?*, paper for the RIIA study group on competition among rules, London, November.

Hosli, M. (1992), *Harmonization versus regulatory competition in the European Community*, mimeo, Centre for Policy Studies, Michigan.

McGee, A. and Weatherill, S. (1990), 'The evolution of the Single European Market: harmonization or liberalisation', *Modern Law Review* **53**, p. 578.

Majone, G. (1990), *Cross National Sources of Regulatory Policy-Making in Europe and the United States*, European University Institute, SPS 90/6.

Majone, G. (1992), *The European Community between Social Policy and Social Regulation*, European University Institute SPS No 92/27.

Majone, G. (1993), 'Mutual recognition in federal type systems', *EUI Working Papers: in political and social sciences*, SPS No 93/1 European University Institute, Florence.

Nicolaides, P. (1991), *Competition among rules*, mimeo, Maastricht, European Institute for Public Administration.

OECD (1992), *Trends in Foreign Direct Investment During the 1980s*, Paris.

Paul, J. (1994), *Economic integration and the race to the bottom*, paper presented at the Workshop on Regulatory Competition and Coordination, University of Warwick Law School.

Sally, R. (1994) 'Theories of the social market and Ordoliberalism: a political economy from Germany', mimeo, London School of Economics.

Siebert, H. and Koop, M. (1990), "Institutional competition: a concept for Europe?, *Kiel Working Paper* No 440, September.

Siebert, H. and Koop, M. (1993), 'Institutional competition versus centralization: Quo vadis Europe?', *Kiel Working Paper* No 548, January.

Steil, B. (1993), *Competition, Integration and Regulations in EC Capital Markets*, RIIA, July.

Sun, J. and Pelkmans, J. (1993), *1992, Regulatory Competition and Business*, paper presented to the ECSA Third Biannual International Conference, 27 May.

Sutherland, (1992), *The Internal Market after 1992: meeting the challenge*, Report to the EC Commission by the High Level Group on the Operation of the Internal Market (Sutherland Report).

Tiebout, C. (1956), 'A pure theory of local expenditures', *Journal of Political Economy*, **64** (5).

Woolcock, S., Hodges, M. and Schreiber, K. (1991), *Britain Germany and 1992: the limits of deregulation*, Pinter/RIIA.

Woolcock, S. (1994a), 'Competition in forms of corporate governance in the European Community: the case of Britain', in R. Dore and S. Berger (eds), *Integration and Institutional Competition in the Global Economy* (forthcoming), University Press of America.

Woolcock, S. (1994b), *The Single European Market: Centralization or Competition among National Rules?*, Royal Institute of International Affairs, London.

5. The Impact of Rules

Keith Hartley, Andrew Cox and David G. Mayes

It is clear from the research of recent years (see Mayes and Burridge, 1993, for a survey) that the impact of the measures implementing the Single European Market has been complex. Firms and markets have responded, but not necessarily in the manner anticipated. In this chapter we focus in particular on the impact of the rules on public procurement, but the problem applies over the whole range of goods, services, labour and capital.

1 THE COSTS OF NON-EUROPE

Although Pelkmans and Winters (1987) set out at an early stage the major mechanisms through which the single market might operate, there has been a considerable reluctance to quantify either actual or expected progress. The European Commission (Emerson *et al.*, 1988) undertook a major exercise with the seventeen volumes of consultants' reports in *The Costs of Non-Europe* but it described the potential for change if a single market were achieved rather than estimating what was actually likely to happen.[1]

One of the great disadvantages of most previous forward-looking quantitative work on economic integration (reviewed in Mayes, 1995c) is that it is based on comparative statics. It describes what the end point is likely to be rather than tracing out the process by which that transformation takes place. One of the most striking insights from the ESRC Single European Market Research Programme has been into the complexity of that process of change and the degree to which that process can affect the outcome.

Thus *The Costs of Non-Europe* painted a scenario of gains attainable through exploiting economies of scale and lowering prices towards those prevailing in the most competitive markets. The Emerson *et al.* report (entitled *The Economics of 1992*), which draws together the ideas from *The Costs of Non-Europe*, approaches this by adumbrating the barriers inhibiting a single market (the physical, fiscal and technical barriers explained in Chapter 1). These relate to differences in technical standards, restrictions on transport, border delays,

---

[1] The well known 'popular' summary of the ideas and findings, *The Cecchini Report*, Cecchini (1988), named after the chairman of the committee overseeing this programme of work, does not contain the more detailed calculations and quantification.

differences in customary behaviour, problems in gaining recognition of skills, difficulties in establishing local operations, differences in tax rules, and so on. The Report then explains what the European economy might look like if those barriers did not exist and the economy operated like a single market. This is achieved by a series of sectoral studies which seek to address the extent of the realizable gains and then a macro-economic simulation of what this will imply if it feeds through the economy as a whole.

It is possible to be critical of this exercise in its own terms (summarised in Mayes and Burridge, 1993). The extent of the distortions may be mis-estimated, the economies of scale attainable may be outdated (Geroski, 1989), the macro-economic feedback may be incomplete – particularly the role of increased investment and competition in increasing the rate of economic growth (Baldwin, 1989). However, the more important concern is that this method of analysis does not address the main issue at stake, namely 'what will the impact of the single market be?' It does not seek to explain what will happen in three main respects. It does not forecast the extent to which the barriers will be removed, it does not explore in any detail how behaviour might respond and lastly, it does not explore the path or mechanism of change in any detail.

Many of the barriers to a single market have not been of a form that is readily removed by the stroke of a pen, unlike the removal of tariffs or quotas. While the legislation thus far enacted may have had a substantial impact, many areas remain largely untouched. In industries, such as insurance (Mayes and Hart, 1994) and leasing (Matthews and Mayes, 1994), the methods of opening up markets offer only limited opportunities for operating across the borders of the member states. In this instance some of the most effective barriers relate to differences in tax regimes, which are not being addressed, at least in this stage of integration. The major form of integration, in some cases, appears to be through ownership across the borders of member states but then operating each market relatively separately. However, it is important not to over-emphasize how long such separation might endure. In securities markets some Australian companies now sell directly in New Zealand using mail and telecommunications links without the need for any local offices or presence at all. Direct insurance selling can also overcome some of the boundaries.

The component chapters in Mayes (1991) suggested that, for many industries, focusing at the European level was largely irrelevant for their strategies which were global. Chemicals and commercial vehicles are clear examples. Indeed, a European level focus might be detrimental to the growth and profitability.

Even looking at the list of measures outlined in the 1985 White Paper does not provide a good indication of the changes as some measures have not been enacted as originally intended and others not fully implemented (see Gold, Matthews and Mayes,. 1995 for illustrations in the social field).

In other instances, although the barriers are being removed they are to be reduced over a much longer period of time than that implicit in *The Costs of Non-Europe* which effectively assumes that the full force of the removal of the barriers comes into effect at the beginning of 1993.

Hence, putting these items together we can more realistically assume that the initial stimulus is rather smaller than that implied in *The Economics of 1992* and combines the effect of a more limited set of measures, limits to the measures themselves and incomplete implementation. Secondly, we should assume that this stimulus will be spread over a considerable number of years, some before 1993 and some lasting out towards the end of the century (this would also include improvements in implementation and enforcement). Thirdly, it seems reasonable that the response to the stimuli will be rather less than a single market because of the ability of firms to continue to segment markets to a considerable extent. Fourthly, offsetting these dampening and delaying factors is the growing dynamic response from more intensive competition and increased investment. This would give a response path rather more like that of RR in Figure 5.1 compared to CC as a characterization of the projection in *The Economics of 1992*. The actual paths are arbitrary. In particular, the second cross-over of the two curves could occur at any time over a wide range of dates from the last part of this century onwards.

The real difficulty is that it is not possible to observe the RR curve, which is the difference between the European economy with and without the single market. We can observe the actual performance of the European economy. The temptation is to speculate what would have happened without the single market measures and the actual growth performance. The counter factual would in, any case, be a highly artificial construct. The European countries would have pressed ahead with measures increasing integration. The 'widening' versus 'deepening' debate might have been resolved more in favour of widening, with a more rapid expansion of the EC to include new members or associates. The list of possibilities is long.

A normal response in these circumstances where the choice is wide is to make one or more simple and transparent assumptions (Mayes, 1978). This is the approach of Buigues and Sheehy (1993), who assume that the EC would have grown at its previous medium-term rate over the years after 1986. However, even this can be a highly misleading procedure. In the first place, using longer run trends has to 'see' right through the business cycle. When Buigues and Sheehy were writing the EU economy was doing rather well. GDP was around 3 per cent above previous performance so they felt able to suggest that around half of the possible gains outlined in the Cecchini Report might already have been realised.

Unfortunately, the business cycle turned down thereafter to the extent that at its lowest points it was below the extrapolation of the previous growth rate. If

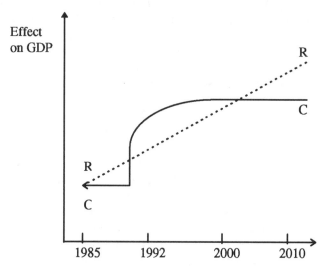

Figure 5.1   Adjustment paths

nothing else, this method confused the cycle with the trend. In the same way that one would not want to ascribe all the improvement in the upturn of the cycle to the impact of the Single Market, one would not want to blame the downturn on it.

It is unlikely to be until we have seen at least a couple of complete business cycles that we will be able to judge if there has been a noticeable change in longer run growth since the mid-1980s. Even then it may be difficult to decide how much of this to ascribe to the completion of the internal market and how much to, say, more effective pursuance of anti-inflationary monetary policies.

Trend extrapolation is, in any case, misleading as some of the previous trend will have been due to the adjustments in response to previous stages in the process of European integration. This would thus tend to increase the base from which the impact of the single market is judged and hence reduce the estimates of its subsequent impact. There are no 'right' answers in undertaking this sort of exercise. The more common approach (see House of Lords, 1985, for example) would be to try to identify the size of the shocks on the system and then trace them through with an econometric model in just the same way that the ex-ante estimates of the shocks were traced through in *The Economics of 1992* (Emerson *et al.*, 1988). Even then it is difficult to provide estimates which will be universally accepted. If the model is (re-)estimated over the period which includes the impact of the shock then some of the result will get bound up in the estimates, as we expect a structural change, particularly one involving a change in public policy, to change people's behaviour (often referred to as the Lucas critique). Hence using a model estimated over the post 1986 period will tend to obscure some of the impact of the single market.

By the same token, ignoring recent years will ignore the impact of influences other than the single market on people's behaviour. This omission will bias the estimates of the impact of the single market. A clearer picture may be obtained by using both models, or by permitting the parameters of the model to change so that the range of plausible outcomes can be explored. However, none of these methods is likely to produce the definitive answers which are sought.

Given these drawbacks, the sensible first step, rather than looking at the overall evolution of the economy, is to explore the extent to which it has approached a single market. Such an exploration can involve determining whether the changes have been as a direct result of the single market legislation but this may prove to be unduly complex. Just noting the changes, irrelevant of cause, would be a considerable step forward.

Unfortunately such an exercise can only be undertaken on a sectoral basis and a comprehensive exercise would involve a rerun of *The Costs of Non-Europe*. This chapter therefore, proceeds by only looking at a section of the internal market. However, it is possible to go a little further at the general level. Mayes and Burridge (1993) suggest that on the basis of initial estimates it is possible to identify some onus of relative loss and gain. This assessment can be categorized in a number of ways. One is to look at the European economy at the industry level. A second is to consider the effects on a regional basis, while a third would be to explore the impact on a micro-economic basis, looking within industries at individual firms and across households and the groups in society.

Industries

The general range of manufacturing industry has been increasingly open to international competition over recent decades. Even though there may have been limited protection in Europe, if major firms were to be successful they needed to be internationally competitive in other markets where they received no special advantage. The main impact of the single market has been occurring in areas where that openness did not previously exist. The two most obvious examples are public purchasing and services and our more detailed focus in this chapter lies in the former category. It is therefore not surprising that attention in the ESRC research programme has focused on these areas including telecommunications, pharmaceuticals and financial services.

In service industries the protection came not through tariffs or taxes on the final products but from other regulatory restraints on the ability to trade, because qualifications were not recognised across borders, because regulatory systems varied, because cross-border trade was not permitted, etc. Thus for a wide range of financial services the European markets were effectively segmented. In insurance, for example (Mayes and Hart, 1994), there was some limited linkage. Some of the major Swiss companies, such as Zurich and Winterthur, had operated across borders, with a presence in Germany, but in general international alliances and takeovers only developed after 1985. Not all such acquisitions have been of one European company by another. The Australian insurer AMP bought London Life and Pearl in 1989, for example. The single market has appeared an investment opportunity on a world-wide basis.

Nevertheless, progress has been steady rather than headlong. It has required a steady stream of legislation in both life and non-life insurance, for example, to provide a genuine opening up of markets. Even so, the tendency has been to operate the various markets separately. Some companies, like Axa-Midi, have sought to combine several facets of their operations, while others have started direct selling without agents.

This last remark emphasises one of the problems for any market entry at the retail level. It is often necessary to have a network of agents or branches. Setting these up from scratch is very expensive and slow. The alternative is purchase of an existing chain. This latter also has a rather chequered history (Mayes and Hart, 1994). UK retailers and insurers have shown that it is possible to buy companies in the US reasonably readily. It has proved much more difficult to operate them profitably thereafter. Genuine integration requires major investment in computer systems. It also entails adequate similarity of products. Marks and Spencer found, for example, that although it could sell readily to tourists in London, nevertheless it had to adapt its style to the local behaviour if it was to operate successfully in France and Belgium.

It has widely been expected (Mayes and Shipman, 1992) that the difference in reported rates of return in retailing in the UK compared with Germany would encourage German retailers to invest in the UK. This has indeed happened to some extent with Aldi at the lower end of the market but the international relationships have remained relatively limited.

Wholesale financial services have proved much more amenable to international opening, with major development, particularly in the London market. Some of this has been co-incident rather than part and parcel of the single market. The dramatic removal of the internal barriers between sectors in the so-called big bang of 1986 in the UK was domestically motivated but it helped encourage foreign institutions to enter the market.

In some cases, leasing is a good example, (Matthews and Mayes, 1993) the regulatory process has not touched the main barriers segmenting the European markets, principally tax rules, but partly accounting standards. Because the new legislation has tried to be generic rather than industry specific some industries are likely to continue to be segmented at the national level.

There has, however, been little if any attempt to document the benefit from these changes. Most studies have documented progress. Brazier, Lovecy and

Moran (1993), for example, show how the regulation of lawyers and doctors has responded. Even though there may not have been much direct requirement to harmonise, nevertheless the national professions have moved somewhat closer together. The benefit is expected to come from a competitive reduction in margins – *The Economics of 1992* places some emphasis on the extent of the differences in the cost of financial services – increased choice, more rapid innovation and possibly economies of scale.

It is the case of public procurement where the gains should be more obvious. In the case of railway equipment (Mayes, 1991) the restructuring of the industry was striking even in advance of the new legislation coming into effect. A small number of large groupings emerged, one headed by GEC–Alsthom and the other by Asea Brown–Boveri, replacing or at least taking over what had been national industries in most of the member states. This process of concentration has continued. Clearly in this case there had been major inefficiencies, particularly in the smaller member states. Even so it has not become apparent that foreign competition has made any real headway in the member states which had major producers, with the exception of the UK. It would not be unduly sceptical to suggest that the UK has been prepared to treat procurement differently, even in industries where it was a major producer. It has been prepared to accept foreign competition and indeed encourage it. Iceland has also been a clear exception in the EEA (Mayes and Albrecht, 1994) with very open tendering. However, in that case there is no local industry in most of the relevant instances.

Privatization of major public entities, including telecommunications, has also meant that a large portion of public purchasing has also moved into the private sector and hence that implicit or explicit pressures for local preferences in purchasing have largely disappeared. The UK has not, however, except in a limited number of cases, gone the whole way and allowed public utilities and former state enterprises to be sold to foreign companies.

One area where the move out of the public sector has been limited is in the field of health. Here the pressure on public procurement has come from ballooning costs. With governments across the European Union facing pressures to control their deficits and borrowing in the run up to EMU, the increasing demand for expenditure on health has provided a serious challenge. The changes in procurement of pharmaceuticals in Germany, for example (Mayes and Hart, 1994), have been driven by the considerations of cost rather than the pressure from the single market. However, these pressures are slowly beginning to emerge. The Medicines Agency and other steps to make the testing and registration of medicines a less repetitive process are likely to have an increasing impact on costs but the costs of developing new preparations will remain.

Taken altogether then, the picture has been one of steadily evolving change. There has not been the sorts of drastic changes that occurred in, for example, New Zealand, when it deregulated in the 1980s, nor even to the extent of the UK, he structure of manufacturing industry changed markedly after 1979 and Soteri, 1994). Cumulatively the change will be very substantial but in the rest of the world have been more influential in many areas of manufacturing industry, such as electronics, clothing and textiles. European industry has had to respond to an external challenge. The single market has in this respect been very much a response to pressures from industry, which has moved its policy focus away from external protection. It is, however, clear that some of the original proponents of the single market in the mid-1980s saw it as a means of increasing domestic competition in Europe behind effective external barriers (Mayes, 1991). This view was also expressed by de Clerq in the Commission (Mayes *et al.*, 1993). In what follows we explain why progress in public procurement is likely to be more measured.

Regions

There has been a well expressed fear (NIESR, 1991) that the development of the Single Market would disadvantage some regions relative to others. Indeed, the fear was that, without offsetting measures, some of the more peripheral regions of the EU might be disadvantaged in absolute as well as relative terms.

It is notable that neither the Cecchini Report nor *The Economics of 1992* devote any real time to the regional consequences of single market. The problem was addressed only afterwards but by the time of the Delors Report on Economic and Monetary Union in 1988 it had been recognised as a key imperative for action (Begg and Mayes, 1993). The structural funds were, of course, in operation at this time and the issue of 'cohesion' had been mentioned in the Single European Act. However, the mere fact that it was felt necessary to double the structural funds shows the change in priorities that had taken place by the time it became clear how the single market was developing.

While there is considerable room for debate it is clear that the more naive models of equalization do not apply, or at least not without very long delays or unacceptable social costs. As the work of Nam and Reuter (1991) illustrates, firms are only partly driven by labour costs in finding suitable locations for production. Proximity to markets and the availability of a network of business services and pool of skilled labour are also important factors. For those reasons alone Nam and Reuter take a more optimistic view of the prospects of Objective 2 regions with declining existing industries than they do of the most disadvantaged, Objective 1, regions, especially where the latter are peripheral in geographical terms. Thus on this basis there is a much better prospect for South Wales, Southern Scotland and Northern Ireland than there is for the Highlands and Islands, Western Ireland, Northern Finland, Northern Sweden and other such remote areas with limited populations.

Undoubtedly the EU's structural programmes are assisting the disadvantaged regions by helping improve infrastructure and the quality of human capital. This should enable them to compete rather better in the single market. However, it is unlikely to make them gainers on a similar scale to many of the core regions. In any case there are many production locations round the world where more 'favourable' labour conditions can be found in the sense of low wages, limited non-wage labour costs and relatively less onerous health and safety conditions than in the EU. Successful regional development will need to be more substantially based (NIESR, 1991).

While there are some decidedly footloose investment projects which follow investment incentives, these present a problem rather than a solution for the less advantaged regions. A zero sum game with the regions competing against each other can readily be the prime result. Furthermore, some of these operations have relatively little impact on the local economy.

Amin and Tomaney (1995) are particularly harsh in their criticism of what they see as the inadequacy of the EU's policies towards the disadvantaged regions. They are strongly of the view that the single market favours the 'advanced' regions. Although O'Donnell (1993), among others, has pointed out that telecommunications and improved transport conditions are reducing the importance of distance in industrial production, Amin and Tomaney stress the extent to which 'learning' plays a key role in the development of products and processes. This tends to place an emphasis on the importance of existing centres of research and knowledge (the 'archipelago' Europe of Hingel (1991) with most of the 'islands of innovation' occurring with the more advanced regions of member states).

This arrangement would tend to concentrate the lower value added parts of production in the less favoured regions, thereby emphasising the split between disadvantaged and the advantaged. This vision is strikingly different from the fears that were expressed at the outset of the development of the single market – that there might be social dumping (Streeck, 1993), with companies moving their operations from the high cost high social benefit centres, such as Germany towards the lower cost lower social benefit regions of southern Europe. Those forces have been weaker than expected and it is not clear that EU policies played a particularly big role in offsetting them.

The threat to the disadvantaged regions is considerably amplified by the prospect of EMU (Begg and Mayes, 1993; Mayes, 1995b). The further constraints imposed by stopping adjustment through the exchange rate and imposing fiscal stringency while these regions are undergoing substantial structural change makes their task of adjustment more difficult and the task of the EU's structural policies even more important.

The Micro-economic Impact

The impact of the single market on individual firms has been widely studied, although without any systematic pattern.   The impact on households has, however, been largely neglected, with one substantial exception – unemployment. One of the main reasons for this latter focus is that there are no obvious groupings of affected households other than those who are concentrated in less advantaged regions, who may enjoy lower incomes and wealth than elsewhere and those who suffer unemployment or poorer working conditions.

The Economics of 1992 addresses the issue of unemployment with some care, while youth and long-term unemployment had already been identified as structural problems for the EC and were being addressed through the structural funds (Objectives 3 and 4). The expectation was that, like all programmes of restructuring or reform which involve increasing the transparency of market signals by removing barriers (Bollard and Mayes, 1993), the initial effect would be a reduction in employment (increase in unemployment).   The relatively inefficient would be driven out of business by the relatively efficient.   The efficient would employ fewer people to produce the same output as the inefficient and hence employment as a whole would fall.   Even if the inefficient were not driven out of business or suffered loss of market share, they would be forced to become more efficient and, as a consequence, shed labour.

Only in the longer run would employment begin to pick up again as this increased efficiency and opportunity was reflected in increased external competitiveness, more rapid investment and an increase in the growth rate. Ostry (1995) describes how the reduction in regulatory barriers appears to be translated into faster growth in a study of some 80 countries by the IMF.   Similar conclusions would be reached from the ideas of endogenous growth theory.

Unemployment has certainly been a serious problem since the mid-1980s reaching 10 per cent in 1985 and above this over 1993–5 (*European Economy*, no. 6, 1995) but this problem has not been unique to the EU.   Other more widespread problems of adjustment to new competition from the newly industrializing countries, rapid technological change and the decline of traditional industries have *inter alia* led to problems throughout the western industrialized world (OECD, 1994).

There is a vigorous debate (see, for example, Gold, Matthews and Mayes 1995) whether the more protected EU labour markets have accentuated that problem. It is important to distinguish, in this regard, between EU policies governing the labour market generally and those which form part of the completing of the single market as such because there are two themes running through these measures. The measures directly related to the single market are concerned with ensuring the freedom of movement of labour. These, if anything, should assist employment and growth as they encourage the movement of people to areas where the relative demand for their skills is greatest. Labour mobility in the EU has remained relatively low despite these measures (Mayes, 1995a) reflecting, among other things, the importance of various social as well as economic constraints such as family ties, language and other local relationships. However, this lack of mobility has also been present within member states with persistent regional unemployment differentials.

The single market also opened up the prospect of labour moving because benefits varied across countries. Thus while social dumping might encourage firms to move to regions where non-wage labour costs were low, the potential employees might be encouraged to move in the opposite direction to regions where the social wage is high. If this had occurred to any large extent it could have resulted in a major rebalancing of the regional problems discussed in the previous section. The second associated raft of labour market policies has been to try to discourage this movement by establishing minimum standards for working conditions.[2]

Thus the pattern of social policy has had two elements to it. On one side there has been the encouragement of the free movement of labour, extending the benefit systems to migrants and their families on a similar basis to that available to nationals and the mutual recognition of qualifications. While on the other there have been measures to encourage employment in the less advantaged regions and to reduce the incentive to move simply because living and working conditions appear better in another part of the EU. (This is in addition to the measures which seek to establish the freedom to provide services and give the right of establishment in other member states.)

Clearly there are contradictions here. The UK government has been particularly outspoken (Department of Employment, 1993) in arguing that there is a danger that the imposition of some of the requirements for working conditions will increase the costs and decrease the flexibility of the European labour market. This in turn will both decrease the ability of European firms to compete on international markets and will limit the effectiveness of the single market in improving efficiency and reaping the potential gains. In Gold, Matthews and Mayes (1995) these measures to improve the operation of the labour are presented in the form of a three dimensional impact on 1) working conditions, 2) unemployment, and 3) efficiency. Ideally the measures would have a favourable impact on all three dimensions. This illustrates clearly the fact that forming the

---

[2] The current Social Action Programme covers thirteen areas: labour market, employment and remuneration, improvements of living and working conditions, freedom of movement, social protection, association and collective bargaining, information consultation and participation, equal treatment of men and women, vocational training, health and safety, protection of children and adolescents, the elderly and the disabled as well as a small miscellaneous category. Appendix 1 of Gold, Matthews and Mayes (1995) sets out the measures developed in EU social policy both before and after the Social Action Programme came into force in 1989. (It took two years to establish the programme after the Single European Act came into force.)

single market in the EU involves not just the removal of regulations which may discriminate against other member states but the creation of new regulations which will themselves have an impact. Thus in assessing the overall impact one must consider the combined effects of the removal or amendment of existing legislation and the introduction of the new.

In the case of much of the labour market legislation in the social chapter, we argue in Gold, Matthews and Mayes (1995) that its impact will be relatively limited. Some legislation, like that relating to workers' councils, does little more than validate existing systems in some member states, while in other areas such as health and safety it is not clear whether the compliance will be equal across the Union on the basis of the mechanisms currently in force. The most sensitive areas of benefit systems remain the competence of the member states. Here the adjustment mechanisms will depend very much on how the European labour force tends to react in practice. If labour mobility were to increase markedly then governments may very well begin to react. Most member states are already under considerable fiscal pressure with the wish to fight inflation and converge to the Maastricht criteria. Although social spending is among the last on the list for limitation it is not immune (Mayes, 1995b).

It is thus clear that the impact of the single market is likely to be considerably different from the more straightforward interpretations in *The Economics of 1992*. As we go on to stress in the remainder of the chapter, which looks at the specific case of public procurement, considerable opportunity remains for the exercise of market power. Amin and Dietrich (1991) emphasise the considerable power of multi-nationals in this framework, while Mayes in chapter 1 of Mayes *et al.* (1993) suggests that non-European multinationals may in fact have most to gain as they can treat the single market as a coherent entity without having to unwind the production patterns of the past which followed the pre-existing national distortions. One main reason which permits market power to be retained is the lack of effective legislation or enforcement mechanisms.

The single market is permissive. Firms may act on a Europe-wide level if they wish to. They are not compelled to. They do not have to break off existing market links just because the rules for public purchasing permit new entrants. Entry by such firms is still to be determined. It is not guaranteed. In the same way the incentive which led the purchasing authorities to let contracts to local suppliers continue to exist. It will depend on both the effectiveness of the directives covering public procurement and their enforcement how much practice will actually change.

2 PUBLIC PROCUREMENT IN THE SINGLE MARKET

Public procurement was seen as a major area for potential gain from the impact of the Single Market as it was characterised by substantial distortions in favour of domestic producers. It remains to be seen how far this favourable impact will be realised but the form of the implementation of the ideas into practice leaves room for considerable doubt.

Although as part of the programme for completing the single market the EU created seven major Directives for European-wide public and utility procurement, it allowed national governments to implement the Directives into national law and create their own national legislative or administrative systems to enforce the implementation of these rules (Cox, 1994a). This provided an opportunity for uneven and ineffective operation. However, notwithstanding this recourse to subsidiarity in action, the EU also agreed to retain the court of last resort role for the European Court of Justice and the European Commission. This provides some degree of centralized backstop, even though the Court is an extremely cumbersome and slow moving institution and the Commission has a very small and under resourced enforcement unit within DG XV.

The interesting question which arises as a consequence of this finding is why did the Union accept the need for procurement rules and then fail to provide any effective centralized system to ensure that the rules agreed could be implemented effectively? To answer this question we must first provide an insight into why the rules were created in the first place and then try to explain why this tension between centralization and subsidiarity was allowed.

Government protectionism in procurement markets formed one of the barriers to the successful completion of the single market. Research in the 1980s found preferential public purchasing reflected in support for national champions and discriminatory practices favouring domestic over foreign suppliers: this meant that public procurement agencies were failing to exploit the benefits from wider competitions. Typically, only part of public purchasing was put out to tender; restricted or negotiated tenders were preferred to open competitions; tenders were not advertised in the *Official Journal*; bidders from other Member States were excluded; governments subsidised some activities; there were widely differing national or exclusive standards; and discrimination occurred in assessing the technical and financial capabilities of the bidders (Cecchini, 1988; Emerson *et al.*, 1988; EC, 1989a; Hartley, 1991b; Hartley and Uttley, 1994).

The 1980s research found that public purchasing was particularly concentrated in construction (building and civil engineering), energy products (electricity, oil, coal), transport equipment and market services. Some high technology areas, such as telecommunications, power generation, railway equipment and defence equipment were characterised by dominant public buyers, few suppliers and little intra-EC trade (Cecchini, 1988). Indeed, an indication of protectionism in public procurement markets was reflected in the fact that the level of imports for public contracts was considerably lower than the general level of import penetration for the EC. For example, in 1987, imports represented under 2 per cent of public purchasing compared with 22 per cent for the economy as a whole (EC, 1989b, p7). For UK defence equipment in 1992, imports were under 10 per cent of equipment purchases compared with import penetration for the UK economy of 20 per cent.

It was estimated that liberalizing or opening-up public procurement markets would lead to substantial savings in the region of 0.5 per cent of Community GDP over the medium- to long-term and the creation of some 350,000 jobs. If defence procurement is included, the estimated savings rise to 0.6 per cent of Community GDP, equivalent to over 22 billion ECU (1989 prices: Cecchini, 1988, Emerson *et al.*, 1988; Hartley, 1991b). According to the official studies, these savings arise from three sources. *First*, opening national markets enables public procurement agencies to buy from the cheapest (for example, foreign) suppliers (the static trade effect). *Second*, increased competition means that domestic firms in previously protected national markets reduce prices to compete with foreign rivals entering the market (the competition effect). *Third*, in the longer run, increased competition will mean that industries will be rationalized and re-structured enabling the surviving firms to obtain economies of scale and learning (the re-structuring effect: Cecchini, 1988). The relative contribution of each of these three sources to the savings were: static trade effect = 32%; competition effect = 16% and the restructuring effect = 52%. In other words, the long-run restructuring impacts accounted for about one-half of the estimated savings which means that the aggregate savings are long-term and sensitive to assumptions about industrial rationalization and the associated economies of scale. In the short run, the benefits of liberalizing public procurement markets will be reflected in the competition effect. Assuming that it is possible to identify and estimate static trade and competition effects separately (that is, that there is no double counting), then increased competition accounts for some 16 per cent of the total savings, which represent the more immediate benefits of liberalized public procurement. Throughout the estimates, it is assumed that reductions in costs and profits are fully reflected in prices.

Broad aggregates, however, conceal substantial variations in the size of the savings available for different products in different EU markets. For example, the price savings from open competition (static trade and competition effects) were estimated at 40 per cent and 52 per cent for pharmaceuticals in the UK and Germany, respectively; and at 40 per cent and 70 per cent for telephone switching equipment in France and Germany, respectively. In addition, protectionism has resulted in national companies operating at relatively small scales so failing to exploit the available economies of scale (restructuring effect). For example, in boilermaking, it was estimated that reducing the number of firms from 15 to around 4, would reduce unit prices and costs by about 20 per cent; and that reducing the number of main locomotive manufacturers from 16 to 3 or 4 would reduce unit costs by about 13 per cent (Cecchini, 1988, p. 22). However, the long-run implication of restructuring is EU oligopolies and monopolies, with the implications of market power for prices, profits, product quality, inefficiency and innovation. This emphasis on restructuring tends to place a disproportionate weight on the supply-side, ignoring demand factors and various national requirements for differentiated products (consumer surplus). Moreover, the estimated savings from restructuring depend on the reliability of the evidence on economies of scale; the assumptions about firm behaviour (profit versus other aims); pricing which reflects (efficient) cost levels and competitive profit margins; and the absence of diseconomies of scale. Nor should it be forgotten that restructuring involves losers as well as gainers and that a socially-desirable change requires potential compensation for those groups made worse-off; and re-allocating resources to alternative uses from firms and regions losing public sector contracts takes time and involves adjustment costs (unemployment and under-employment of resources: Hartley *et al.* 1993). On this basis, the estimated savings could be maximized taking an optimistic view of the benefits and under-estimating or neglecting the costs of liberalizing public procurement markets.

One can legitimately ask that, if the benefits of opening-up public procurement markets are so large, why the EU member states have apparently failed to exploit such obvious opportunities for making their citizens better-off? One possible explanation is that protectionist procurement policies are believed to be socially optimal so that change is not worthwhile. Governments can use procurement policies to pursue a variety of policy objectives concerned with strategic aims and independence (for example, aerospace, defence, telecommunications); with supporting employment in declining industries and regions (for example, coal, steel, shipbuilding); with promoting high technology industries (for example, telecommunications; nuclear power); and ultimately with seeking re-election (for example, via awarding contracts to firms in marginal constituencies). Such behaviour is possible since governments and public procurement officials have discretion in interpreting the 'public interest' and in obtaining 'good value for money'. As a result, inefficiencies in public procurement markets could be policy-created.

3   THE RULES FOR LIBERALIZING PUBLIC PROCUREMENT

Creating open public procurement markets is a classic example of the problems of translating economic models into a set of legally-enforceable rules. Problems arise with the economist's interpretation of competition which starts with simple models of competitive markets which assume large numbers of suppliers, free entry and firms acting as price-takers. Such an approach fails to recognise the role of contestability (the threat of entry), the relevance of transaction costs (for example, the costs of organising competitions), the role of uncertainty and markets in continuous change (tending towards but never achieving equilibrium) and more recent developments which incorporate economies of scale and oligopolistic markets (Krugman, 1989). More generally, problems arise because utility-maximizing agents on both the demand and supply sides of public procurement markets will pursue self-interest subject to any constraints imposed on their behaviour (that is, they will collude and seek to thwart the aims of legislation and regulations).

The Single Market legislation aimed to create open, liberalized public procurement markets, often expressed in terms of non-discriminatory purchasing, and a level playing field (Arrowsmith, 1993). However, Community rules affecting public procurement are not new. During the 1970s, the EC adopted specific legal Directives including requirements for purchasing organisations to advertise contracts above specific thresholds on a Community-wide basis. But the 1970s initiatives had their limitations. Only about 20 per cent of eligible contracts appeared in the official Bulletin (that is, many countries failed to advertise public contracts); and there were other loopholes resulting from the application of national standards, discriminatory purchasing, non-tariff barriers, vague awards criteria together with some public authorities which were corrupt and had poor staff: all of which created opportunities for ignoring or thwarting the rules. Furthermore, there was little in the way of legal penalties to force compliance and there were a number of excluded sectors (Cox, 1993).

After the experience with the 1970s initiatives, the single market Directives (rules) aimed to remove the remaining barriers to open public procurement markets for civil goods and services. These Directives embraced *public works* (for example, building work for hospitals, schools, and so on), *public supply* (supply of physical goods and equipment such as office equipment, furniture, computers, and so on), *the utilities* (energy, transport, telecommunications, water) and *public services* sectors (for example, accounting, advertising, architectural, financial, insurance, maintenance and repair, computer services: Trepte, 1993). The Directives specify:-

(i) **Contract thresholds** above which all contracts must be advertised on an EU-wide basis in the *Official Journal*.

(ii) **The awards procedures**, which comprise open, restricted and negotiated procedures. The norm is expected to be open or restricted tendering, with negotiated tendering regarded as exceptional.

(iii) **Technical standards.** The aim is to apply European technical standards where possible, so minimizing opportunities for using special national standards (which might be discriminatory).

(iv) **Transparency and time limits.** Contracting authorities are required to provide an indication of their future contract awards by estimated value and there are minimum time periods for firms to respond to advertised contracts (ie, to ensure proper and fair competition).

(v) **The awards criteria** specify that contracts must normally be awarded to the lowest price or 'most economically advantageous tender' which allows consideration to be given to such non-price factors as artistic and technical merit, delivery dates, running costs and after sales service. (However, such broad criteria provide obvious opportunities for public buyers to exercise discretion in their procurement choices.)

(vi) **Reporting and monitoring requirements.** Member states are required to inform the Commission annually of any regional and other preferential schemes and to provide annual statistical reports on contract awards (for example, number and value of contracts above the threshold; procedure used; nationality of the contractor; the products purchased: Spachis, Mardas and Stampoultzi, 1993).

In total, the Directives aimed at transparent and non-discriminatory purchasing embracing all civil works, supplies and services contracts awarded by the public sector and the utilities. However, defence equipment remains a major excluded sector in EU public procurement markets (Sandler and Hartley, 1995).

Compliance with the Directives is achieved through national legislation implementing the rules into national law and through the Remedies Directives (Arrowsmith, 1993; Cox and Lamont, 1993). The national legislation can be enforced through the two conflicting routes outlined earlier. *First,* an aggrieved party in the public procurement process can now take legal action against an offending authority through the national courts or tribunals created by national governments. If this fails private parties have a problem because they cannot bring an action before the European Court of Justice themselves (ECJ). The *second,* centralizing route of enforcement through the ECJ, is only open to the Commission and other member states (Arrowsmith, 1992). Typical public procurement cases which have been brought to the European Court have included the failure to advertise in the *Official Journal*; the failure to implement the Directives within the specified time period; disputes about the awards criteria, contract specifications, the financial and economic standing of eligible contractors and the criteria for contractor selection (for example, requiring contractors to allocate work to the long-term unemployed: Arrowsmith, 1992). In such cases, action might be taken to suspend a contract already concluded, to require an authority to re-open the awards procedure, to require the amendment of national regulations or to award damages (but it can be difficult for a firm to prove that it would have won a contract and to assess the monetary estimates of any loss – for example, lost profits: Arrowsmith, 1993).

4　THE IMPACT OF COMPETITION AMONGST RULES IN EUROPEAN PUBLIC AND UTILITY PROCUREMENT

It should be clear from this brief discussion of the procurement rules that there is a tension between the national implementation approach adopted by the EU and the apparent need to have a fallback position of centralized enforcement.　In practice, as shown above, the centralized enforcement of the rules will be very difficult because private parties have no effective direct recourse to this route and the system is in any case cumbersome and poorly resourced within the Commission (Cox, 1993).　This implies that for the rules to work successfully it is at the level of national implementation that integration of procurement practice will have to take place.　The evidence so far does not indicate, however, that the new rules are having any significant impact on the behaviour of public sector contract awarding bodies.

Cox and Furlong have undertaken extensive research into the impact of the procurement rules on contract awards behaviour in the 12 member states (Cox and Furlong, 1994).　Table 5.1 provides some illuminating evidence about the apparent lack of success of the procurement rules to achieve their intended effect.

As the 1993 data indicate, almost all of the EU countries still continue to source their public and utility requirements from nationally based contractors or suppliers. While there is no directly comparable historical data about previous contract awards behaviour to work on, and even though the data are incomplete because not all contracts awarded are reported in the *Official Journal of the European Communities*, the results are somewhat depressing given the expected scope for change.

The evidence demonstrates conclusively that, as of 1993, only those countries – like Ireland, the Netherlands and Belgium – which lack indigenous industrial capacities of their own seem prepared to source outside their domestic economies. Some countries – like Greece, Portugal and Spain – which lack indigenous capacities still source almost everything domestically.　The low figure of 76.2 per cent for Spain is clearly masked by the fact that for the remaining 23.8 per cent of contracts awarded the Spanish authorities refused to disclose the nationality of the successful contractor.　Our assumption is that this was almost certainly Spanish and that the Spanish figure is likely to be at or very close to 100 per cent of contract awards to Spanish based companies. The evidence has been supported by additional work undertaken on statistical performance indicators by the European Commission (Mardas, 1992) and by (Cox, Hartley and Uttley. 1994).

Whilst statistical indicators are a valuable policy tool, there are major data problems which mean that they should be used carefully (for example, not applied mechanically and uncritically). In addition to the work by Cox and Furlong, there is a need for up-to-date and reliable disaggregated data, for data on public sector purchasing by product groups and by imported products, and data on the involvement of small and medium sized firms and foreign enterprises in public procurement. For example, data are needed on the extent of import penetration of police and Government motorcar fleets in those countries with sizeable national car industries: casual empiricism suggests that these groups buy from their domestic industries.

The empirical work which has been undertaken on the impact of the public procurement Directives alongside that undertaken by Cox and Furlong shows the following:

(i)   Within the EC, in 1990 public procurement of supplies, services and public works was almost 560 billion ECU, equivalent to 15 per cent of the Community's GDP. Over 35 per cent of this total reflected purchases by the utilities, mostly energy, telecommunications and railway transport (Mardas, 1994).

(ii)   Within the Southern Region (Greece, Portugal, Spain and southern Italy), low productivity in the mechanical and electrical engineering sectors means that unless productivity can be increased, these industries are likely to be uncompetitive once their markets are opened to foreign competition (Mardas, 1994).

(iii)   A study of various statistical indicators for measuring openness in public market in Denmark, Germany, Ireland, the Netherlands and the UK found evidence of preferential public purchasing in a variety of industries including electricity and gas, medical equipment, printing, pharmaceuticals, railway rolling stock, shipbuilding and tele-communications (none of which were unexpected: Cox, Hartley and Uttley, 1994; Mardas, 1992).

(iv)   An increase in the number of tendered contracts, although it is not clear whether such an increase reflects increasing compliance with the Directives and/or inflation so that more public contracts exceed the threshold levels (Uttley and Hartley, 1994).

(v)   An increase in the proportion of all EC contracts tendered under open procedures and a substantial decline in the share of negotiated contracts. However, there are major differences between member states. For example, in 1992, open competitions accounted for about 11 per cent of contracts in Italy and some 80 per cent in the Netherlands (Uttley and Hartley, 1994).

Table 5.1 European Union public and utility procurement: the nationality of suppliers in relation to the nationality of contract awarding bodies (1993) (Percentage of total contracts awarded in OJEC by country)

Country Awarding Contract	Nationality of Suppliers Winning Contracts													
	Belgium	Denmark	Germany	Greece	France	Ireland	Italy	Lux	Neths	Portugal	Spain	UK	Others – Non EU	Not Reported
Belgium	87.8	–	2.0	–	2.0	–	0.7	1.4	1.4	–	–	0.7	2.6	1.4
Denmark	–	91.6	1.3	–	0.8	0.2	–	–	0.2	0.2	–	1.5	1.9	2.3
Germany	0.1	0.1	91.9	–	0.2	–	–	–	0.2	–	–	0.1	0.8	6.6
Greece	–	–	–	100.0	–	–	–	–	–	–	–	–	–	–
France	–	–	0.8	–	93.7	–	0.1	–	0.1	–	–	0.1	–	5.1
Ireland	–	–	3.2	–	6.3	71.6	2.1	–	–	1.1	1.1	9.5	3.0	2.1
Italy	–	0.1	–	–	4.8	–	85.6	–	–	–	0.1	–	–	9.4
Lux	3.1	–	–	–	3.1	–	–	89.2	–	–	–	–	1.5	3.1
Neths	9.6	0.6	8.6	–	1.3	–	–	–	76.4	–	–	1.3	0.3	1.9
Portugal	–	–	–	–	–	–	–	–	–	94.6	–	–	5.4	–
Spain	–	–	–	–	–	–	–	–	–	–	76.2	–	–	23.8
UK	–	–	0.2	–	0.1	0.3	–	–	0.1	–	–	95.3	0.1	3.9

(vi)   For a sample of UK supplies contracts, an average number of 14 firms submitted bids which suggests that purchasing authorities are creating competitive conditions. However, for the same sample, foreign firms with no UK presence accounted for some 3 per cent of total tenders (Hartley and Uttley, 1994).

(vii)   A survey of over 350 award notices found only 30 per cent of notices contained details consistent with the reporting requirements of EC supplies legislation (that is, transparency requires tendering and contract award information to be published and open to scrutiny: Hartley and Uttley, 1994).

(viii)   A survey of over 200 contract award notices found that 70 per cent of contracts were awarded to large companies (that is, over 250 employees), the balance to small and medium-sized enterprises (SMEs: under 250 employees). On this basis, the proportion of contracts obtained by SMEs is significantly less than the number and share of SMEs in UK manufacturing industry. This may reflect various impediments to SMEs participating in public contracting such as the threshold levels being too high for SMEs; or the costs of bidding; or an information gap (Hartley and Uttley, 1994: Furlong, Lamont and Cox, 1994).

5   CONCLUDING REMARKS

There are good reasons for expecting the actual impact of the single market programme to be substantially different in terms of both timing and extent from the implicit theoretical paradigm set out in *The Costs of Non-Europe*. There is very substantial variation by both sector and region and reference to overall totals can give very misleading impressions for individual components but some generalizations are possible. While there are plausible grounds for suggesting that the dynamic impact of the changes may be underestimated, most of our discussion has focused on aspects which suggest smaller and more drawn out impacts. There are three main sources of caution over the impact. The measures being implemented do not tackle all of the barriers to a single market. Some of those measures themselves, even if implemented fully, are unlikely to remove the barriers they aim at. It is not clear that the plans for implementation, monitoring and enforcement will ensure compliance and hence the desired changes in behaviour. While by all accounts there will be a substantial net gain, there will be losers as well as gainers and it is not clear how far the mechanisms which have been put in place will provide compensatory payments.

Our analysis has focused on the case of public procurement. Here it appears that the route used for implementation with the use of the principle of subsidiarity is resulting thus far in relatively limited change and will tend to make genuine openness difficult to enforce. There are several plausible explanations for this approach.

The theory of clubs, for example, would indicate that expanding the club size and making it work was of more importance to the EU than providing clearly workable and enforceable procurement rules. To have provided rules which would have forced the member states to change their behaviour more comprehensively might well have created irreparable damage to the consensual relationships within the existing club.

Subsidiarity provides a way in which everyone could appear to be agreeing to integration while still retaining control over the effective implementation and enforcement of the procurement rules.

Rent seeking theory and the notion of distributional coalitions allows us to understand the subtle and complicated way in which particular interest groups in the member states were able to limit the size of the reductions in the threshold levels to minimise the impact of the rules of their market behaviour and, failing this, to create anti-third country reciprocity clauses, derogations and easements in the rules – especially the utilities Directives – to minimise the impact on the market. Finally, it appears that the Commission and the national bureaucracies in each member state have fallen into the trap of equating policy success with the enactment of Directives and national implementing legislation rather than with any real concern for the direct impact of the rules on market performance and behaviour. The evidence so far gathered indicates that the performance of the new rules leaves a great deal to be desired if one of the primary goals was the integration of the market through an increase in the incidence of cross-border contract awards.

There are clearly problems with the procurement rules in this respect. However, it must be remembered that the rather damning evidence about the success of the current approach, shown in Table 5.1, may not be entirely fair to a proper analysis of the efficacy of this approach to European integration. Even if it is true that there has been little impact on the nationality of firms winning public contracts in each member state this cannot, alone, be taken as conclusive evidence that the approach has failed. The reasons for this are that the Single Market initiative may assist European integration in two ways which are unconnected to the clearly observable phenomena of the nationality of cross-border contract awards.

First, there has clearly been an anticipated reaction by leading companies about the impact of the rules, which may well be observable at the level of financial ownership and sourcing rather than through the nationality of awards. There is evidence that many of the companies winning contracts which appear to be nationally specific may well be increasingly owned financially by holding companies from other member states or from third countries. Secondly, there is evidence that the sourcing of components by nationally based firms may well be far more integrated and/or regionally and globally based than initial contract award data indicates. Work by the Commission on the sourcing by, and ownership of, member states' companies in the utilities sector as part of a combined study on utilities procurement with the USA in 1994 indicated clearly that integration may well be more firmly developed at the first, second and third tiers of supply than the initial *Official Journal* data indicate.

For this reason, we must remain agnostic about the true impact of the present approach to achieving a single European market. There is little doubt that as far as cross-border contract awards are concerned the rules have not worked. On the other hand, it may well be that there is far more integrated purchasing through regional sourcing at sub-component levels than these data indicate. Whether or not these developments are a consequence of deregulation and increased competition as a general consequence of the programme for completing the single market initiative or due to the knock-on effects of changes in ownership and sourcing as a direct result of the perception that public and utility markets will be more open is hard to say. More research on the complex patterns of relationships in European sourcing and supply markets is clearly required before a proper conclusion can be reached about the efficacy of the approach. For the time being, however, the available evidence does not indicate that the approach is achieving substantial results.

REFERENCES

Note: * = part of the ESRC SEM Programme

Amin, A. and Dietrich, M. (1991), *Towards a New Europe*, Aldershot: Elgar.
*Amin, A. and Tomaney, J. (1995), *Behind the Myth of European Union: prospects for cohesion*, London: Routledge.
*Arrowsmith, S. (1992), *A Guide to the Procurement Cases of the Court of Justice*, South Humberside: Earlsgate Press.
*Arrowsmith, S. (ed.), (1993), *Remedies for Enforcing the Public Procurement Rules*, South Humberside: Earlsgate Press.
Baldwin, R. (1989), 'The growth effects of 1992', *Economic Policy*, **9**, 248–70.
*Begg, I. and Mayes, D.G. (1993), 'Cohesion in the European Community: a key imperative for the 1990s?', *Regional Science and Urban Economics*, **29**, 427–48.
*Bollard, A.E. and Mayes, D.G. (1993), 'Lessons for Europe from New Zealand's liberalisation experience', *National Institute Economic Review*, February, pp. 81–97.

*Brazier, M., Lovecy, J. and Moran, M. (1993), 'Professional regulation and the single European market: a study of the regulation of doctors and lawyers in England and France', University of Manchester, mimeo.

Buigues, P. and Sheehy, J. (1993), 'Recent developments and trends of European integration', paper prepared for seminar in Latin America's Competitive Position in the Enlarged European Market, Hamburg, March.

Cecchini, P. (1988), *The European Challenge 1992. The benefits of a single market*, Aldershot: Wildwood House.

*Cox, A. (1992), 'Implementing 1992 public procurement policy: public and private obstacles to the creation of the Single European Market', *Public Procurement Law Review*, **2**, 139–54.

*Cox, A. (1993), *The Single Market Rules and the Enforcement Regime After 1992*, Public Procurement in the European Community, vol. I, South Humberside: Earlsgate Press.

*Cox, A. (1994a), 'Derogation, subsidiarity and the Single Market: the case of energy exploration and extraction under the EC utilities procurement rates', *Journal of Common Market Studies*, **32** (2), (June), 127–47.

*Cox, A. (1994b), 'The future of European defence policy: the case for a centralized procurement agency', *Public Procurement Law Review*, **2**, 65–86.

*Cox, A. and Furlong, P. (1994), 'The impact of the public procurement directives on EU contract awards in 1993', Paper to ESRC Single Market Initiative Conference, Exeter University, September 1994.

*Cox, A. and Lamont, F. (1993), *The Texts of the Community Directives, Recommendations, Proposals, Decisions, Resolutions and Communications in Force*, South Humberside: Earlsgate Press.

*Cox, A., Hartley, K. and Uttley, M. (1994), *Statistical Indicators for Keeping Watch Over Public Procurement: Country Studies of Denmark, Germany, Ireland, The Netherlands and UK*, Report to EC, unpublished, Brussels.

EC (1989a), *Research on the Cost of Non-Europe: The Cost of Non-Europe in Public Sector Procurement*, vol. 5, Luxembourg, Commission of the European Communities.

EC (1989b), 'Public procurement in the excluded sectors', *Bulletin of the European Communities, Supplement 6/88*, Luxembourg, Commission of the European Communities.

Emerson, M. *et al.*, (1988), *The Economics of 1992*, Oxford, Oxford University Press.

Department of Employment (1993), *Growth, Competitiveness and Employment in the European Community, Paper by the United Kingdom*, July, London.

*Furlong, P., Lamont, F. and Cox, A. (1994), 'Competition or partnership?' *European Journal of Purchasing and Supply Management*, **1** (1), 37–43.

Geroski, P.A. (1989), 'The choice between diversity and scale' in Centre for Business Strategy *1992: Myths and Realities*, London: London Business School

*Gold, M., Matthews, D. and Mayes, D.G. (1995), *The Implications of the Evolution of European Integration of UK Labour Markets*, NIESR Report for the Department of Employment.

Hartley, K. (1991a), *The Economics of Defence Policy*, London: Brasseys.

Hartley, K. (1991b), 'Public purchasing' in D. Gowland and S. James, (eds), *Economic Policy After 1992*, Aldershot: Dartmouth.

Hartley, K. *et al.*, (1993), *Economic Aspects of Disarmament: Disarmament as an Investment Process*, New York and Geneva: United Nations and UNIDIR.

*Hartley, K. (1994), 'The independent appraisal of an aerospace sefence project: the economics of Eurofighter 2000', *The Economic Appraisal of Aerospace Projects*, London, Royal Aeronautical Society: June.

*Hartley, K. and Uttley, M. (1994), 'The Single European Market and public procurement policy: the case of the United Kingdom', *Public Procurement Law Review*, **3**, 114–25.

Helm, D. (1993), 'The assessment: the European internal market: the next steps', *Oxford Review of Economic Policy*, **9** (1), (Spring), 1–14.

Hingel, A. (1991), 'Archipelago Europe – islands of innovation', Monitor/FAST prospective dossier, No. 1 (April).

House of Lords (1985), *Report from the Select Committee on Overseas Trade*, HL238 I-III, London: HMSO

Krugman, P. (1989), 'Economic integration in Europe: some conceptual issues', in A. Jacquemin and A. Sapir, (eds), *The European Internal Market: Trade and Competition*, Oxford: Oxford University Press.

Mardas, D. (1992), 'Statistical performance indicators for keeping watch over public procurement', Conference paper at CEDECE, Univeriste Paris II.

Mardas, D. (1994), 'The profile of the industries supplying the utilities sectors in the Southern Regions of the EC', *Public Procurement Law Review*, **2**, 87–97.

*Matthews, D. and Mayes, D.G. (1994), 'The evolution of rules for a single European market in leasing', National Institute Discussion Paper no. 35.

Mayes, D.G. (1978), 'The effects of economic integration on trade', *Journal of Common Market Studies*, **17**, no. 1, pp. 1–25.

*Mayes, D.G. (1991), *The European Challenge: industry's response to the 1992 programme*, London: Harvester Wheatsheaf.

Mayes, D.G. (1995a), 'Factor Mobility', chapter 19 in A. El Agraa (ed.), *Economics of the European Community*, 4th edition, Oxford: Philip Allan.

Mayes, D.G. (1995b), 'The distributive implications of economic and monetary union', Europa Institute Forschungsbericht 9507, University of Saarland, October.

Mayes, D.G. (1995c), 'Quantitative estimation of the effects of integration', ch. 4 in A.M. El Agraa (ed.), *International Economic Integration*, London: Macmillan.

Mayes, D.G. and Albrecht, I. (1994), *Statistical Performance Indicators for Keeping Watch over Public Procurement in EEA Member Countries: Iceland*, NIESR for European Commission.

*Mayes, D.G. and Burridge, M. (1993), *The Impact of the Internal Market Programme on European Economic Structure and Performance*, European Parliament, Economic Series E-2.

*Mayes, D.G. and Hart, P.E. (1994), *The Single Market Programme as a Stimulus to Change: Comparisons between Britain and Germany*, Cambridge University Press.

*Mayes, D.G. and Shipman, A. (1992), 'The response of UK retailers to the single European market', National Institute Discussion Paper no. 6.

Mayes, D.G. and Soteri, S. (1994), 'Does manufacturing matter?', ch. 17 in T. Buxton, P. Chapman and P. Temple (eds), *Britain's Economic Performance*, London: Routledge.

*Mayes, D. G., Hager, W., Knight, A. and Streeck, W. (1993), *Public Interest and Market Pressures: Problems Posed by Europe 1992*, London: Macmillan.

*Mayes, D.G. *et al.* (1993), *The External Implications of European Integration*, London: Harvester Wheatsheaf.

Nam, C. and Reuter, J. (1991), *The Impact of 1992 and Associated Legislation on the Less Favoured Regions of the European Community*, European Parliament Research Paper no. 19, Luxembourg: Office for Official Publications of the European Communities.

*NIESR (1991), *A Strategy for Social and Economic Cohesion after 1992*, European Parliament Research Paper no. 19, Luxembourg: Office for Official Publications of the European Communities.

O'Donnell, R. (1993), 'Ireland and Europe: challenges for a new century', ESRI Policy Research Services Paper no. 17, Dublin: ESRI.

Ostry, J. (1995), Draft Paper on 'New Zealand's Medium-Term Growth Potential', IMF, Washington.

OECD (1994), *Jobs Study. Facts, Analysis, Strategies*, Paris.

Pelkmans, J. and Winters, L.A. (1987), *Europe's Domestic Market*, London: Pinter for Royal Institute of International Affairs.

*Sandler, T. and Hartley, K. (1995), *The Economics of Defense*, Cambridge Surveys of Economic Literature, Cambridge: Cambridge University Press.

*Shipman, A. and Mayes, D.G. (1989), 'Changing the rules: a framework for examining government and company responses to 1992', *NIESR Discussion Paper*, no. 199.

Spachis, A., Mardas, D. and Stampoultzi, (1993), 'Bibliography on public procurement', *Public Procurement Law Review*, **2**, 257–309.

Streeck, W. (1993), 'The social dimension of the European economy', ch. 4 in Mayes *et al.* (1993).

Tiebout, C.M. (1956), 'A pure theory of local expenditures', *Journal of Political Economy*, **64** (October), 416–24.

Trepte, P.A. (1993), 'Extension of the EC procurement regime to public services: an overview of the services directive', *Public Procurement Law Review*, **1**, 1–12.

*Uttley, M. and Hartley, K. (1994), 'Public procurement on the Single Market: policy and prospects', *European Business Review*, **94** (2), 3–7.

*Woolcock, S. (1994), *The European Single Market: Centralisation or Competition Among National Rules*, London: RIIA.

6. Socio-economic Environments and Rule-making in the EU[*]

Robert M. Lindley

The purpose of this chapter differs somewhat from others. It is concerned more with the socio-economic context in which rules are evolving rather than with a specific aspect of the process of evolution, as captured under the other themes: setting and influencing, implementing, competition and conflict between, impact of, evolution of, political legitimacy of, and the external (that is, extra-EU) impact of rules for the Single European Market (SEM). In this respect, the chapter relates to a field which is complementary to that covered directly by the projects of the ESRC's SEM research programme.

Socio-economic environments are partly conditioned by rule-making, and rule-making is partly a response to the perceptions that key actors have of current and future socio-economic situations. At the same time, the study of different elements in the evolutionary process and of different substantive areas of policy making and behaviour inevitably touches to some degree upon the underlying assumptions being made by the different actors as to political, social and economic objectives and upon the *styles* of rule-making and implementation thought to be appropriate for the different areas of policy (at local, regional, national and Union levels).

Such views will in turn be dependent on the nature and scale of a problem: priorities among objectives and preferences for policy styles may change under the pressure of major imperatives. These imperatives may derive from within a country or region as the consequences of previous decisions and events which work their way through into the future, by which time they may appear to be purely exogenous influences. Imperatives may also come from external forces

[*] This paper draws particularly on work undertaken by the author as a member of the 'Groupe de Réflexion Prospective' of DGV of the Commission of the European Communities (CEC) and for the project 'Human Resource Regimes and the Single European Market' (No. L113251018) of the ESRC's SEM Research Programme. Thanks for helpful discussions are due to Arnold Calon, Luigi Frey, Antoine Lyon-Caen, Heinz Markmann and Spiro Simitis; to Terence Hogarth, Linda Luckhaus, Graham Moffat and Christopher Whelan of the University of Warwick; and to Luis Fina and Jean-François Lebrun of the CEC. Responsibility for the views expressed, however, lies with the author. I am also grateful to William Wells (UK Department of Employment) for permission to use his data in preparing the charts relating to regulation of the labour market and to Professor Jacques Zighera (LAEDIX, Université Paris X-Nanterre) for permission to reproduce figures from his study of regional labour costs.

that are largely unrelated to the behaviour of the system in question but impinge upon it.

How the analysis of current and possible future socio-economic environments is conducted and presented to those involved in the evolution of rules is likely to affect their judgment at various stages in the evolutionary process. This chapter deals with selected aspects of the links between socio-economic context and rule-making, focusing more on the characterization of the context and its implications for the orientation of the regulatory process, rather than working through how this affects the evolution of specific rules.

The chapter begins at the broadest level with the powerful metaphor of 'globalization' and the importance that different interpretations of this phenomenon play in the definition of problems placed on the agenda for reform. In the light of this discussion, a brief resume of the probable *qualitative* impacts of the SEM programme on sectors and countries is given, as revealed by the main studies available.

The following section turns to the link between the SEM and developments in the labour market, for it is here that economy and society meet and where the so-called 'social dimension' to European integration begins.   Scenarios are presented which capture differences in the approaches taken to the social dimension according to alternative diagnoses of the principal problems facing the EU. This section also looks at the differences between member states in some of the key labour market features likely to play a part in the integration of the Single Market.

Powerful injunctions to 'labour market flexibility' were issued during the 1980s (OECD, 1986) and reiterated thereafter. An industry of social scientists working on the interpretation of this notion grew up, somewhat ahead of those scrutinizing the meaning of 'globalization', the phenomenon most responsible for the calls for labour market flexibility in the first place. Section 3 thus remains largely concerned with the labour market area of the socio-economic environment, dealing with two elements: first, the relationship between objectives, constraints and policy styles relating to labour market reform; and, second, the notion of social policy found in a European context and how this relates to ideas of European regulation and convergence among member states.

Concluding comments are given in the last section.

1   GLOBALIZATION, REGIONALIZATION AND THE SINGLE MARKET

1.1 Global Imperatives

Developments in the internationalization of the world economy have sometimes been presented as inevitable, almost as if 'globalization' were a natural phenomenon. We might wonder if it were in our interests, but there is no stopping it. Energies should be devoted to adapting to the new economic environment and to the realistic assessment of what governments individually and collectively can do to prepare their people to compete in the new economic game.

But as to the nature of the game and the evidence on how far it has proceeded, there is much confusion (Jones, 1994); indeed, enough to question how far it is inevitable or desirable and whether or not globalization is occurring to the extent claimed. 'Regionalization' then appears partly as a potentially more convincing representation of the internationalization of the world economy, and partly as a more desirable outcome which it is within the power of political actors and institutions to deliver.

Analyses of globalization come in many different forms. Some stress a collection of phenomena of a more or less global nature: geo-political change marked especially by the gradual decline of US economic power and the sudden collapse of the communist experiment; the globalization of multi-national corporate behaviour; the globalization of financial markets; and the recognition of global environmental issues.

Debate in the security and environmental arenas is preoccupied with how market forces need to be controlled in some way so as to promote understanding of the interdependent nature of national or supra-national regional behaviour. Debate in the socio-economic arena is preoccupied with how national or regional market forces need to be harnessed in order for the countries and regional groups concerned to face the imperatives of global market forces. Technological change and globalization are seen to be mutually reinforcing and neither can nor should be slowed down to meet the preferences of particular groups or nations or social groups. Intervention to correct market forces on environmental grounds is acceptable to ensure sustainable development but *existing* intervention on social welfare grounds is seen to have gone well past the point at which it might have been justified in order to maintain the cohesiveness of the *economic* system.

Other analyses of globalization start from the behavioural processes at work which underlie the more macro phenomena and/or are stimulated by the political-economic conditions to which those phenomena give rise.

Elements of globalization are examined at the micro level, relating them to the macro level context at the same time produced collectively and endured individually by the corporate actors. Globalization is then a process in which certain linkages based on space and nationality become progressively weaker.

(i) Companies make choices about the location of supply, production and investment with less reference to historical, political and social ties, other than those which have economic value to the company. One might add the qualification *long-term* economic value, but such well-considered behaviour need not be dominant even if it may be in the interests of the company, its employees, shareholders and the 'home' or 'host' countries.

(ii) The parameters which come into corporate decision-making are sufficiently different in spatial terms for this to generate a wider range of actual choices once behaviour is conditioned as in (i).

(iii) A progressive weakening of consumer loyalty occurs with respect to the goods and services of national producers and those of regionally linked economies.

(iv) Beyond the willingness of financial capital to sustain the plans of industrial capital on the global basis implicit in (i), a global market in financial assets develops.

(v) Human capital becomes more mobile because there is unlikely to be a coincidental supply of appropriate skills available in locations preferred in other respects. So carrying out production and investment intentions is likely to require skills which are supplementary to those available locally and to present opportunities for switching geographically, via the internal labour market, at least some company personnel who are needed more in one location than another. It may even stimulate greater cross-national recruitment via the external labour market.

Regionalization may be seen as a qualification to the spatial range of actual decision-making brought about by the patterns of costs and benefits attached to the diversity of options theoretically available. This micro-level perspective has, however, a counterpart at the macro political–economic level in that certain activities may be promoted by particular regional international agreements. The latter provide a framework conducive to more intense intra-regional activity, thought this may in fact strengthen the base from which some companies are able to launch global strategies.

For a specific regional block, therefore, regionalization may be a strategy which is essentially defensive, even if it is also dynamic in that it is seen as a step in securing macro-level success in a global economic environment.

The implications of the internationalization as globalization or regionalization debate are thus quite profound for the stance of socio-economic policy. Deregulation of socio-economic space in order to survive in the high seas of irresistibly extensive trade, large-scale FDI and financial capital in perpetual motion is one thing; de-regulation in order to implement a liberal democratic vision of the way economies should be run when other visions would also be viable is quite another matter.

Regionalization may be seen as a means of constructing a much bigger raft capable of remaining at sea and weathering global capital storms, or a sea wall behind which it will be possible to get the best out of the development opportunities facing societies which are geographically proximate, structurally converging and culturally similar but still diverse. The former view accepts that persistent underlying forces are working towards globalization but may be mitigated at national level through the formation of regional political-economic alliances. The latter is more tentative, hoping that the SEM, EMU and more political union will themselves together become an underlying force, enabling the EU to choose models of working and living which are anchored to 'European values' rather than drawn from an identikit for global economic success.

Reflections on global scenarios

Globalization and related forces take many forms although they are usually characterized by the use of the same words. The particular form has a major impact on the context in which the SEM might operate and hence on its operation.

The ambiguity over characterizations of international economic development may also be found in the analytical frameworks of applied economics devoted to the preparation of scenarios. The regular periodic assessments of the global economy or selected regional economic blocs produced by international agencies quite often fall into this category, especially when providing the introduction to what is essentially a labour market assessment, as, for example, in OECD (1993, 1994). These reports frequently pass over the problems or interpretations, concentrating on the broad description of the 'global trends' to which labour market actors need to respond.

A further related ambiguity arises when in those studies that deal more clearly with the globalization–regionalization issue. In their particularly thoughtful assessment, the Dutch Central Planning Bureau (CPB) (1992) offers three perspectives on the different approaches taken towards economic policy. An evaluation of the past policies and performances of the main regional country groups alongside the threats and opportunities facing them then yields four global scenarios suggestive of the constellation of future choices and outcomes.

The three perspectives encompass the following basic sets of conditions and the responses to them enunciated by the CPB (1992, pp. 115–4).

(a) The 'equilibrium' perspective derives from consideration of an economy with an effective price mechanism and well-informed individuals who face circumstances enabling them to be reasonably good at predicting the future context likely to affect their own decisions. So imbalances between supply and demand appear but can be resolved.

(b) The 'co-ordination' perspective derives from a situation in which the economic actors are not well-informed and subject to a high degree of uncertainty about the future. Co-operation between government, business and labour is engendered within a macroeconomic framework of counter-cyclical policies and a regulatory framework to promote stable product and labour market conditions in the face of de-stabilizing tendencies. Government institutions and/or funding are made available for the creation of human capital and intellectual property and its effective deployment. Uncertainty is reduced by fixed exchange rates and trade agreements of various kinds embodying restrictions in some cases and open trading in others.

(c) The 'free market' perspective represents a different strategy for dealing with poor information and inherent uncertainty. Unfettered entrepreneurship is the hallmark of this approach.

> Man in general is viewed as vital, creative and intuitive, provided he is assured of picking the fruit of his efforts. This requires a well-developed system of property rights, autonomy in the economic sphere, low taxes and a frugal system of social security. There is a profound distrust of government policies. Government is no better informed than individuals and is not corrected by the market when it makes wrong decisions. Policies may make the future even more unpredictable and cripple the dynamics of the economic process. ... In the field of international trade and exchange rates, the free market is advocated without reserve.

Scenarios (even such as those conceived by the CPB) tend to emphasize patterns of behaviour by the economic actors, the nature of the economic environment and policy responses in the macroeconomic, industrial and trade areas. So, whilst reports may reach policy conclusions that call for major social change both in the labour market and the wider society, their treatment of complex socio-economic relationships is more or less non-existent in the *construction of the scenarios* in the first place.

The place for social cost–benefit analysis is later if, indeed, it ever comes. Moreover, its position in the sequence of analysis limits it more to the secondary evaluation of possibly awkward consequences rather than as an inherent part of the process of choosing the overall strategy. The Foreword to *The OECD Jobs Study* (OECD, 1994, p. 3) provides a recent prominent example of this:

> The many benefits to be expected but also the human and economic costs which could be involved, especially in the short term, are noted in the report but have not been analysed in detail at this stage.

The equilibrium perspective outlined above, for example, assumes that economic equilibrium is somehow sustainable when the economic conditions favourable to stable and efficient trading combine with an institutional framework and government policy style that achieve efficient markets. They do not, however, contain explicit recognition of social behaviour. Yet conclusions based on a scrutiny of economic scenarios often involve policy recommendations with quite fundamental implications for social regulation. The difference between the equilibrium perspective and the co-ordination and free-market perspectives stems from the incomplete information and uncertainty which are missing from the former but with which the latter seek to grapple. Without these phenomena, the equilibrium perspective is, in effect, advanced as a viable if stylized solution to the economic development problem. There are no social dynamics: no progressively changing aspirations and expectations, no patterns of social behaviour which unfold to de-stabilize the economic system. It is assumed simply that 'economic subjects [who] are rational well-informed and have accurate expectations of the future' combined with the provision of public goods and appropriate adjustments for externalities by a rational government will generate sustainable economic development.

So whilst the expositional value of the equilibrium, co-ordination and free market perspectives as ingredients present in different proportions in real economies should be recognised, there is a case for complicating the mix to allow for a 'socio-economic perspective'. This perspective gives separate representation to the dynamics of social behaviour deriving from a number of influences at inter-generational, social group and individual level. In economic terms several of these influences may be rooted in economic changes: rising real incomes and access to a wider range of goods, services, working practices and lifestyles through greater trade, communication, foreign direct investment and foreign travel. But, leaving aside reservations about what is meant by 'economic', other influences seem rooted as much in the area of social relations and power and the interactions between changes in economic and social conditions. So we should, perhaps, add a fourth element (d) to the CPB's stylized analysis.

(d) The 'socio-economic' perspective represents a society in which 'activities' are located and re-located within the institutional, industrial and occupational structure according to political, economic and social factors. Reform and experimentation proceed with reference to notions of equity and efficiency that search for solutions which allow for their potentially mutual reinforcing behaviour, as well as recognizing the presence of trade-offs between them. Democracy in the economic sphere, the full acknowledgment of the need to address problems of patriarchy throughout the socio-economy, and the recognition of and response to chronic social exclusion are high on the political agenda.

The CPB consider the three perspectives and the degree to which the major regional economic groupings reflect different and changing mixes of them over the post-war period, the extent to which certain general long-term trends are likely to push those groupings into situations for which their experience and recent social innovation have prepared them, albeit with a need to adapt it to changing circumstances, learning from others and altering the combination of attitudes and approaches which have governed the past. The trends considered cannot literally be exogenous but are presumably deemed to be sufficiently robust that they are unlikely to be nullified through endogeneity. They concern the availability and use of non-renewable resources: the environment; technology, internationalization and market structures; world food supply; demographic change; social and political trends; the growing need for international co-operation.

In some ways the treatment of such trends as exogenous is an expositional device, reflecting also the technical limitations to global macroeconomic modeling and long-term projections. To a degree, however, this inevitably raises the danger of assuming away what is supposed to be under investigation: the case of socio-economic behaviour has already been mentioned.

Accepting this caveat, the constellations produced as overall scenarios are revealing. They are briefly summarized below, together with their implications for Europe.

Global Shift (CPB, p. 22)
... characterized by the strong dynamics of technological change. In order to benefit from the dynamics, vigorous entrepreneurship, incentives and market competition are essential preconditions. The gale of creative destruction continuously threatens market positions and vested interests.

European Renaissance
... new entrepreneurship encounters more barriers than in Global Shift. Huge funds are needed for research and development, involving large risks and uncertainties. Increasing returns to scale in finance, production, marketing and R&D, continue to be very important. As a result, global competition increasingly leads to the emergence of world-wide oligopolies and strategic alliances. These 'conglomerates' seek support from governments in order to reduce the degree of uncertainty. Consequently, strategic technology, together with industrial and trade policies become more important.

Global Crisis
Despite the optimistic beginning of the nineties, the United States does not really seem to break away from the trends of the eighties, while in Western Europe high expectations about Europe '92 are not met. Although no dramatic

set-backs take place, the process of economic decay is, slowly but surely, settling in to stay.

Balanced Growth

A revived and ever stronger striving towards sustainable economic development combined with continuously strong technological dynamics ... This calls for a new balance between the economic perspectives.

During the next years the weak points of the major industrial countries are corrected. The United States government reduces the budget deficit and improves education and infra-structure, while American business changes its attitudes and practices. Western Europe strengthens incentive structures and Japan liberalizes and opens up to the world economy. At the same time, reform processes continue or gain new strength in regions like Latin America, the former Soviet Union, India and China. As a result, during the second half of the nineties, world-wide economic growth picks up strongly.

These positive developments on a regional level also stimulate an open and co-operative attitude on the international level [in trade, security and the environment].

Needless to say, balanced growth is the more optimistic scenario, but how might the European Union fare under the different visions?

Under *global shift*, the free market orientation is at an advantage and an extended EU fails to meet the Asian-Pacific threat. As the CPB envisages (p. 23):

Economic reforms intended to promote or restore market competition are not realised or are implemented half-heartedly, due to effective resistance by pressure groups. This applies particularly to the labour market. The European bias in favour of security, stability and risk-aversive behaviour prevails once again. As a result, economic growth recedes, and important industrial sectors quickly lose ground. A number of countries will make the shift towards protectionism by awarding subsidies to vital industries and introducing non-tariff barriers, for example. Other countries oppose this, however. The Community is once again split. Fortress Europe is in the making. Eurosclerosis has returned to the stage.

Under *European renaissance*, the co-ordination experience of the EU member states individually and collectively, combined with improvements in market flexibility, is at a premium. Assuming the SEM *and* EMU proceed as intended the language is one of reconciling Western Europe as we know it with the intensified pressures of competition:

> The European process of integration is an important stimulus toward strengthening incentive structures on the Western European product and labour markets. A far-reaching process of reform of the West European welfare state is set in motion, especially in north-western Europe. In this, attempts are made to combine the European tradition of social equity, with an increased sensitivity to economic incentives. By 2000 the European Free Trade Association (EFTA) countries will already be full members of the Community, while a special status will have been granted to the Central European countries. Based on the European Energy Charter, the European Community also quickly initiates a Pan-European Energy Community. This subsequently becomes the focal point of close co-operation with regard to environmental and energy issues, including the introduction of a limited CO_2 tax.

The echoes of this outcome found in the CEC's (1993) *White Paper on Growth, Competitiveness and Employment* are particularly strong, though the latter links the taxation of pollution more strongly to the reduction of taxes on employment.

In *global crisis*, Europe would share in a widespread malaise represented by a continuation of the economic climate of the 1980s and early 1990s. Perhaps better described as 'global doldrums', this is clearly the most pessimistic scenario for European countries and the United States, but there is also no gain to be had from this by other regions.

Finally, under *balanced growth*, the richer regions attend to their principal inadequacies, and all regions benefit. Success with international environmental policy moves centre-stage, and GDP grows overall at an average of 3.5 per cent annually.

The discussion of this section and illustrations by reference to the CPB's study has been very schematic. The principal points, however, are, first, that the status of 'global imperatives' in commentaries and analyses of the political economic environment for the EU should not be accepted uncritically – there is much theoretical and empirical confusion over what they mean; second, the socio-economic perspective is systematically played down in the analysis of the problem of EU economic development whilst being played up in the proposed solution; third, the EU's ability to influence the extent and nature of these global imperatives should not be underestimated.

1.2 The Impact of the Single European Market

The integration programme
European integration is happening through economic and social forces which have a momentum of their own but which may be reinforced by concerted political action at European level. The European Community is engaged in such

action through three broad initiatives: completion of the Single European Market (SEM), promotion of economic and monetary union (EMU), and development of deeper political union. The first of these initiatives is well under way having passed the target date of the end of 1992 for the formal removal of 'physical, technical and fiscal barriers' to trade between member states. The second and third initiatives, even after the ratification of the Maastricht Treaty, are the subjects of continuing debate about the nature and pace of reform thought to be appropriate.

Further European integration beyond completion of the internal market seems likely, at first sight, to have even greater impacts upon European employment than will completion itself. The removal of national control of monetary and exchange rate policy may have potentially profound effects upon the conduct of short-run and medium-run policy. However, it has been argued that the development of international financial markets has meant that even short-run discretion is, in practice, very limited and that, in the long-run, it is illusory to believe in the notion of national sovereignty in manipulating the supply of money and the level of the exchange rate. So, having accepted the liberalization of capital movements and a competitive market in financial services, member governments have endorsed a market structure that precludes forms of national control which historically have provided scope for ameliorating the effects of structural adjustment. It is argued that EMU would amount to a recognition of this and provide an orderly sustainable framework within which EU economies could advance to meet their North American and Pacific Rim competitors (CEC, 1990b).

The European Union (EU) produces about 30 per cent of world GDP with only 7 per cent of the world's population of working age. Regional (EU) exports amounted to over 40 per cent of world exports in 1990, and 60 per cent of them were to other member states. Whilst the EU is in the process of both deepening and widening the extent of its integration, there are some disagreements about how far deepening and widening should go and about the degree to which the pursuit of one may inhibit the achievement of the other. All member states supported the SEM programme but not all support EMU to the same extent. All member states supported the addition of the rich economies of the European Economic Area (EEA) (notably, Austria, Finland, Norway and Sweden) but there is much less consensus over the possible membership of countries of Central and Eastern Europe which are in transition to becoming market economies.

The medium-term prospect, nonetheless, is for a continued institutional strengthening and extension of the EU as a regional economic bloc. Whether the institutional strengthening will lead to a much stronger overall economic performance compared with that achieved since the late 1970s or as compared with what would have happened in the absence of the SEM and progress towards EMU, is a moot point. Detailed analysis of the effects of the creation and enlargement of the European Communities upon activity and employment within EU member states and outside the EU is beyond the scope of this paper. As far as the re-launching of the European vision during the 1980s is concerned, (for example, Cecchini, 1988), it is still probably true that the various *a priori* assessments of the impact of the integration programme are better guides to the possible consequences of further integration than is any attempt to extract preliminary answers from the experience of the transition period, beginning with the early stages of completing the internal market. This is because of the extraordinary conditions under which the SEM and EMU initiatives have been launched. The major recession at the beginning of the 1980s was traumatic enough to leave forecasters and sectoral commentators hard pressed to identify the underlying trends from cyclical fluctuations whose depth and duration was so exceptional. Without taking the latter into account, it was difficult to assess whether or not and in what sense growing integration was taking place specifically because of the SEM measures and what effects completion of the internal market was having on the key economic indicators.

The downturn at the end of the 1980s put paid to the prospects of any successful attempt to monitor quantitatively the impact of the SEM in the short run, simply because it, too, was of major proportions, coming after a period of painful economic adjustment which governments had hoped would avoid precisely the debacle of depression which has been inflicted upon the 1990s. If there was not, at the turn of the decade, enough 'noise' in the economic information system to discourage the model builders from too much confidence in tracking the evolving impacts of the accumulation of SEM measures, the uncertainty produced by the stalling of the Maastricht ratification process and the collapse of the European exchange rate mechanisms (ERM) should have been enough to discourage even the boldest technocrats.

Moreover, whole the recent statistical evidence has failed to yield unequivocal evidence on the likely *long-run* impact of the SEM *per se*, there has also been little recent work improving on the earlier *a priori* assessments, including those produced by the Commission itself such as Cecchini (1988) and the 'costs of non-Europe' programme summarised by the report, Emerson *et al.* (1988) and Buigues *et al.* (1988, 1990). The NIESR (1993), for example, in its extensive review of the relevant research, points out that very limited empirical analysis has been carried out which meets the criticisms made of the essentially partial economic analysis characterizing the earlier work.

So no attempt will be made here to sum up EU experience in ways which attach magnitudes, first, to different institutional influences (changes in rules for the SEM and in the parameters – tariffs and tax rates, and so on – embodied within those rules) and, second, to their effects on activity. The emphasis of this section and the one to follow is on relevant structural conditions and the perceptions that have arisen during the integration process, focusing on the SEM rather than EMU, and the threats and opportunities it appears to offer both enterprises and the labour force.

Potential impacts on specific sectors

In examining the impact of the completion of the internal market upon different industries, attention has been paid particularly to those industries protected by relatively high non-tariff barriers behind which price dispersion has flourished (Buigues and Ilzkowitz, 1988; Buigues, Ilzkowitz and Lebrun, 1990). Not only do such barriers raise the cost of trade between member states but they also tend to fragment the market and this could lead to potentially inadequate exploitation of economies of scale and to a tempering of competitive forces which might otherwise help to lower prices and costs and improve allocative efficiency.

Buigues and Ilzkowitz (1988) identified 40 sectors likely to be significantly affected by completion: they cover approximately half of the Community's industrial value added and employment. Employers in these sectors will be particularly affected by the SEM initiative. Four principal groups can be discerned, allowing for the extent to which the markets concerned are open to foreign trade by third countries and have been fragmented from the point of view of European producers (Table 6.1).

However, from the social dimension perspective, it is important to distinguish the source of the additional competitive pressure. In one group of industries producing high technology products, competition is already high from American and Japanese multi-nationals operating at global level and price dispersion is low. The SEM is seen principally as an opportunity which will stimulate rationalization of the European industry so that it may reap greater economies of scale and compete more effectively in Europe and elsewhere with the currently more efficient non-European producers. It is hoped that technical co-operation between European enterprises and the creation of a common labour market for scientists and technologists will facilitate this strengthening of the European position. The Community's strategy should be to promote high levels of training, research and development so as to boost the output of intellectual property and ensure its successful incorporation into advanced processes and products.

A second group of industries consists of those where the European market is highly balkanised particularly through the influence of public procurement policies. Third-country competition has here been discouraged leaving high price dispersion reflecting low market penetration by non-European producers whether they are rooted in high or low cost economies. In these cases the reduction in non-tariff barriers is more likely to stimulate the re-structuring of the European industry, leading to changes in its corporate organization and in the location of its various functions. It may also provoke higher levels of import penetration from non-European transnational corporations but a more likely effect is higher foreign direct investment. This could make for a significant

Table 6.1   Sectors especially sensitive to completion of the SEM

Category	NACE code	Branches
Group 1	330	Computers and office equipment
	344	Telecommunications equipment
	372	Medical and surgical equipment
Group 2	257	Pharmaceuticals
	315	Boilermaking
	362	Railway equipment
	425	Champagne, sparkling wines
	427	Brewing
	428	Soft drinks
Group 3	341	Insulated wires and cables
	342	Electrical plant and machinery
	361	Shipbuilding
	417	Spaghetti, macaroni
	421	Chocolate and sugar confectionery
Group 4	247	Glass
	248	Ceramics
	251	Basic industrial chemicals
	256	Industrial and agricultural chemicals
	321	Agricultural machinery
	322	Machine tools
	323	Textile machinery
	324	Food processing and chemical machinery
	325	Mining and related plant
	326	Transmission equipment
	327	Wood, paper and leather machinery
	345	Other electronic equipment
	346	Domestic electrical appliances
	347	Lighting
	351	Motor vehicles
	364	Aerospace equipment
	431	Woollen goods
	432	Cotton goods
	438	Carpets
	451	Footwear
	453	Clothing
	455	Household textiles
	481	Rubber goods
	491	Jewellery
	493	Photographic, cinema, labs
	494	Toys, games and sports goods

Source: Buigues *et al.* (1990)

extent of footloose investment from both the reorganization of European producers and entry of non-European companies.

As with the first group, a third group of industries also tends to exhibit relatively low price dispersion because of third country competition but here the pressure comes from newly industrializing countries with low wage and non-wage labour costs reinforced by high levels of productivity. Completion *per se* will be less important in these cases than will the conduct of Community external trade policy. For some industries, completion will speed up the process of reducing spare capacity and restructuring is likely to occur on a wider European basis than if national governments had as much power to favour domestic producers through public procurement or direct state aid as applied pre-completion. It is possible that this process may intensify corporate search for lower cost European locations, assuming that Community trade policy makes continued existence viable by limiting the penetration of European markets by third countries. If trade policy reduces the quotas or tariffs on non-European producers this could add further pressure upon employees of European-based producers to accept lower conditions of employment in order to protect their jobs.

A fourth group consists of industries where intra-Community trade is already high and completion will bring about a reduction in administrative and technical barriers. This would not only cut the costs of distribution but may provoke changes in distribution channels themselves. This should apply especially to the consumer goods which dominate this group. Such effects could be particularly important where price dispersion is quite high and provides sufficient incentives to wholesalers and retailers to switch to suppliers in low cost locations. Competition between final manufacturers may also shake up producer supply chains as manufacturers seek to defend their markets. The industries involved tend to have a higher proportion of smaller companies than is the case for the other three groups. From the employer perspective, therefore, this will tend to increase the significance of the effects of completion because small companies are less able to relocate partially across countries in response to changes in demand. But in other respects this group is likely to be affected only modestly by completion.

The above groups of industry are involved in international trade in goods. There are, however, other sectors which will be affected by completion, either directly through trade or indirectly through the knock-on effects of product market changes and the potential application of the social dimension across the whole economy. Those trading in financial business services are especially important because, along with telecommunications services, they provide the 'financial and informational infrastructure' of the economy. Concentrations of high quality services in these areas will reinforce other locational advantages which countries may have for foreign as well as domestic producers in particular sectors.

In addition, considerable interest attaches to three other sectors: construction (both because of its potential gains from new industrial and office building stimulated by the higher business activity and greater locational movement involved with it, and because of its traditional association with difficulties in regulation of atypical work forms); tourism and leisure (because of the scope for a substantial improvement in the value-added position of an industry which hitherto has been associated with low quality jobs which escape the regulatory framework already in existence); and wholesale and retail trade (because of the potential disruption to distribution networks described earlier and because these industries cover a particularly wide range of forms of employment).

Potential impacts on countries

The measures taken to complete the internal market are intended to provide not only a once-off stimulus to economic growth raising European GDP by about 5 per cent but also a source of dynamic gain which builds on itself (Cecchini, 1988). However, greater efficiency and adaptability in the labour market are seen as prerequisites for the return to low levels of unemployment. Combined with education and training systems which facilitate social as well as economic innovation, this would establish a foundation for long-run improvements in both the quantity and quality of jobs available to the people of the Community.

Similarly, in considering the sensitive sectors, there are quite marked differences in the implications for different countries. Space does not permit a full discussion of this but a summary of the overall implications is given in Figure 6.1. This shows the extent to which member states at the start of the SEM initiative were placed in strong, average or weak positions *vis-à-vis* those sectors most likely to be affected by the SEM. In the case of Germany (the FRG), over 70 per cent of employment in the sensitive sectors (which cover about 55 per cent of total employment in the production sector) was in sectors where trade performance was strong. In Greece, Spain and the UK, only about a third of employment in the sensitive sectors could be said to be in highly competitive industries.

The contrast between Ireland and the UK is an interesting one in this respect. Despite its poorer economy and location, a higher proportion of Irish employment is in the more competitive sectors; this can be attributed to a high level of transnational investment in Ireland. The UK's position indicates a failure to switch employment from low to high value-added manufacturing. Note also that the two poorest countries, Greece and Portugal, had exceptionally high proportions of their industrial employment in the sensitive sectors (amounting to 70 per cent in the case of Portugal) but Portugal had a significantly higher proportion in competitive sectors.

Of course, the crude analysis given above does not identify the dynamic positions of the countries concerned where improved performance may already

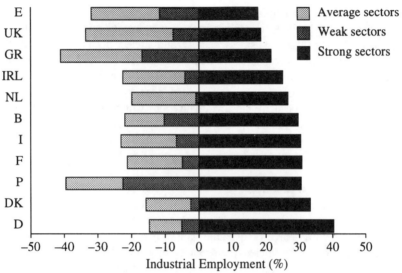

Source: CEC (1990a). Estimates are based on 1987 data.

Figure 6.1   Share of industrial employment in sensitive sectors

have been under way or, indeed, the scope for improving upon those positions over the longer term. The reference to Ireland touches upon a key issue, however: that of the potential impact of foreign direct investment (FDI). This process has assumed considerable significance from the labour market policy perspective on the analysis of the effects of the SEM.

2   SEM REACTIONS AND THE LABOUR MARKET

2.1 The Ingredients of Change

Foreign direct investment
The principal *long-term* gain from foreign inward investment is qualitative. It is unlikely that the resources used by foreign companies would have remained idle. However, the co-existence of high levels of unemployment and capital utilization indicates a shortage of both capital investment and the organizational capacity to bring about a fully occupied labour force in the short term and medium term. Foreign direct investment adds to the stock of physical capital available to an economy. It can also add to the stock of human capital available, in terms of foreign company management and technical skills involved in projects. Depending on the nature of the investment, it can provide a long-term dynamic stimulus through its role in demonstrating and diffusing product and process

innovations, showing new organization styles and strategies, intensifying competition in domestic markets and opening up better access to overseas markets.

National economic policies, therefore, usually include measures to encourage foreign direct investment which will enhance both the quantity and quality of economic activity.

Completion of the internal market will affect foreign direct investment, first, because it is expected to increase European GDP and gross fixed capital formation. Part of this increase is likely to be in the form of a cross-national creation of fixed assets which forms part of FDI. Second, the nature of the completion process is that firms will examine their business strategies in the light of the momentum towards greater European integration and ask whether or not they should consider a greater degree of international investment. This would involve options such as foreign acquisitions, licensing, joint ventures, creation of new subsidiary companies abroad, and greater investment in existing subsidiaries.

Third, the scope for achieving economies of scale once companies are unfettered by tariff and non-tariff barriers will lead to a rise in the size of plant. Other things being equal, this is likely to increase the significance of locational decisions because the number of plants will be fewer. It is also likely to increase the need for certain locational characteristics, notably, scope for expansion and an infrastructure capable of handling the physical and communications traffic.

Fourth, the reassessment of business strategy mentioned above is likely to extend not only to product market involvement and location of establishments but to the definition of the business – which functions it should perform itself, the balance between in-house and external provision. This may have locational consequences for both the firm and its current or potential future suppliers. Fifth, over and above the locational implications which stem from firms re-evaluating strategies regarding scope and the geographical distribution of their establishments, there will be impacts on suppliers.

Thus the above factors suggest that the completion process will be accompanied by and will probably give rise to in the long term a higher proportion of 'footloose investment' in the aggregate European total. The initial adjustment to the Single European Market will involve a large element of once-off transition but there will be a dynamic change tending to increase the range of organizational and locational options seriously considered and this will tend to increase the range of choices actually made and the changes consequent on that.

Responses to completion of the single market

Overall, then, it is intended that there will be greater co-operation between companies, a higher level of foreign direct investment between European countries, and more competitive organizational structures. Whilst these are seen as an essential part of achieving a Single European Market, there is less agreement about the creation of European 'social space' and the introduction of a 'social dimension' to the completion process.

One approach favours an extension to the process of deregulation of product markets to encompass labour markets as part of the economic integration agenda. This view stresses that Europe collectively will not be able to compete internationally if many labour market rigidities are not removed. Vigorous product market competition within Europe will help to do this by undermining national product market protection for inefficient labour market customs and regulations. This is the '*efficiency scenario*'.

However, two broad groups are concerned about the risks of this scenario. The first see problems of structural adaptation and market failure (especially in the training, research and development fields), which call for more significant institutional change in both the monetary and labour market areas. A bigger dose of deregulation given to more national labour markets is not regarded as being sufficient. The second group has a somewhat deeper programme of change in mind encompassing the promotion of economic democracy as part of political and social development at national and international level.

Both groups, nonetheless, see the spectre of low age competition accompanied by a shift in power towards transnational corporations and capital in general. In this scenario, companies would have free rein to depress wages, non-wage labour costs and other conditions of employment towards their lowest European common denominators. The foreign direct investment process would play a particularly important role in effecting this with national governments claiming competitive imperatives as a justification for dropping a variety of regulations. The outcome would be a '*cost-cutting scenario*' with fierce labour cost competition among member countries driving down first quality of jobs, then quality of labour and eventually quality of products. At its gloomiest, this prognosis points to the prospect of obsessive intra-European cost competition still failing to match the unit cost levels of newly industrializing countries whilst at the same time undermining Europe's capacity to develop its position in high value-added product markets, especially those dominated by Japan and the United States. To counteract the fear of 'cost-cutting' there has emerged what might be called the '*economic and social cohesion scenario*' which tries to reflect what its proponents would regard as the spirit as well as the letter of the Single European Act. This is wide-ranging but includes the aim of raising the legislative floor underpinning the individual and collective rights and social welfare provision for the labour force.

In addition to these three scenarios, there is a fourth option which seeks to achieve two objectives: first, the balancing of consumer and producer interests and, second, the creation of a virtuous circle of European economic development based on high human capital, high productivity, high wages, profits and investment. This view regards the curbing of monopoly power in both labour and product markets as essential but argues that changes in the regulation of the labour market beyond a certain point make virtually no contribution to that aim – they merely make weak workers weaker. Increases in the regulation of trade unions or decreases in the regulation of employment contracts to protect employees create political and social problems which distract attention from pursuing the second objective, namely, entry to the virtuous circle: we shall term this option the '*quality scenario*'.

The quality scenario lays much stress on improving the quality of human capital in its widest sense and deploying it fully in work, leisure, and in the production and maintenance of human capital itself (that is, education, training, health care and community support). In terms of policy on foreign direct investment, this strategy seeks to attract investment requiring high levels of complementary human capital and involving high specific expenditure on the training and development of the work force by the inward investor.

The four scenarios – 'efficiency', 'cost-cutting', 'economic and social cohesion' and 'quality' – are obviously somewhat stylized but correspond to those European scenarios which capture the main aspirations and anxieties accompanying the completion debate.

The actors
Turning now to the principal labour market actors involved in the process of integration and structural change, much concern has been expressed, especially by trade unions, about the extent to which the creation of the Single Market and liberalization of capital flows provide transnational corporations (TNCs) with enormous discretion over the conduct of their activities and plenty of incentive to exploit situations of weakness on the part of national or regional governments and the labour force. An alternative view is that TNCs are now so concerned with operating at the high quality end of the value-added spectrum that the benefits from exploiting the cost and quality of labour differentials available in Europe are minimal compared with those which arise in comparisons between the EU and third countries. From this point of view the transnational question is seen to be less relevant to the internal structure of the EU economy and much more important in relation to the rest of the world.

Nonetheless, the notion that TNC behaviour will put pressure on individual member governments to de-regulate further their labour markets in order to compete for FDI against Community and non-Community countries is a resilient one. In an extreme case, following the earlier terminology, this would initiate the 'cost-cutting strategy' which the 'economic and social cohesion strategy' is intended to oppose.

Evidence on the long-term development of TNCs does, however, seem at variance with the cost-cutting strategy becoming a major phenomenon *within* the

EU. The future appears to be dominated by complex organizational models producing high value-added products in which the 'service' or 'software' element assumes increasing importance, even when the product is a physical good. The momentum of this development seems to rule out any widespread, cost-cutting pursuit of locations in the weaker EU labour market segments.

Whether we can trust the 'efficiency strategy' to evolve into the 'quality strategy' without requiring some element of the 'economic and social cohesion strategy' is a moot point, the answer to which does depend crucially on the national perspective adopted. Could it be, though, that the fuss over the social dimension will prove to be much less important economically and socially than both sides of the debate currently seem to think? The 'quality strategy' will be critical to the success of any company based in a western industrialized country and engaged in international trade. How optimistic is it to argue that part of this strategy will be high levels of pay, participation and protection? Arguments about minimum standards would then not affect TNC behaviour very much at all, though they will probably complain to some degree since few organizations (or individuals) like to give up elements of discretion.

Alongside concern over the strengthening of the position of large multi-national corporations, there is anxiety that the creation of the Single Market will both intensify the disadvantages that small and medium-sized enterprises (SMEs) already experience and open up national industrial structures such that some SMEs will lose market niches within which they have hitherto operated very successfully. It is for these enterprises that the strategic choices are sharpest as they negotiate a path towards greater competitiveness through a landscape of progressively harmonized product market conditions but still highly differentiated labour markets.

The role of the social partners is also potentially subject to considerable change as a result of the completion of the Single Market. This concerns the level at which collective bargaining takes place and the range of issues covered by bargaining. It also involves the role of the social partners specifically in the regulatory process at EU level. Differences of style between countries are so marked in this respect that behind the formal structure of social partnership built into EU institutions lies a quite disparate pattern of relative influence between employers and trade unions *vis-à-vis* national governments and the EU according to country and sector.

Labour market factors and location
The impact of completion will depend partly on existing differences between national labour markets and their responses to the process of completion and partly upon other developments in the European and world economic environment. The latter are beyond the scope of this chapter.

The lowering of physical, technical and fiscal barriers may create situations in which it makes sense for companies to take advantage of better labour market conditions in one country compared with another. These relative conditions may have been known for some time but were not themselves sufficient incentive to justify investing in (or, at least, to a higher degree in) the preferred country. The conditions will include especially those which relate to:

(i) legislative constraints on management's ability to adopt working conditions and practices and to adjust employment levels and hours of work to match corporate requirements;
(ii) the extent of cooperation to be expected from trade unions in turning labour force potential into actual performance;
(iii) the availability and potential productivity of labour (demographic and labour force participation patterns, educational and training provision, and the supply of specific skills, notably, in managerial and technical occupations); and
(iv) the costs of labour, including statutory and customary (voluntary) non-wage labour costs. Underpinning all of these elements is the role of the state in regulating, on the one hand, the *process* of education, training and employment, on the other hand, the rights and obligations of *participants* involved in them.

Whilst companies may thus find themselves in better positions to exploit *existing* labour market differences, an awareness of this and other aspects of international economic change may lead countries to try to *alter* their positions in the labour market rankings. Various combinations of legislation, administrative measures, corporatism and exhortation can be deployed at national, regional or local levels, depending on constitutional and customary arrangements. The drift to de-regulate the labour market during the 1980s has been observed to some degree in almost all member countries of the European Community, though admittedly from very different starting points. Completion of the internal market could accelerate this process for those countries that 'lag behind'.

2.2. Labour Market Variations

The impact of technical change, the emergence of strong forms of global competition and transnational organization, the dramatic recession and recovery of the 1980s, followed by recession in the early 1990s and the impact of demographic change, have all contributed to the tensions and trends found in the labour market. Sectoral adjustment is disruptive and, when combined with macroeconomic policies which give priority to reducing inflation, it is unlikely to occur without a rise in unemployment. As regards employment, however, Figure 6.2 summarizes the changes in its level and sectoral structure during the last decade (see Table 6.2 for a key to the sectors). The principal feature is that virtually all the growth in employment has taken place in market and non-market services, whereas most of the debate about the SEM has related to the prospects for output and their implications for employment amongst the production industries. This feature is, of course, particularly marked for women.

The development and diffusion of new technology in processes and products, the restructuring or production, and an opening up of decisions regarding overall corporate and product market strategies provide a potent environment for change. The mutually interacting organizational and technological trends mean that decisions regarding the spatial location of economic activity are particularly coming under focus. Such decisions depend on a variety of factors: political factors; macroeconomic factors; corporate financial and legal considerations; infrastructure characteristics; national government and EU fiscal policies; market characteristics, including proximity to other market areas; and labour market factors.

With the greater integration of the EU, political, macroeconomic and financial conditions might expect to be 'Europeanized' with greater stability being achieved for all member states compared with situations of less integration but relative improvements being especially important for the weaker economies. Infrastructure characteristics and fiscal policy environments are more susceptible to national differentiation. The use of European fiscal policy via the Structural and Cohesion Funds is an attempt to offset some of the advantages of more developed and dynamic regions by way of infrastructure.

As regards market characteristics, including nearness to market and size of market considerations, the significance of these has been substantially intensified with the removal of barriers of trade, capital mobility and the entry of foreign ownership.

Considerable structural change, has therefore, been taking place interacting with changes in policy regimes. This has led to alterations in sectoral boundaries. The changes in manufacturing and service sector employment partly reflect shifts in the relationship between the two sectors. These involve particularly the externalization of some service functions previously performed within manufacturing enterprises and their incorporation as independent businesses within the service sector. Connected with this is the stronger manufacturing demand for high level service functions. The organization-market interface has shifted in favour of more externalization and more sophisticated service sector companies have evolved. As a consequence, a weaker locational link between services and manufacturing has developed, facilitated by improvements in communication and travel systems.

Male sectoral employment in EUR10 (excl GR,I), 1982 and 1991

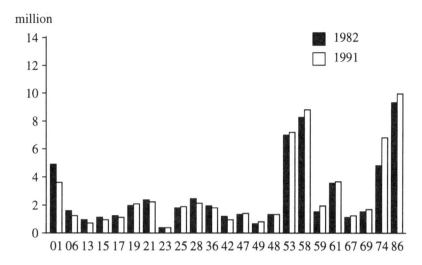

Female sectoral employment in EUR10 (excl GR,I), 1982 and 1991

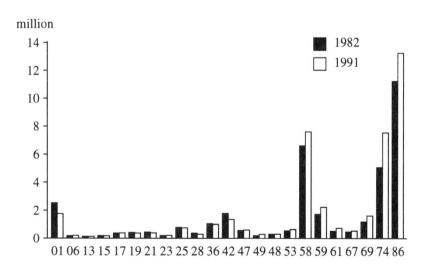

Figure 6.2   Sectoral employment in EUR10 (excl. GR,I), 1982 and 1991

Table 6.2 Classification of sectors shown in figure and allocation of 'sensitive sectors'

NACE-CLIO R25		NACE Sensitive Sectors
01	Agriculture, forestry and fishery	
06	Fuel and power products	
13	Ores and metals	247-8 (4I)
15	Mineral products	251 (4I), 256 (4I), 257 (2)
17	Chemical products	315 (2)
19	Metal products	321-7 (4CA)
21	Agricultural machinery	330 (1), 372 (1)
23	Office and dp machines	344 (1), 345-6 (4CO), 347 (4CA), 341-2(3)
25	Electrical goods	351 (4CO), 361 (3), 362 (2), 364 (4CA)
28	Transport equipment	417 (3), 421 (3), 425 (2), 427-8 (2)
36	Food, beverages, tobacco	431-2 (4I), 438 (4CO), 451 (4CO), 453 (4CO), 455 (4CO)
42	Textiles and clothing, footwear	
47	Paper and printing products	481 (4I)
49	Rubber and plastic products	491 (4CO), 493 (4CO), 495 (4CO)
48	Other manufacturing products	
53	Building and construction	Key to the above: Figures in parenthesis relate to the sensitive sector
58	Recovery, repair, trade services	group covered;
59	Lodging and catering services	4CA, CO or I denote capital, consumer or intermediate groups within
61	Inland transport services	group 4.
63	Maritime and air transport	
65	Aux. transport services	
67	Communication services	Note: '61*' appearing in the Figure 6.2 represents 61, 63 and 65
69A	Credit and insurance	together.
74	Other market services	
86	Non-market services	

The research evidence on factors affecting the location of industry has, indeed, highlighted a number of key elements of economic activity whose accumulation produces a dynamic effect, the presence of each being reinforced by that of others. The 'dynamic stratum' of economic change appears to consist of specialised high-tech manufacturing companies, research and development organizations, telecommunications companies, corporate and regional head-quarters of large enterprises, and high level business services. An agglomeration of these activities places a region or nation in a much strong position to cope with the threats and opportunities of European-wide socio-economic change.

Turning to the labour market factors likely to affect investment decisions, some indication according to the variations in the above characteristics among member states is given briefly below, recognizing that within member states there can also be large variations which exceed average national differences.

As regards the *industrial relations and legislative environments*, Figures 6.3-8 capture some of the differences in regulatory regimes and their effects on management's prerogative to deploy personnel in line with corporate requirements. The charts are more or less self-explanatory, tending to show that the UK and Denmark (where included) have by far the most de-regulated labour markets. Spain tends to be among the most regulated whereas the other three poorest economies usually either appear in the middle of the regulatory range covered by the remaining member states or move about within it.

Accompanying the structural trends noted above are changes which affect the nature of the employment relationship. First, part-time employment and the use of more 'flexible' contractual forms and working patterns are increasing in many countries, involving different degrees of attachment between employees and employers and more temporary work. Second, even for those with conventional full-time contracts, the obligations placed upon or voluntarily accepted by employers as part of the employment relationship are being reduced in range and/or depth. This is not so much an endorsement of the 'core-periphery' model of the firm's personnel structure as a dominant influence in organizational change but a recognition that increasing the number of paid employees who are clearly at the margin of the particular workforce is not a guarantee of protection for the majority. Third, a weakening of social partnership through changes in the legal framework or through employer-led rejection of custom and practice has occurred at various levels in many countries. Conditions are gradually being created in which more workforce adjustment will be externalized by enterprises rather than contained as far as possible within the internal labour markets of their organizations.

These three aspects of change do not occur together in all countries, however. The futures of trade union movements and of corporatist practices will not be determined merely by the experiences of the 1980s. But certain features have already established themselves or are likely to emerge in whatever situations

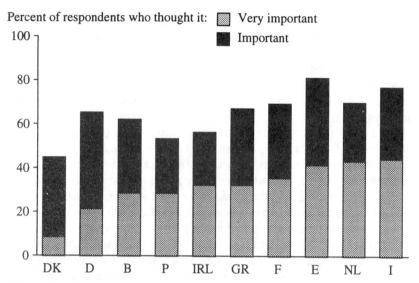

Percent of respondents who thought it: ▨ Very important   ■ Important

Note: Manufacturing industry. Denmark and Luxembourg were not surveyed.
1989 EC Survey adjusted for non-response.

*Figure 6.3 Importance of hiring and firing laws as an obstacle to
employing more people*

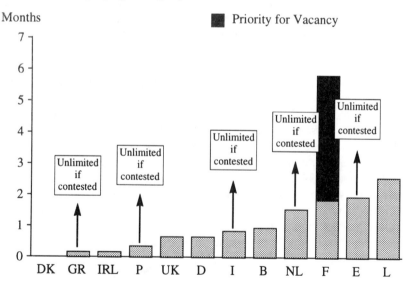

Months   ■ Priority for Vacancy

Note: Covers redundancy through dismissal for economic reasons.
Source: Emerson (1988), Wells (1992)

*Figure 6.4 Time taken to carry out redundancy of a 'blue collar'
worker with 9 months service*

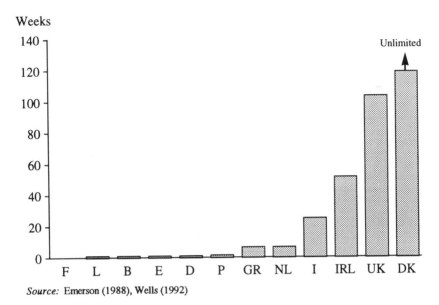

Source: Emerson (1988), Wells (1992)

*Figure 6.5 Statutory duration of probation or qualifying period
for 'blue collar' work*

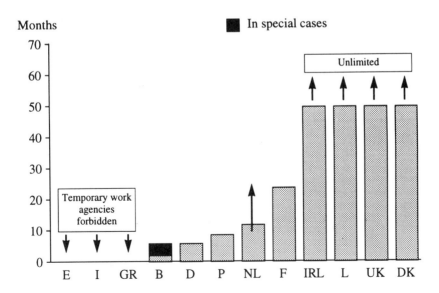

Figure 6.6 Maximum duration for temporary work

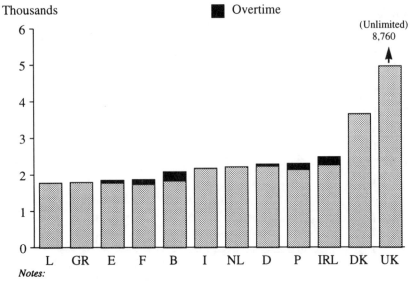

Notes:
(a) Maximum hours permitted without authorisation
(b) Estimates for 1989. Maximum weekly hours are being reduced in Portugal.

Figure 6.7   Maximum statutory hours per year for a 'standard' worker

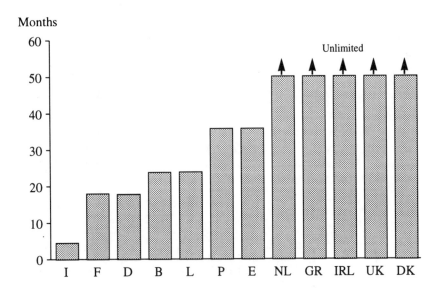

Figure 6.8   Maximum duration for fixed term contract

evolve at national or European level: for example, the notion of 'flexibility' will continue to grip the debate on industrial relations and the notion of 'insider versus outsider' will progressively increase its influence.

Turning to *labour supply conditions*, although most of the EU's projected growth in the labour force will arise in northern Europe, the highest rates of growth are in poorer countries of the south, together with Ireland. The likely scale – 30–40 per cent increases over the period 1990–2010, according to CEC (1993) – must be seen against a background of current high unemployment rates in the four key countries: Greece, Spain, Portugal and Ireland. Only in the last of these is the labour force growth substantially due to population effects; the principal factor in the other three cases is the rise in participation rates.

So it is in the poorer member states that the actual labour surplus and socio-demographic potential for its continuation appear to be the greatest. Unfortunately, the surplus is of such an extent that it may be argued that it is more a disadvantage than an advantage with respect to attracting domestic and foreign investment, because of the socio-economic burden it implies for the national governments concerned.

Moreover, when considering educational and training provision, all four poorer countries turn out to have less than average educational attainment. However, whereas Ireland and Greece are only just below average, with over 40 per cent of those aged over 25 in the labour force having had post-compulsory or university level education, the figures for Spain and Portugal were 30 per cent and 15 per cent, respectively. In contrast, Germany and Denmark record about 80 and 70 per cent, respectively. Whilst these figures rise substantially for the younger cohorts within the group (gaining, on average, 10 percentage points if restricted to 25–34 year olds), the same country ranking tends to be reproduced. Similar results apply if the educational attainment of those in *employment* is examined; the results are shown in Figure 6.9, to which reference will be made later in relation to sectoral-country differences.

A somewhat more complicated picture arises when turning to occupational structures as an indication of the skills embodied in the labour force through occupational work experience, notably in the managerial, professional and associate professional/technical occupations, that is, those most associated with the growth areas of employment. This is because with such occupations there is room, especially in international comparisons, for wide ranges in the matches between occupation on the one hand and the qualifications resulting from education and training, whether possessed by the individual (as measured here), required specifically for the jobs as initially designed by the organization, or used in stipulating recruitment standards. Not only do the data capture differences between classifications, but they also reflect the social construction of skills. However, the provisional calculations shown in Figure 6.10 do point to the low position of Spain and Portugal (with Spain recording the lowest proportions in this case in contrast to the findings for educational attainment) and the much more average pattern for Greece and Ireland.

The presence of different industrial structures among member states can be allowed for in the aggregate summary of educational attainment and occupational structure. If each country is given the average EU industrial employment structure but retains its own educational attainment rates and occupational proportions by sector, hypothetical national rates and proportions can be derived. The effects of this in all four poorer countries is to increase attainment and skill levels substantially and, in more human capital-intensive countries, to reduce the values of these parameters. However, the disparities between the two groups remain significant, indicating that the weaker economies generally apply lower education and skill intensities to activities sector by sector. This is apparent from the disaggregated data.

For the EU as a whole there are very large differences between sectors in these respects. The highest rates of educational attainment are found in non-market services (no. 86 – education, health, research and development, and other public services), 'other market services' (74 – business services, recreational services), credit and insurance services (69A), fuel and power (06), and other electrical goods (25). Chemicals (17) and communications services are also quite high in the ranking. There is a similar pattern of occupational attainment though other sectors also feature, most of which show reasonably high educational attainment: agricultural, industrial and office machinery (21 and 23), and paper and printing products (47).

The *relative costs of labour* may be analysed in a variety of ways (Table 6.3). Essentially, the important elements are the unit labour costs that result from any system and the extent to which enterprises have the scope for negotiation over the different parts of the labour cost-productivity package. There are very wide differences in (i) the size and the employer and the net income received by the employee and (ii) the relationship between net labour income, other income, the prices of goods and services in the market place, and the availability of other goods and services to which there is access via non-market processes.

In simple theoretical terms, how the tax element of the wedge is treated, that is, what proportions of tax are paid by the employer and employee, and whether they are deemed to be income tax, national insurance against unemployment or other social security charges does not greatly matter. Certainly, structural factors can mean that the composition of both the tax element and the voluntary non-wage cost element – and the way in which they impinge on different members of the labour force – can introduce significant variations in consequences for incentives to employ and be employed. Nonetheless, the major point often overlooked is that the enterprise and employee are both likely to receive some 'return' from the tax wedge taken by the state. How that return is structured, for example, in terms of state support for education, training, health, redundancy payments, employ-

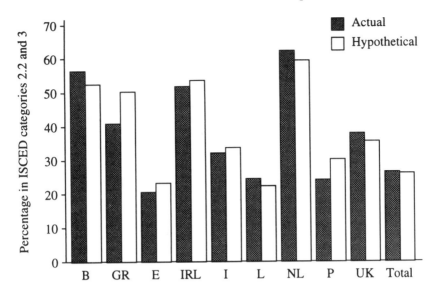

Note: These data are provisional; adjustments for significant differences
in classification between countries are not yet complete.

Figure 6.9   Educational attainment by country and EUR 9, 1991

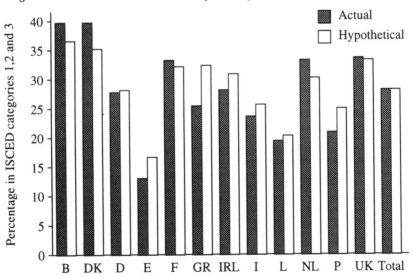

Note: These data·are provisional: adjustments for significant differences
in classification between countries are not yet complete.

*Figure 6.10   Higher and intermediate occupations by country
and EUR 12, 1991*

ment subsidies, unemployment benefit and social security and how it interacts with other transfer payments will affect the competence and motivation of the labour force and the relative costs of labour force adjustment borne by the employer, employee and the state.

The labour costs debate in the EU has fluctuated somewhat, the evidence cutting across the fears expressed by those who envisage a cost-cutting scenario and apparently giving neither confirmation nor reassurance. Two quite different though related issues have hinged on the labour costs concern. The first is that national governments such as the UK's have, in effect, sought to bring down labour costs and encourage vocational education, training and better human resource management in order to increase productivity. Together these gains would then provide a firm basis for initially low labour costs, leading to an attractive climate for domestic and inward investment, high profits and eventually higher wages once these had been earned by the achievement of low *unit* labour costs. At the same time, the official UK view taken is that many other member states should be doing the same thing because they are also unable to justify such high costs, especially those deriving from social security charges and paid holidays (Table 6.3).

This second perspective is not particularly intended to help those with relatively high labour costs to compete with those with low costs but to strengthen the capacity of Europe as a whole to compete alongside each other with third countries. Indeed, it is apparent that there is little expectation of the cost-cutting scenario being generated at all through intra-EU cost and regulatory competition. Buigues, Ilzkowitz and Lebrun (1990, p. 4), for example, believe that the SEM will 'neither upset the mix of sectoral specializations across member states nor lead to massive transfers of economic activities between geographic zones'. This may indeed be the case with intra-industry trade which involves countries introducing new or substantially reformed sectors into their industrial structure is unlikely to be so conveniently inclined towards maintaining the status quo. Even in the case of intra-industry trade, the notion that each country will specialize according to comparative advantages (for example, regarding high/low intensities of capital/skilled labour/unskilled labour) settling for their current position in the quality – value added league for the various sectors flies rather in the face of promoting social (meaning usually regional) cohesion.

Finally, it is worth stressing once again that labour market variations may not be decisive in determining location decisions. A survey by Prognos, for example, gave most weight to the 'institutional framework' which referred to the environment of economic regulations, market potential and the political and social climate. Production costs were no more important than the 'technological-economic infrastructure'. The quality of the labour force was much less important (see Table 6.4). Great care must be taken in interpreting such survey

Table 6.3 Average hourly industrial labour costs in the EC, 1988

| | Actual | Re-weighted for industrial structure[a] | Non-wage costs as % of actual[b] | | | |
			Total	Social Security	Paid Holidays	Other
Belgium	17.0	15.1	46	24	9	13
Denmark	15.5	14.7	17	6	8	3
Germany	18.4	17.5	44	21	11	12
Spain	9.1	9.3	–	–	–	–
France	15.3	15.2	48	28	9	11
Greece	5.3	5.2	38	18	7	13
Ireland	10.6	10.0	30	15	12	3
Italy	14.2	13.1	47	33	11	3
N. Italy	14.5	14.3	–	–	–	–
S. Italy	13.5	11.9	–	–	–	–
Luxembourg	13.6	11.9	31	15	11	6
Netherlands	16.4	16.0	44	24	10	10
Portugal	3.0	3.3	41	18	5	18
United Kingdom	10.9	10.7	29	14	10	5
CE 12	14.1	14.8	–	–	–	–

Note: Industries include manufacturing and construction only. Data have been converted using average ECU exchange rates for 1988.

Sources: (a) Zighera (1993) (b) Eurostat Labour Costs Survey.

Table 6.4 *Factors influencing the location of activity within the EC*

Weight	Institutional framework 35%	Infra-structure 25%	Qualification of workers 14%	Production costs 26%
B	0	–	+	+
DK	–	++	+	– –
D	++	++	+++	– –
E	0	– –	– –	+++
F	+	++	+	0
GR	– –	– –	– –	+++
IRL	0	– –	++	+
I	0	–	0	0
L	0	0	0	0
NL	0	++	++	0
P	– –	– –	–	+++
UK	++	++	0	+

Source: Walwei and Werner (1993), based on a study by Prognos.

responses but they serve to indicate that the practical significance of large differences between countries in labour market parameters may be quite modest.

3   SOCIAL POLICY RATIONALES AND REGULATORY STRUCTURES

The evidence cited in the previous section suggests that labour markets differ significantly and that these differences are likely to have a greater effect on the distribution of employment and income within the EU as internationalization proceeds in one form or another and a greater proportion of production, sourcing and investment decisions are open to market forces. Governments in the pursuit of investment, a broader tax base and a larger concentration of corporate power operating out of the national economy have become increasingly concerned about labour market regulation and labour force quality. This section looks at the rationales for policy and the notion of regulatory convergence.

3.1 Objectives, Scope and Style of Labour Market Policy

If European labour markets consist of actors, it is clear that not all are using the same script. Expectations differ for several reasons but particularly because of ambiguity about the following:

(a) the objectives of the different actors;
(b) their rights;
(c) their responsibilities;
(d) the appropriate scope of the employment contract;
(e) the role of the labour market in a modern economy.

Government attitudes are especially important because they condition both the socio-economic environment and the policy response to it. This section focuses almost exclusively on national government and EU policy rationales, though other actors, notably trade unions, have found themselves faced with difficult decisions about how to adapt to change in the last quarter of the 20th century.
   The principal objectives of government have been to:

• promote long-term efficiency,
• promote long-term equity,
• mitigate short-term social hardship.

It has become increasingly important when considering the equity objective, particularly in discussions at EU level, to distinguish between individual equity, workplace/enterprise solidarity and wider social cohesion.

Major constraints relating to the markets for labour and training arise from regulations governing, especially:

- compulsory education;
- state and occupational pensions;
- recruitment and redundancy;
- health and safety;
- equal opportunities;
- social security and related benefits;
- minimum wages;
- access to and provision of education and training.

The 'free' operation of the 'market' has, therefore, been thoroughly compromised. From this perspective, policies across Europe differ only by degree. 'Convergence' has occurred and the values inherent in the labour market systems of different countries are similar. From this point of view, attention should be paid not so much to the inter-EU variation but to the gap between the constellation of national policy mixes currently observable and the needs of the next decade and beyond.

The scope of policy – the impact of constraints

Some of the constraints on the market process actually make more effective certain types of intervention which seek to promote employment whilst working with the remaining elements of the market mechanism (Lindley, 1991a). For example, the presence of a binding minimum wage constraint will enhance the effectiveness of employment subsidies targeted on low paid, unskilled workers (Johnson, 1980). Note that the subsidies in this case are not intended to generate improvements in the operation of the labour market which would ultimately make them unnecessary. They reflect an acceptance on the grounds of equity, of the presence of minimum wages and social benefits but accompanied by a recognition that they can have some negative effects which the employment subsidy is intended to counteract.

Some constraints limit management freedom to hire and fire according to the needs of the organization as they perceive them. There is clearly considerable variation in the recruitment and redundancy provisions across Europe (Figures 6.3-8). Some limit the freedom of both management and the individual, as in the case of compulsory education.

Other constraints appear to represent a widening of the role of the labour market, rather than a limitation upon the operation of the market mechanism. Their effect is, nonetheless, to lock together transactions that need not be connected. The provision of housing for employees, medical insurance, childcare, pensions and, even, training all tend to create barriers at the same time as creating benefits. Ostensibly, they enrich the employment relationship, but they do so by manipulating the benefit package (often by exploiting tax advantages) in ways which tend to tie certain groups of employees to the organization.

This blurring of the boundaries between the labour market and other markets can also have important effects upon the other markets which may in turn have further implications for individuals, both for those 'benefiting' and other workers. The provision of childcare via tax concessions only to employer-based schemes may not only discriminate against those form whom that kind of provision is unsuitable but also distort the availability of childcare in ways which undermine the potential supply of childcare in the locality concerned, and hence the conditions governing the labour force participation of other groups.

In the pension field, too, the element of coercion in some occupational systems and the familiar elements of gender discrimination found in many state and occupational schemes, together crate winners and losers on quite arbitrary grounds.

The sort of constraints identified above may be very common across Europe but this does not meant that they are found to the same degree or in the same form. The rights and responsibilities accepted by or imposed upon employers and individuals/households or assumed by the state or regional authority are clearly seen in different lights (Lindley, 1991b). Why this should matter at the EU level is considered in the next sub-section. What is worth noting at this stage is that the general motivation behind each 'constraint' can give rise to rather different outcomes regarding the four potential objectives.

Moreover, the form of regulation which underpins the constraint may introduce its own effects upon the outcome. Legislation and legal organization affect access to the law,, the system for promoting compliance, and the ultimate practical significance of the constraint; self-regulation by employers, or joint regulation by the social partners within a framework established by the state will produce further variants. Attitudes towards and expectations of the effects of regulatory and fiscal labour market policies will depend upon perceptions of the rigour with which they will be implemented.

Thus the notion of 'active' labour market policies can be related both to the 'enabling' of the market mechanism and the 'enforcement' of measures to temper its effects.

'Enabling' the market mechanism to function more effectively

The efficiency of any market will be impaired if participants are poorly informed, operate under great uncertainty, are slow to make decisions, are subject to very restrictive contracts, or encounter high barriers to energy; it will also be impaired if the market interacts with other markets which are themselves inefficient (see below). The impact of low labour market efficiency will depend upon the strains being placed upon the labour market mechanism. In a period of steady growth accompanied by modest cyclical fluctuations these will not be great. But in a period of considerable structural change the inefficiency of the labour market can seriously impede the adjustment of the whole economy.

The general notion of a labour market is familiar to many participants in the debate about the economy and employment. Some think that the labour market does exhibit certain elements of competitive behaviour quite strongly, some argue not so much that the market is fairly competitive but that it should be made to work that way, and some feel that the main impediment to achieving such a change is the lack of competition in product markets rather than the inherent limitations placed upon labour market behaviour by institutional and social factors. Others take a more skeptical view of the possibilities of achieving a labour market which performs its functions of allocating available skills to jobs more effectively through the pay structure. In that case, the most that can be hoped for is that by some means the aggregate rate of wage inflation can be brought within reasonable bounds leaving the wage structure to the mercies of whatever compromises were required to get agreement on overall wage increases in firms and across industries.

Much of the debate about labour market policy has dealt only very indirectly with the basic issue of what functions we should realistically expect the labour market to perform. This makes it difficult to provide a satisfactory economic rationale for policy, for example, that concerned with promoting occupational mobility through stimulating industrial training. Policy makers on the labour market front have operated within a framework of limitations placed upon them by imperatives often created in national negotiation over such matters as the practice of industrial relations, prices and incomes control, industrial and regional policy, and the evolution of the public sector.

Of central importance, therefore, to the style of labour market policy is to decide where the evidence points to the need to *bypass* the market mechanism and where it suggests that measures should be adopted to *make the market work more effectively*. Judgments of this kind are difficult to make. They depend not only upon an assessment of the practical problems facing decision-makers in the labour market now and in the past but also on a view of the sort of environment likely to arise in the future. Moreover, they will differ according to sector, skill and geographical location, for the labour market is really a multiplicity of partly interacting sub-markets.

Market-oriented policies and reality
If the idea of making the labour market work more effectively is to acquire more substance than has been evident in debates over the last decade or so of considerable policy activity, then we need to know much more about the feasibility of introducing a greater degree of market-orientation and the advantages and disadvantages of doing so.

Nonetheless, the notion of making the market work better seems to imply the use of a package of measures or approaches along the following lines:

(a) Foster greater efficiency in each labour market, whether locationally or occupationally defined, largely through providing better information to participants in the market, and a brokerage service designed to reduce the time and resources involved in job search by individuals and recruitment by firms.

(b) Encourage wage settlements which produce average pay levels and pay structures which reflect economic conditions in the labour and product markets concerned.

(c) Reduce imperfections in parallel markets (leaving aside the question of product markets), such as the housing market and the capital market available to individuals to finance mobility. These imperfections otherwise undermine attempts to promote greater mobility.

(d) Seek to circumvent inefficiencies which may arise where the labour market has taken over a considerable role in the provision of services which need not necessarily be tied so firmly to a particular employment contract, notably in the supply of training and in pension provision – this may be done partly by pursuing a greater separation of these markets.

(e) Promote competition in product markets (including 'product-labour' markets found amongst some of the professions); failing which, act to weaken the link between product market power and collusive agreements between employers and trade unions/professional associations.

(f) Recognize that, in a segmented external labour market accompanied by highly structured internal labour markets in some sectors of the economy, attempts to make the market more efficient must be made in each segment – otherwise a considerable imbalance is likely to arise which will operate to the disadvantage of those workers with least influence in the labour market and will cause inefficiency through the presence of occupational barriers.

The above deal with improving the infrastructure of the labour market and removing distortions which would tend to lead to a mis-allocation and under-utilization (whether in the form of low productivity or open unemployment) of the labour force. Such measures might also promote greater equity, particularly if item (f) were pursued with commitment. Much of labour market policy in the areas mentioned above implicitly assumes that reducing the inefficiency and inequity is desirable and reducing the former will help to reduce the latter.

Stepping over the boundary to 'help the market along' may also involve other actions at the margin to stimulate more efficient contributions from the education and training systems and to facilitate more mobility.

(g) Ensure that education and training programmes correspond with the needs of new entrants to, those returning to, and existing members of the labour force in order for them to be able to respond to the evolving pattern of job opportunities in the economy.

(h) Speed up adaptation to structural change by promoting inter-market movement through increasing the financial provision for geographical and occupational mobility.

However, experience since about the mid-1970s suggests that governments have come to recognize that tackling imperfections in the labour market, as in (a)–(h), is a long-term exercise with limited short-term benefits to those social groups most seriously affected by high levels of unemployment. Moreover, it is quite likely that the political will to push through more competition at all levels of the labour market will falter at the very point where the action taken so far exposes the most vulnerable members of the labour force to more competition without affecting the more advantaged members.

As a consequence, a variety of experimental schemes has been tried in most European countries with the aim of reducing unemployment at minimum public cost and least risk of increasing inflation. Four sets of initiatives can be distinguished which partly overlap with each other and, as some of them take on a semi-permanent status, begin to overlap with the longer-term measures summarised above.

(i) Introduce measures to stimulate the demand for labour. These fall broadly into two groups: (1) those which aim to provide temporary employment outside the conventional labour market arrangements, with some opportunities for training where possible; and (2) those which work more through the market system by subsidizing the retention of existing employees and the recruitment of new people.

(j) Promote the redistribution of employment opportunities by providing financial incentives for short-time working schemes, job sharing and job splitting, and/or by encouraging changes in general hours of work, holidays, and so on, through collective agreements or by further restrictive legislation.

(k) Attempt to reduce the supply of labour (in terms of people seeking employment) by providing incentives for early retirement, prolonged periods of initial education and training, and greater opportunities for mid-career training, and so on.

(l) Seek to improve the positions of particular groups of disadvantaged people, first by combating irrational and ill-informed discrimination against them and, second, by introducing positive action programmes to tilt the balance of costs and benefits in favour of employing, training and promoting such workers.

Governments who start with a firm notion of promoting the market process as far as possible are then driven progressively to vary their approaches according to precise function concerned (for example, training) and the political and economic imperatives at the time, weighing objectives and constraints. Policy styles have thus exhibited various mixes of four generic approaches to government–market relations:

- use the market as it stands;
- make the market work better;
- bypass the market;
- extend the market.

The most important example of extending the market is in areas where government has sought, in effect, to strengthen the external training market so that access to training is not so conditional on obtaining a job, that is, on the state of the labour market. For women and older workers, this is a potentially crucial improvement in the market structure serving both long-term efficiency and equity objectives (Lindley, 1991b). Moreover, it serves not only individuals but also some enterprises. Part of the impact of product market conditions and new technology upon organizational design is to increase the skill content of jobs, especially in the white collar sector; better qualified entrepreneurs, engineers, technicians, secretaries, and so on are required. Given their more limited internal labour markets, the capacity of small and medium-sized enterprises (SMEs) to provide initial and continuing training alongside attractive career development opportunities is much more restricted than is the case of larger organizations. Moreover, this problem is likely to increase as the skill-intensity of production and service activities increases.

More effective labour and training market structures will need to evolve in order to promote more efficient training so that access to training by individuals and to skilled employees by SMEs is not impeded by the lack of 'economies of scale' in training and career development when conducted in the context of a particularly SME.

3.2 Convergence and EU Social Policy

The language of European social–economic policy

The notion of European social policy is not without difficulty. Most discussion within the European policy community associates 'social' policy with a much narrower field of policy than might have been expected from a context in which 'social' is implicitly the complement of 'economic'. Much of EU usage does not cover areas of social policy that would commonly be recognised as relating to 'social life'. Whilst this partly reflects the difference between the scope of national government policy and that of EU competence, it has a deeper significance which colours the nature of the policy debates in the EU. One way of looking at this is in terms of efficiency, individual equity, workplace solidarity and social cohesion.

Essentially, European social policy corresponds to those areas of economic policy which relate to human resources, except when it relates to regional policy, part of which deals not only with human resources but also with investment in physical capital and industrial development. The first usage arises in discussions of the 'social dimension' of the SEM, especially the Social Charter and its derivative, the Social Chapter of the Maastricht treaty; the second usage arises in discussion of social cohesion in the context of EMU. In each case, however, a third usage is to be found. This extends the coverage of policy to include areas where, through the legal process notably the European Court, and evolution takes place in interpretations of the original intentions lying behind the law and the applicability of the law to present day issues brought before the Court. This has had particular importance in the field of social policy which is concerned with equal opportunities for women.

In whatever context, however, anything which relates to the institutional framework of the labour and training markets is treated as 'social'. The implication is that these activities are somewhat suspect in the contribution they can make to economic objectives. They are, therefore, allocated to a category which groups together a wide range of functions with more or less connection with social welfare issues.

Thus the term social policy has become a residual category which covers those parts of EU policy which raise issues relating to either the development and deployment of human resources or to equity between individuals or groups identified by social and/or spatial characteristics.

At the same time, the terms social dimension, social cohesion and social policy have, in a sense, become so elastic that they cease to provide an adequate indication of the subject matter involved. This has helped to distort the discussion of European economic integration in a way which has allowed market liberals to claim that the 'social dimension' will undermine progress towards achieving the central overriding objective: competitiveness of the EU economy on a par with that of North America and the Pacific Basin.

In particular, the social dimension has been seen to introduce into a process of economic integration, which is based on promoting EU-wide product market competition, an element of back-sliding; not only does it appear to compromise the integration-competition agenda by introducing more 'politics' but it also threatens to place 'social obligations' on employers which many may not be able to afford.

Despite paying lip-service to the importance of education in promoting long-term economic growth, it has been common in macroeconomic policy analysis to regard education purely as a consumption good; training and 'social partnership' have tended to receive the same treatment.

This confusion or carelessness in applying the epithet 'social' to activities which manifestly contribute directly to 'economic' growth would not necessarily be removed by identifying a middle category of 'labour market and training policy' or 'human resources policy'. For the problem is to avoid presumptions which separate 'economy' from 'society' rather than to find a bridge between them. Economic activity is social activity; social life is economic life.

The concept of convergence
Despite the ambiguity of the term 'social policy' discussed above, the analysis of the objectives, scope and style of policy given above provides a basis for clarifying the concept of convergence. The policy models evolving in different countries may be said to be converging if the following characteristics are becoming similar:

- the balance struck between the four objectives: increasing efficiency, individual equity, workplace/enterprise solidarity, social cohesion;
- the constraints on the market mechanism which are accepted as the framework within which labour market policy must do its best to promote the four objectives;
- the choice of policy style as it relates to market structure and process: especially as regards working with or bypassing the market.

If a state of convergence is represented by the above trends, under what conditions will convergence be necessary for EU economic growth to be both substantial and sustainable? That is, when is an EU-wide social policy embodying the notion of convergence likely to be justifiable?

Overall, many EU member states face continuing problems of achieving productivity growth and competitiveness on a par with the leading countries, the re-emergence of high unemployment, persistent shortages of key skills, failure to integrate women into the labour market, restricted choices available to older workers both in relation to redeployment and retirement, aging of the population, concern about social exclusion and a potential problem of migration into the EU from central and eastern Europe and from north Africa. However, this does not itself justify the pursuit of an EU-wide social policy or the harmonization or various delivery systems. The need for such collaborative thinking and co-ordination derives from other perspectives.

The case for EU social policy

Clearly there are many facets to the case for developing an EU social policy and the labour market component within it. Only some of the key aspects are considered below.

First, where the problem has its origin in a phenomenon which is essentially European-wide but not evenly distributed, there is a case for considering a sharing of the burden and this requires appropriate mechanisms at Community level. Examples of this category are the likely influx of migrants to the EU and major disparities between member states in the effects of the single market programme upon employment and unemployment, particularly in already depressed regions. The EU structural funds are, of course, intended to follow consistent principles in assisting projects submitted for support and in evaluating the outcomes.

Second, under EMU, as opposed to the SEM, fiscal restraints by those governments whose budgetary positions and inflation records are weak will require the setting of a social framework which, whilst respecting the different values and cultures of different countries, will inevitably embody a certain view of the priority groups whose protection from the worst effects of fiscal restraint is to be regarded as legitimate. Examples are fiscal obligations deriving from the implementation of EU equal opportunities legislation, measures to reduce the long-term social and economic effects of current restraint, and supply-side investments relating to the labour market.

Third, to the extent that labour market situations might lead to an undermining of the Single Market, there is a case for EU policy to prevent this happening (Lindley, 1991a). However, the notion of 'social dumping' is an awkward one when applied to the relations between producers within the EU as opposed to the relations between EU and third country producers. One of the basic ways in which poorer regions might close the gap between them and richer regions is to invest more in efficiency than in equity or social cohesion. Arguments about the economic benefits of programmes to promote equity and a 'regulatory floor' are not easily resolved in this context and deserve more rigorous research.

Fourth, there is a political–economic case for EU–level policy which begins with an assumption that member states share the judgment that the SEM and EMU are critically important to the long-term growth of the EU. Concern over the social dimension is then seen from a number of perspectives but may be summarised as follows:

(a) if economic differences between countries get too large, this will lead to resentment and political instability in the EU;
(b) all countries should benefit absolutely from integration;

(c) in counter-factual terms, (b) may be true even if a country actually experiences a lower growth rate (or even an absolute drop) in GDP during and after integration when compared with the period before;

(d) poor countries should benefit relatively from integration;

(e) in counter-factual terms, (d) may be true even if a country actually experiences a worsening of its relative position after integration;

(f) but in both (c) and (e) the counter-factual argument is probably too subtle to be plausible – people will not believe that their national performance would have been even worse;

(g) so Europe must achieve faster growth overall than has been the case in 'the past' and poorer countries should catch up with richer countries to some degree;

(h) without the latter, poorer countries will be disillusioned and, without the former, richer countries will be disillusioned;

(i) however, four key issues are:

(1) will poorer countries catch up best by competing on costs (including financial and non-financial costs of labour) whilst moving to the quality scenario in particular industries or will the former actually discourage the latter?

(2) will 'raising the regulatory floor' then be better for all countries?

(3) how crucial will be the scale and distribution of the structural funds in off-setting the transitional competitive disadvantages for poorer countries?

(4) should structural funds operate more closely in conjunction with private sector investment so as to increase the leverage of structural fund expenditure on the introduction of the 'quality' strategy?

The above factors deal with situations in which certain labour market problems are inherently European; or are given special attention when resolving arguments about the fiscal stance of countries with weaker economies operating within complete or quasi-monetary union; or are seen to have a very direct effect on the integrity of the Single Market; or are part of a more general threat to European political–economic stability arising from continuing or increasing divergence of national economies. Thus, all fall within a framework based on consensus about the critical importance of a long-run commitment to an integrated Europe.

To return to the scenarios of section 2, we might ask which completion scenario is evolving. This will depend, of course, on the industry and country or region. The quality scenario, for example, may characterize the German clothing industry but an incipient cost-cutting scenario may threaten the British industry. Can EC and national policies encourage the quality outcome or will the efficiency scenario lead to that anyway? What parts must the different actors play in such developments: what is the appropriate division of responsibility between the EC, member governments, employers, trade unions and individuals?

A particular key issue relates to regional development and the so-called 'dynamic stratum' mentioned earlier. A major question is whether or not new patterns of comparative advantage can, indeed, emerge to compete with existing ones based on the location of natural resources, position in the European transport and distribution network, and current concentrations of dynamic activities which favour further momentum of development.

The notion that supply-side policies can foster enhanced comparative advantage in relatively poor regions implies, of course, the further assumption that such policies can be introduced in a sufficiently differentiated manner with respect to poor rather than rich regions and the policy return in the former will be good enough to maintain the relative benefit.

In the labour market area, especially training, the scope for targeting poorer regions is considerable but there is also a strong need for complementary initiatives in infrastructure and sectoral economic development in order to capitalize on the improved education, training and potential productivity of the workforce. Better infrastructure and economic momentum are already features of rich regions and even without national or Community assistance, there are autonomous mechanisms that can work to produce attractive human resource regimes in those regions.

In the case of the human resource environment, it is thus important to examine how far supply-side policies in this field can act as a major continuing stimulus to inward investment and regional economic regeneration rather than as short-run supplementary measures to help to improve the competitiveness of existing industry. In the former case the economic base of the region is *extended*, in the later case the existing base is *defended*.

It remains to be seen whether strengthening Europe's competitive position by promoting research, design and development can be tackled partly through the creation of new regional patterns of comparative advantage based on technology and human resources, harnessing education and training programmes to the expanding occupations of the future. This would be the ideal scenario, achieving growth and regional convergence objectives at the same time.

Thus the treatment of public spending on the 'human resource environment' could emerge as an increasingly important element of quite specific state aid to industry as the skill-intensity of employment rises and the need for continuing vocational education and training develops further. If this does, indeed, happen it will be necessary for the EU to consider how to deal with the mix of arguments regarding state aid and competition policy, economic and social cohesion from the Community-wide perspective, and job quality and equal opportunity at the level of the individual.

Finally, alongside the concern that some countries or regions might lose out, there is the fear that certain groups of the labour force, indeed, possibly even labour as a whole, may be disadvantaged by a process which gives primacy to market forces that not only ignore wider values of equity and community but also tend in practice to have short-term preoccupations. Moreover, whilst capital is more mobile than labour, financial capital is more mobile than industrial capital. Combine the rigours of the SEM and those of free capital movement and there arises a situation in which financial markets have apparently been handed much greater power to impose their judgments of performance and priorities upon the workings of the other constituents of the EC economy – see, for example, Notermans (1993).

Reform and experiments

There are two other classes of factors, however, that can be invoked in favour of EU social policy: those which relate to situations where improvements across the EU in a particular aspect of the labour market would generate major economic gains, and those which relate to the political and social rights which are already in the Treaties or are the subject of clarification and development by the Court. In both cases, objections on the grounds of the principal of subsidiarity can apparently be lodged.

On the face of it, the first group arises from judgments about what the actors in the labour market could be doing if only they realised how valuable particular actions could be for the conduct of economic activity: examples are the fostering of more effective 'social partnership', increasing commitments to training, greater recognition of the economic benefits of measures to provide women with better access to higher quality jobs, and the gains from more flexible retirement arrangements.

In all the above cases, there is evidence of market failure of one kind or another (for example, in training) or of institutional inadequacy (for example, in worker participation) which persuades some governments that intervention is necessary, usually involving imposing requirements on employers. Their assessment of the situation is that if employers or, indeed, trade unions cannot see what is good for them collectively and the economy, they must be 'encouraged' to change behaviour. But the evidence is not usually decisive and not all governments agree that intervention is required or that a particular form is appropriate.

Probably the most important example of this is the wide range of views held regarding 'social partnership'. The enriching of the employment relationship through greater participation of the workforce can be seen as a prerequisite for entering or remaining within the virtuous circle of higher productivity, higher wages and profits, higher investment, leading to further productivity gains. It can also be seen as being desirable mainly as a reward for better performance rather than as a factor contributing to the improvement. So, if greater incorporation of employee representation is thought likely to damage performance, greater participation is avoided like an expensive 'perk' which cannot be afforded and which cannot easily be withdrawn later.

At this point, the risk apparently attached to fostering employee involvement can be seen to be more acceptable if the right to economic democracy at the enterprise level is, in any case, a principle embodied in the integration programme. In other words, it is regarded as being part of the culture of the economic and social system. Thus, if the social scientific evidence is inconclusive on the subject of which, if any, forms of macro and micro social partnership are most effective from the economic point of view, the debate reverts to one which is more concerned with the style of the new Europe.

There does arise the possibility, however, that the evidence differs across countries and historical periods: some arrangements that work well during one period in one country may not work in another period in the same or a different country (see Henley and Tsakalotos, 1992; Boyer, 1994; Marshall, 1994).

These difficulties may arise in other areas of policy apparently closer to being shown to be unequivocally good for the economy concerned. Even here, however, there can be debate about how far it is desirable and legitimate to use EU instruments to impose on all member states regulations which restrict the rights of labour market actors to ignore what may be good for them or for the economy and society as a whole. Attitudes to placing obligations on governments and/or employers to provide a certain minimum level of training for members of the labour force fall into this category. On the other hand, whilst it is generally recognized that more investment in training would benefit virtually all EU economies, this still leaves plenty of room for argument over the appropriate form of training. The balance between formal education and vocational training, initial and continuing training, off-the-job and on-the-job training, enterprise-based and college-based training or other provision are all a matter of judgment.

The same is true of the economics of policies to promote the interests of disadvantaged groups. It may be an attractive strategy to argue for EU anti-discrimination measures on the grounds that they would pay for themselves, but the fact is that the economics of personnel is a much-neglected field of applied labour economics. It would be better to recognize this and put the principal stress on individual rights rather than social scientific evidence.

Thus, whatever political convenience might be served by confusing arguments based on rights with those based on judgments that considerable economic benefits would ensue, the contributions of social scientists should try to separate the two.

First, there need to be clearer understandings of the different objectives being pursued by member states, the constraints they encounter or impose upon themselves, and the policy styles adopted. Second, rigorous evaluations of particular regulatory and fiscal programmes need to be carried out so that the comparative analysis of labour market experiments in different countries can proceed from good micro studies and the maximum insight can be extracted from the experimental variation afforded to cross-national studies.

In a world of uncertainty, it is also worth distinguishing further between convergence around rights to be granted to labour market actors, convergence in the allocation of responsibilities for giving effect to those rights, and convergence in delivery mechanisms. Social cohesion does require substantial agreement on the rights of individuals and, indeed, organizations. But the process of implementation needs to be open to experimentation within a transparent system of evaluation. Different market structures and allocations of responsibilities to the labour market actors may be equally successful in achieving certain economic and social objectives. Where they are not, the case for 'managed convergence' may eventually be strengthened by marshalling the evidence of Community-wide experience. This would be better than the periodic exchanges of fire which have accompanied the evolution of the social dimension so far.

4   CONCLUDING COMMENTS

Some of the key hypotheses explored in this paper, together with related concluding comments, may be expressed as follows:

(i)   Globalization is not a natural phenomenon but a collective policy choice by richer states – the full implications of this are only now becoming apparent and they will present a further menu of choices in the field of international economic regulation with sharper recognition of social and political factors.

(ii)   Moreover, the metaphor of 'globalization' is itself somewhat confused in public policy debate, especially regarding the relationship between 'regionalization' of the world economy and globalization. In particular, which imperatives facing regional systems such as the EU stem from globalization and which from choices made implicitly or explicitly about the kind of economic union being created?

(iii)   Overall, it can be argued that the product market measures in the SEM programme are compatible with most interpretations of the globalization/ regionalization issue. Where it becomes more important to discriminate between interpretations in order to orientate the search for appropriate regulatory responses is in tackling the issue of social dimension and in the approach taken to further economic, monetary and political union.

(iv)   The evidence available for which socio-economic systems at the macro- and meta-levels and which organizational forms at the micro-level perform best does not point unequivocally towards the deregulation of socio-economic space. In that sense, we have not reached the 'end of economic history' – there is more to learn and different approaches can be taken towards the learning process and the treatment of different social actors within it.

(v)   The relationship between political democracy and economic democracy has not yet been settled in favour of the schizophrenia evident in liberal democracies between the individual as citizen and the individual as seen in several separate roles: worker, consumer, investor, dependent, etc.

(vi)   Demographic and social trends in the EU will place increasing pressures on rule-making processes to accommodate both a more comprehensive understanding of long-term 'economic' policy, incorporating aspects that have tended to be given very secondary treatment under the 'social' heading, and a more rigorous analysis of the social consequences of the design of economic institutions and the policies enacted through them.

(vii)   However, alongside the choice between regulation and fiscal policy measures, more attention needs to be given to promoting a more rigorous learning and dissemination process based on the 'experimental variation' available from among the member states.

(viii) This goes beyond the need for more *ex ante* and *ex post* evaluation of proposed/implemented EU rules and expenditure programmes. It encompasses the experience of relevant national initiatives and organizational forms employed.

(ix)   The *promotion* of this process of learning and experimentation and the *regulation* of it when it relates directly to EU initiatives is a potentially very important role for the European Commission in order to foster more effective social innovation. This should raw as much upon wide-ranging ideas of the patterns of rights and responsibilities thought to be desirable at different socio-economic levels, as upon those derived form current interpretations of macroeconomic imperatives.

REFERENCES

Boyer, R. (1994), 'Le retour des politiques des revenus?', in *Les Politiques des Revenus en Europe*, R. Boyer *et al* (eds).

Buigues, P. and Ilzkowitz, F. (1988), 'The sectoral impact of the internal market', DGII (11/1334/88), Brussels: CEC.

Buigues, P., Ilzkowitz, F. and Lebrun, J.F. (1990), 'The impact of the internal market by industrial sector: the challenge for member states', *European Economy – Social Europe*, Special Edition, Brussels: CEC.

Cecchini, P. (1988), *The European Challenge 1992: The Benefits of a Single Market*, Aldershot: Gower.

Commission of the European Communities, (1990a), *Employment in Europe, 1990,* Luxembourg: CEC DGV.

Commission of the European Communities, (1990b), *Economic and Monetary Union,* Luxembourg: CEC.

Commission of the European Communities, (1993), *Growth, Competitiveness and Employment,* Luxembourg: CEC.

Dutch Central Planning Bureau (CPB), (1992), *Scanning the Future,* The Hague: Sdu.

Emerson, M. (1988), 'Regulation or deregulation of the labour market', *European Economic Review,* **32,** 775–817.

Emerson, M. *et al.* (1988), 'The Economics of 1992: an assessment of the potential economic effects of completing the internal market of the European Community', *European Economy,* no. 35, Luxembourg: CEC.

Henley, A. and Tsakalotos, E. (1992), 'Corporatism and the future of the European labour market', Fourth EALE Annual Conference, University of Warwick, September.

Johnson, G.E. (1980), 'The theory of labour market intervention', *Economica,* August, 309–30.

Jones, R.J.B. (1994), 'Globalization, regionalization and the political economy of the European Community: empirical and theoretical issues', ECPR Workshop on the Single Market and Global Economic Integration, Madrid, April.

Lindley, R.M. (1991a), 'Politica fiscale, strategie sul mercato del lavoro e il 1992', in *Mercato del Lavoro Disoccupazione e Politiche di Intervento,* Bengamino Quintieri and Furio C. Rosati (eds), Rome: Franco Angeli, pp. 187–213.

Lindley, R.M. (1991b), 'Individuals, human resources and markets', in *Training and Competitiveness,* J. Stevens and C. Mackay (eds), London: Kogan Page, pp. 201–28.

Marshall, R. (1994), 'Perspectives on the employment relationship: the US Commission for the Future of Worker–Management Relations', Round Table on Social Dialogue, Brussels, April.

NIESR, (1993), 'The Impact of the Internal Market Programme on European Economic Structure and Performance', Directorate General for Research, Economic Series E–2, no. 7, Strasbourg, European Parliament.

Notermans, T. (1993), 'The abdication from national political autonomy: why the macroeconomic policy regime has become unfavorable to labor', *Politics and Society,* **21** (2), 133–67.

OECD (1986), *Flexibility in the Labour Markets: the Current Debate,* Paris: OECD.

OECD (1993), *Employment Outlook,* Paris: OECD.

OECD (1994), *The OECD Jobs Study,* Paris: OECD.

Walwei, U. and Werner, H. (1993), 'Employment and social dimensions of the single European market', *IAB Labour Market Research Topics*, no. 1.

Wells, W. (1992), 'Does the structure of employment legislation affect the structure of employment and unemployment?', UK Presidency European Labour Market Conference, Glasgow, November.

Zighera, J.A. (1993), 'Regional dispersion of industrial labour costs in the European Community (1988)'. (Revised version of paper to EALE Annual Conference, University of Warwick, 1992. Available from Laédix, Université Paris X-Nanterre.)

7. The Evolution of Rules

Duncan Matthews

The notion that the evolution of rules provides an appropriate strategy for the development of European Community (EC) policy is implicit in the whole concept of a single European market programme. Through the combined techniques of 'essential' harmonization, mutual recognition and reference to standards, the Commission's 1985 White Paper to complete the single market by 31st December 1992 not only laid down a coherent strategy for adopting Community rules to remove legislative barriers to the free movement of goods, services, capital and labour but also set in motion a continuous process of change to define and re-define what rules would evolve and govern the behaviour of agents across all twelve member states of the European Community.

With Community regulation limited to those measures deemed necessary to set minimum requirements to ensure basic levels of safety, health and environmental protection, the intention was that differing national standards would be mutually recognized and allowed to persist, should market conditions so demand. New rules would evolve through a process of 'competition among rules', or be subject to negotiation and voluntary agreement via standard setting bodies. As competition and negotiation took place, realignment would result in some national systems dominating others, the latter member states then revising their own rules to attract new business activity and capital. This process was intended to be continuous, competition among rules and negotiation resulting in convergence towards of a common set of Community rules according to the 'best practice' available. In effect, with firms operating under different rule systems coming into direct competition with one another, 'the market' would decide what rules are required, with no presumption that the new dominant rules would be welfare enhancing and, in some instances, rule changes supporting the producer rather than the consumer interest.

Through harmonization and competition among rules, each of these changes represents an evolution of the 'rules' by which national governments, firms, trade unions, consumers, groups and individuals operate. Assessing the likely impact of these changes has been the object of the ESRC's Research Programme on the Evolution of Rules in the Single European Market.

ESRC's Research Programme is a range of projects which examine different aspects of rule-setting, institutional frameworks, specific policy areas, responses to rule change and evaluations of the impact of the single market. Each stage of the process in which rules are set, influenced and implemented is an explicit theme of this book. This chapter adopts a broader view, providing an interpretive framework for the empirical results emerging from the projects at all stages of the process of change. It does so in the context of one of the main themes of the ESRC's Research Programme: how rules for a single market evolve.

By focusing on the notion of an 'evolution of rules' in the single market, this chapter examines the key components in the process of change and considers each in relation to the specific issues likely to determine the future pace and direction of the single market project as a whole. The chapter therefore addresses the following related set of issues:

- what institutional structures are required to 'manage', control and guide the process of change?
- how do differences in applying the rules influence the evolutionary process?
- how should the principle of subsidiarity be applied?
- what do agents other than regulatory institutions contribute to the evolution of rules?
- do some rule systems dominate others?
- what forms of change are actually taking place?

But before these questions are addressed, the primary task must be to define more clearly what is meant by the 'evolution of rules'.

1 A FRAMEWORK FOR EXAMINING THE EVOLUTION OF RULES

What are 'Rules'?

In its widest sense a 'rule' is any instrument which controls or alters the behaviour of an agent (a government, regulatory agency, firm, employer, worker, consumer or individual) by influencing that agent's decision-making processes, limiting its objective-setting ability and the range of possible options open to it. Rules may be of a legal kind, in that they are the result of legislation or judicial interpretation, or of a behavioural kind, in that they are codes or conventions followed by one or more agent. Under this broad definition, a rule might be seen as an operation or function which modifies the likelihood of potential outcomes, determines the selection and implementation of actions, and influences the way that behavioural options are assessed. This explanation of a rule is, however, on its own probably too broad: bad weather may influence an agent's behaviour, but the weather is not a 'rule'.

More appropriately, a rule might be seen as a written or unwritten prescription which influences decision-making processes, simplifies choices and controls or alters an agent's behaviour by setting out commitments which are either agreed or imposed by an outside agent, or even imposed on oneself voluntarily. This is the definition that Shipman and Mayes (1991) adopted in constructing a rule framework to explain company responses to the single market process, drawing on the seminal work of Nelson and Winter (1982).

Within this framework, rules govern economic and political behaviour. But rules are also modified by agents' rule-governed conduct itself, that conduct in turn being conditioned by the results of past actions (Sah and Stiglitz, 1990). An agent may deliberately break a rule, seek to change it or exploit others who choose to follow it.

Rule-based decisions are usually contrasted with 'rational' decisions, in which a rather more complete process of identification, evaluation and ranking of possible alternatives occurs prior to selection of the 'optimal' action (Watson and Buede, 1987). Yet there are strong arguments that the dichotomy may be a false one because in many cases 'rational' decisions cannot be made. Problems of inadequate information, which make the 'rational' decision process hard to engage in, have been well rehearsed elsewhere (Loasby, 1991) and, based on the premise that problems of 'rationality' cannot easily be solved, Nelson and Winter (1977) assert that it is actually rule-based decisions which guide an agent's actions.

This approach identifies three possible functions of rules: the simplification of decision processes, the co-ordination of actions in situations of interdependency, and the establishment of 'credibility' in commitment to future action (Shipman and Mayes, 1991).

A further extension of the rule framework arises from the categorization of 'decisions' as rules. Where an agent is an organization or a firm, the 'external' rules set by the outside environment are converted into 'internal' rules by members of the organization (March and Simon, 1958; Leibenstein, 1987). The individual actions that result build up into an 'organizational' action. The distinction between 'external' and 'internal' rules is an important one.

External Rules

Some external rules are of a legal kind, the result of negotiation or imposition by legislators (such as governments or parliaments) or by regulators (such as competition task forces at the national or European Community level). Rules, such as planning restrictions, are also set by local level, while in some member states regional governments (such as the German Lander) also have a strong tradition of legislative rule-setting of their own. In other instances, external rules are set through the establishment of legal precedent by national and international courts, or by the way these courts interpret and modify legislative rules. These are the legally enforceable 'external' elements that are most commonly understood to be 'rules' in the single market context.

There are, in addition, other types of external rules, unenforceable in a judicial sense but nonetheless important components of the single market rule framework. Some of these are behavioural rules with a moral or ethical basis (Matthews and Mayes, 1994). Others are administrative rules, such as those set by national labour inspectorates as guidelines on how best to conform to Community law on health and safety at work, which are important enabling mechanisms that operationalize many of the provisions laid down in national or Community rules. Breaching guidelines may result in a failure to meet legal obligations, but will not necessarily do so if these obligations are met by other, equivalent means.

In some cases, technical standards set by national or European institutions are legally enforceable external rules where they are designed to attest conformity with minimum requirements necessary to ensure the health and safety of individuals who come in contact with a product. In other instances, standards set by industry may become the norm in the sense that they become external 'rules' which govern market behaviour as the result of technological or economic change. As the experiences of the consumer electronics sector with rival formats of audio cassettes and VCR tapes have shown, technological or economic pressures for common standards can prove more important than formalized agreements in generating the 'rules' that determine what the market standard will actually be. Although not legally enforceable, inter-industry competition and collusion may lead to an industry standard that is entirely the result of market behaviour by dominant economic agents. In this way, market-driven external rules condition the behaviour of economic agents.

Economic agents do not act in isolation. Instead, informal agreements, codes of practice and behavioural conventions are all followed, either deliberately or unknowingly, as a means of interpreting the information provided by the external environment and responding in the form of co-ordinated action: Marshall's (1920) 'integrated' activity. These behavioural conventions might also be considered 'rules'. Although not enforceable in a legal sense, the possibility of financial sanctions imposed by the rule followers on those who deviate from the accepted norm is a powerful incentive to comply.

Internal Rules

While agents seek to integrate their responses to the external environment, some economists have argued that firms also operate 'internal' rule systems in response to externalities (Schumpeter, 1934). In this sense, technological, managerial and commercial progress may all be seen as what Marshall (1920) characterized as manifestations of 'differentiation', each firm seeking to benefit from its own interpretation of the conventional wisdom in that sector. Internal rules of this type would include managerial practice, use of technology, or employment policy. In this way, internal rules set by management condition decision processes (March and Simon, 1958; Leibenstein, 1987) and build into organizational responses designed to enhance performance.

The link between external regulation and internal practice – the interaction between new formal rules and resulting behaviour – however, remains elusive. There is no guarantee that changing legal rules will alter behaviour in the way intended. New rules may initially result in only marginal or non-committal responses, not least because rule followers may have good reason to be cautious in their response to change.

Although some rules may require a particular response from an agent, most simply alter the range of actions available and the way the preferred response is selected. Giddens (1979) noted that agents generally tend to retain discretion within the rule, even ignoring the rule where the costs outweigh the benefits of complying. A rule may either assist, constrain or modify an agent's ability to set objectives, assemble a set of possible actions, select the most appropriate action, identify the outcome and assess its implications for future decisions.

This rule framework definition of 'rules' as any operation or function which restricts or modifies the information entering an agent's decision process is, however, unlikely to satisfy all lawyers, political theorists, public policy specialists and sociologists who will have their own ideas about what constitutes a 'rule'. The rule framework described above is nevertheless a useful attempt to accommodate each discipline, adopting a multi-disciplinary approach and integrating elements of economics, organization studies, sociology, politics and law. In doing so, it risks offending everyone and satisfying no-one. Yet in the way that it takes account of the interactions between rule-setters and rule-followers, between legally enforceable and self-enforcing rules, and between 'external' and 'internal' rules, the framework does offer a sufficiently broad definition of rules for consideration in the remainder of this paper. The next task must be to consider how rules evolve and change over time.

What is the 'Evolution of Rules'?

What, then, is meant by 'evolution' in the context of rules and how does this help to explain what is happening in the single European market?

Essentially, what we are concerned with is a process of change – not only one type of change, but a whole range at different stages of development at any one given time. Shipman and Mayes (1991) identified four types of rule change. Their categorization provides a useful starting point for this paper:

(i) rules imposed by a governmental authority;
(ii) rules introduced by a governmental authority on the basis of negotiation and consensus among those agents likely to be affected;
(iii) rules originating through a process of Darwinian evolution, with competing agents adopting different patterns of action with different survival chances until, over time, all survivors are conforming to one set of rules;
(iv) rules resulting from a more Lamarckian evolutionary process, with competing agents starting from different patterns of action, the most successful of which is then imitated so that agents converge towards an efficient set of rules.

The latter two characterizations involve an evolutionary explanation of the origin of rules in the sense that they involve a continuing process of change in a developing system in a given environment over time (Boulding, 1982).

The Lamarckian explanation of evolutionary change in particular has proved popular in certain areas of economic theory, such as in the market-structure simulations of Nelson and Winter (1982). The Darwinian approach to the evolutionary process of rule change, on the other hand, has generally been regarded as unsuited to explaining how rules change since it relies on a decentralized environment within which only self-enforcing rules and conventions operate (Shipman and Mayes, 1991). This is primarily because a Darwinian explanation is seen as allowing no scope for explaining the existence of imposed or negotiated rules. Yet even in the sense, Darwin's belief that evolution is a continuous process has tended to be superseded by a theory of punctuated equilibrium, shocks and major changes leading to evolution.

Attempts to provide an evolutionary explanation of how markets develop are not a recent trend. Alfred Marshall suggested a link between economic co-ordination and biological evolution in 1920, although his views on Darwinian evolution were never developed at any great length. Schumpeter (1934) considered that economic evolution could in some way be attributable to changes arising as a result of 'creative destruction' when new economic behaviour, policies and theories destroy existing equilibria and change agents' views of how economic life should operate. Within this framework for understanding change, expectations and the quality of information available to economic agents determine the pace and direction of economic development.

That the process of change may be described as 'evolutionary' need not, therefore, presume any biological or Darwinian explanation of a continuous process, or even of convergence towards some optimizing point. Punctuated equilibrium and divergence away from optimal results may equally apply. Nor should there be any presumption of convergence towards a single point at all since sub-markets can emerge.

Rules themselves are not even always a stimulus for change. They also have the potential to protect agents from having to change their behaviour. In the single European market, for instance, national governments, particular industries or individual firms all have a vested interest in seeking EC level rule changes which maximize the benefits of any EC rule change for its domestic market, while minimizing the need for change to a new 'European' rule system. These agents, we assume, are all in the business of ensuring that imposed or negotiated rules will require other national rules to converge towards their preferred system. The question of how and why some rule systems dominate others will be specifically addressed later in this chapter.

Despite some notable attempts to account for rule change entirely through evolutionary explanations (Hayek, 1973; Nozick, 1979), imposed or negotiated rules are equally important. Legal rules which are imposed by a governmental authority or introduced on the basis of consensus among those likely to be affected by a rule also have an impact on how rules evolve.

The distinction between rules which originate through imposition or negotiation and rules which evolve is not clear cut. Once imposed or negotiated rules have been introduced, they subsequently become exposed to evolutionary pressures for change and modification. Statute law, for instance, is inevitably clarified by case law or, in the light of experience, modified by subsequent legislation. Unwritten behavioural rules which determine the actual practice of agents in a market are, meanwhile, by their very nature undergoing a constant process of change as firms in particular adapt to new regulatory and commercial environments. The significance of sociological interpretations of market behaviour and attitudes towards regulation have also been recognized (Wilks and Cini, 1991), as have inter-firm relations, codes of conduct, conventions and commercial practices which are all 'rules' that constrain the behavioural options open to a group of agents (Matthews and Mayes, 1994).

How, then, can an evolutionary explanation of how rules change provide a suitable framework for assessing what is happening in the single European market?

2   STAGES OF THE EVOLUTIONARY PROCESS IN THE SINGLE MARKET

Different elements of the single market programme will pass through stages of the evolutionary process at different times. One possible sequence of evolutionary change in the single market (although there may be others) involves rule-setting, subsequent competition among rules, a resulting alignment of associated rules and, by way of a second round of rule changes, revision and consolidation of the rules.

Rule-setting

Chapter 2 specifically addresses the process of setting and influencing the rules for a single European market. Yet because rule-setting is the critical first stage in the EC policy process which determines both the form and the substance of new Community rules, it is also a crucial issue for this chapter if we are to understand how and why rules for the single market evolve.

Despite the growth of intergovernmentalism since the founding of the Community, the Commission retains the sole right of initiative in proposing those EC legislative measures considered necessary for the establishment of a single market in goods, services, labour and capital. Community rules are thus defined, developed and formulated through a standard format of agreement among the member states on the basis of proposals by the Commission, taking into account the views of the European Parliament and the Economic and Social Committee.

The earliest stages of the policy process actually take place before this, within the Commission. This stage of policy formulation has been characterized as informal and fluid (Gold, 1993), the informality of the process allowing the Commission to choose, on a pragmatic basis, whether to ask a working party or an individual to assist in the preparation of an initiative, or indeed whether to bother at all.

The informal and fluid nature of this process has been accounted for largely in terms of the Commission's responsibilities within the EC, particularly its requirement to propose rules which reflect the complexity of existing law, practice and traditions across all twelve member states (Gold, 1993). In achieving this task, the distinctive approach of the Commission towards policy formulation has traditionally been viewed (Wallace, Wallace and Webb, 1983) in terms of its openness to new ideas and its accessibility to client groups.

By announcing the intention to initiate a general rule change, but not specifying the detail of new measures, the Commission is not only acting within the spirit of its guiding principle of 'transparency' but also opening itself up to outside influence from those covered by existing rules and those outside them who may be affected by new rules.

While the roles and responsibilities of Community actors, national governments and interest groups vary depending on the nature of the issue at stake (Nugent, 1991), during this process of rule-setting national governments, firms and other actors generally seek to influence the form and content of proposed new single market rules. For national governments, pressure is exerted through negotiation, either by direct links with the Commission or at an intergovernmental level in the Council of Ministers (Lodge, 1989). Because the rules under which the Commission and the Council engage in negotiation are constantly evolving, Weale and Williams (1994) have noted that the interpretation and application of Treaty provisions are themselves an important stimulus for the formulation of Community policy. Assessing the evolution of Community environmental law, Weale and Williams have suggested that the extension of Community competence over environmental policy via the Single European Act led the Commission to promote its own procedural authority in that area. Because the application of procedural rules always remains open to interpretation and revision, institutional actors will always seek to advance their own interests in the evolving policy framework.

For firms, trade unions and other interested parties pressure is exerted by lobbying (in either a pre-emptive or reactive way) targeted directly at the Commission or indirectly at national governmental negotiators (Matthews and Mayes, 1993). During this rule-setting phase, Mazey and Richardson (1992a) have noted that lobbying styles may be as important as the content and objectives of the lobbying itself. The way that business is conducted will affect policy outcomes, as it plays a significant part in shaping the perceptions of participants and, therefore, their willingness to listen to each other and to make concessions during the processing of issues. If, as they suggest, the Commission is not yet sufficiently mature as an organization to have developed widespread 'standard operating procedures' for processing policy issues, the lobbying styles and lobbying strategies of groups will potentially have profound implications for the character of new single market rules which eventually emerge from the EC policy framework.

Competition Among Rules

As new single market rules take effect, the removal of barriers between countries exposes previously segmented markets to new competition, not just from competitor firms in other countries, but from firms operating under different rule systems in the same market. As firms seek to take advantage of remaining differences in national rules, competition between different national rules may result. This dynamic learning process of adjustment is the subject of Stephen Woolcock's chapter 4 on competition among rules.

As a means of accommodating different national rules under conditions of economic interdependence without these being allowed to form the basis of protection, competition among rules is also an important facet of the 'evolutionary' explanation of change addressed in this chapter.

Firms want Community rules to increase markets and assist their business practices. Since segmentation is a normal means for firms to increase profitability and protect market share it is by no means clear why there should be strong pressures for achieving all aspects of the single market. The perceived optimum for firms is presumably to gain access to other markets while having others' access to their own restricted (Matthews and Mayes, 1993). Only in the case of external regulation is wider welfare taken into account.

Access to other financial markets, for example, is generally permitted because under the Second Banking Directive a financial institution may operate a branch in another member state subject to home country control. Its branch does not have to comply with the host country's rules. The result is that firms operating under different rule systems compete directly in the same market. In the case of leasing, for example, Matthews and Mayes (1993) have noted that because firms licensed to operate in a home market can operate its branches in other member states subject to home control, those leasing companies covered by the Second Banking Directive are subject to different rule systems yet compete directly with each other in the same national markets.

If one set of national rules is more favourable, firms may respond in a number of ways, with competition among locations to find the most competitive leadership by dominant firms in a process akin to dynamic games, such as collusion to set up new codes of behaviour. The process of development then involves a second round of responses from national governments in the face of industry's actions. Member states with less favourable rules may seek to modify and improve their own regulations.

George McKenzie (1993) has explored the degree to which competition among rules is likely to result in the internationalization of financial markets. Although member states are sovereign in that they set national regulations subject to EC minimum standards, McKenzie suggests that an independent rule system for securities markets is unlikely to persist if other national systems adopt less restrictive forms of regulation. McKenzie acknowledges that it is difficult to predict whether such competition among rules will result in 'regulatory arbitrage': 'bad' regulatory systems driving out the 'good', in effect a 'race to the bottom' as the most permissive systems drive out the safest, the worst case scenario being that wide disparities in national interpretation of capital adequacy rules will cause competitive distortions, not only within the EC but also between the US and Japan.

Because financial trading is carried out not only within the EC but in third countries, the globalization of financial markets suggests that the most appropriate level for regulation should be much wider than Europe. In practice, because the EC cannot implement financial rules without consideration of what is happening elsewhere, particularly under US and Japanese regulatory regimes, wider harmonization through international institutions such as the Bank for International Settlements (BIS) has already emerged as the most appropriate means of preventing 'regulatory arbitrage'. With the US already taking an active part in BIS deliberations of a proposal very similar to the EC's Capital Adequacy

Directive which would set similar standards for banks operating in international securities markets, the evolution of internationally recognized rules for securities markets becomes a distinct possibility.

But market-led competition among rules may not be appropriate in all instances. Rules imposed by institutions may be preferable. The possibility of sub-optimal outcomes from tax policy under a process of competition among rules, for example, led Stephen Smith (1993) to advocate the evolution of EC tax rules through a process of institution-led co-ordination, along the lines of current Community policy which specifies minimum tax rates which member states can apply. This would, in effect, limit 'destructive tax competition' and leave individual member states free to set higher rates of taxation if they wish.

Alignment of Associated Rules

While attempts to create the appropriate regulatory environment to achieve completion of the single market have involved the introduction of a wide range of new and far-reaching legislative measures, many of the adjustments actually taking place in the single market are not legally binding rules at all. Instead they are changes in arrangements between firms, developed at local or EC level without recourse to legal structures or intervention from outside agents. These co-ordinated behavioural responses to single market rules are the codes of conduct, 'gentlemen's agreements' and conventions which underpin commercial activity throughout the Community and create the reality of the single market. They are specifically discussed later in the paper in the context of the role of firms in the evolutionary process.

Revision and Consolidation of the Rules

Some rules may require strengthening, some may need modification, while others may require new institutions to monitor and co-ordinate enforcement activities across the Community. The need for appropriate institutions capable of ensuring effective co-ordination and monitoring of enforcement activities is addressed in the next section.

3   PRECONDITIONS FOR THE EVOLUTION OF RULES IN THE SINGLE MARKET

Creating the appropriate conditions in which the evolution of rules for a single market can take place requires the effective operation of a number of mechanisms and processes. Community level and national institutions, and other agencies such as standard setting institutions, all play a role in this process.

Appropriate Regulatory Institutions

The single market comprises a multiplicity of actors with distinct economic, political and social interests, each actor displaying behavioural characteristics which are conditioned by the quality of information they have access to, and their subsequent interpretation of that information. To manage these often competing interests appropriate regulatory regimes, judicial structures and administrative agencies are required.   They are essential components of the institutional framework necessary to determine how rules and markets will evolve.

The task of institutions is two-fold: first, to govern the competitive relations between agents; and second, to set and enforce the most appropriate rules. Institutions must be capable of managing market relationships in the single market, monitoring implementation and compliance with EC rules and being sufficiently flexible and responsive to adapt the rules where the evolutionary process of change results in their impact being nullified or where the effect of rules is other than that intended.

Community regulatory institutions

Simon Bulmer (1993) has examined the reality of Community governance from a new institutionalist perspective. By dissecting governance structures, comparing policy substructures and reassessing the range of economic, political and legal instruments available at the supranational level, Bulmer suggests that a distinct mode of Community governance can be detected across a range of policy regimes. His view is that institutions matter in the sense that political struggles are mediated by prevailing institutional arrangements.   Bulmer adopts an institutionalist focus, based on regime analysis, to suggest that economic, political and administrative-legal elements all contribute to the evolution of rules for a single market.

Francis Snyder (1993) has also considered the legal and administrative preconditions necessary to ensure the effectiveness of Community law. These comprise the interrelationships between Community institutions, member states, corporatist arrangements, pluralist politics, policy networks and individuals. Snyder suggests that, in coordinating these disparate interests, the Community has worked best where it has created legal principles and dealt with national administrations through negotiation and adjudication. Embedded in the process of administrative negotiation between the Commission and member states and the development of a judicial liability system by the Court of Justice, Snyder finds an evolving system of elaboration and refinement of Community rules.

For Bulmer, institutional structures that influence the rule process extend beyond the formal organs of government. 'Soft law' codes of conduct and conventions between institutional actors also contribute to the evolution of an emerging pattern of behaviour in the single market.

Although not legally enforceable, it is often soft law rules that determine how institutions, member states and firms conduct their affairs in practice. In its application of the Merger Control Regulation, for example, Bulmer suggests that non-binding Commission guidelines have provided the principal means of putting into operation this aspect of Community competition policy.

Snyder also describes how the Commission, with expansion of its rule-setting competence restricted by the member states, has resorted to informal soft law rules which determine conduct. Since the Cassis de Dijon case in 1980, the Commission has developed soft law through a quasi-legal form of communication which may be of an informative, declaratory or interpretive kind, explaining Court of Justice judgments and spelling out their implications for member states and private individuals (Snyder, 1993).

For Snyder, the question of appropriate regulatory institutions capable of ensuring the effectiveness of Community rules must involve a fundamental review. It must involve basic questions concerning the political bases of the Community, its legitimacy, the scope for institutional change and its likely future development. Any meaningful discussion of how to improve the effectiveness of Community rules therefore requires due consideration of the potential for development of Community institutions, the relation between the Community and member states and, more fundamentally, the purpose of the Community and possible alternatives for the development of Europe.

Stephen Wilks (1992), undertaking a thorough evaluation of comparative competition policy in the Community setting, has also noted that institutional factors are crucial in determining the character of Community rules. For Wilks, it is the distribution of institutional power which determines how the various policy priorities and legal pressures are articulated, and ultimately determines the pace and direction of EC rules. Administrative procedures established under Regulation 17 give the Commission extensive powers to police, interpret and apply EC competition policy rules. The degree of policy choice and administrative discretion exercised by the Directorate-General responsible for competition policy (DG IV) is considerable.

Wilks explores how DG IV has evolved as a regulatory institution and attributes the gradual development of Commission competence over competition policy to three historical cycles. These are, first, a legal cycle, during which DG IV became increasingly sure of how to define and apply articles of the Treaty as a result of the growing body of case law from the European Court of Justice; second, an economic cycle, during which the period 1972–82 was punctuated by pressure from national governments towards a pragmatic use of industrial policy;

and, third, a generational cycle, during which DG IV personnel have evolved as a cadre of 'regulators' (in the American sense) capable of interpreting their jurisdiction in a broad manner which is neither rigid nor defensive, but instead uses regulatory means to secure general policy objectives.

From the 'metamorphosis of European competition policy' which Wilks describes it is clear that effective and appropriate institutional structures capable of managing market relationships in the single European market will themselves take time to evolve. In the case of competition policy these structures evolved in line with legal and economic developments, through the strong personalities of successive Commissioners and through the burgeoning departmental culture of 'rule-setting' policy makers. The evolution of appropriate regulatory institutions will be essential if the consequences of single market rules are to be those originally intended.

Community institutions not only manage market relationships, but may themselves provide the impetus for change. David O'Keefe (1992) has described how the European Court of Justice plays a key role in interpreting Treaty articles concerning the free movement of persons and has created a jurisprudence which goes far beyond the original intentions of the Treaty. O'Keefe notes that the Court's views are themselves evolving, not constant. It is the development of EC case law, for instance, which led to a migrant worker, a self-employed person or a provider of services becoming an individual capable of invoking the right of free movement in a context which is not necessarily related to an economic activity or status, but more to do with human rights or constitutional expectation. Through an evolving system of judicial rules, O'Keefe suggests that we may be witnessing the development of an embryonic Community citizenship by the Court of Justice.

National regulatory institutions

While Community level institutional structures and administrative mechanisms are crucial in determining the conditions under which the evolution of rules takes place, the necessity for appropriate administrative, legislative and judicial bodies to 'govern' the evolutionary process is not only a matter for Community level structures. The national regulatory institutions are also central to the single market process. Brazier *et al.* (1993) have examined the mechanisms of institutional control and the dynamics of regulatory reconstruction in the field of professional services. Focusing their analysis on two professions (doctors and lawyers) in Britain and France, Brazier *et al.* examined the degree of self regulation permitted to the professions as a result of the historical traditions in each country.

Self-regulating professional institutions, they found, were particularly important in Britain, where the role of professional associations has altered in recent years as competitive practice rules governing the occupations has evolved and administrative intervention from national government increased. Doctors and lawyers have both faced exposure to structural changes which in each case necessitated internal rule changes within the profession (lawyers, especially barristers, being more successful in preserving professional autonomy in the face of these pressures than doctors).

Brazier *et al.* found that British professional associations representing doctors, solicitors and barristers each operate regulatory systems on a 'tightrope' stretched between the market and the state, simultaneously seeking to protect themselves from competitive forces and, having allied themselves with the state in order to acquire some protection, in turn seeking to keep the state at a distance. Operating under these conditions, self-regulation has governed relations with the state and determined how the professions have each adapted to the new conditions of enforced market competition.

The ability of national regulatory institutions to exhibit markedly different behaviour in the single market will clearly remain a key factor in determining the form common rules are likely to take.

Standard setting bodies
Through the mutual recognition route, the prospects are that harmonization and evolution will be a slow and difficult process, the result of unpredictable outcomes from competition, negotiation and compromise. Where harmonization is likely to occur, Weale and Williams (1992) suggest, is through the 'low politics' of committees of experts in particular fields negotiating over standards.

Much of the convergence of standards actually taking place is in an incremental fashion since the single market process delegates the maximum possible level of competence to standard setting bodies. At the European level standards are set by the various CEN/CENELEC committees, on which representatives of the national standards institutes sit, the most influential being DIN (Germany), BSI (UK) and AFNOR (France). Attestation and conformity certification bodies then ensure compliance with harmonized standards in each member state.

The complex interactions between public agencies, responsible for the legislative aspects of technical harmonization, national and European standard setting bodies, with a private status which have to fill in the detail of essential safety requirements laid down in directives, and companies whose products have to meet these essential requirements, are discussed at length elsewhere (Woolcock, Hodges and Schreiber, 1991). The role of standard setting bodies in negotiating technical rules is, however, clearly important in the context of this chapter in guiding and facilitating the evolutionary process of change.

Implementing and Enforcing the Rules

Community law is designed to have an intended outcome on how single market rules evolve. The impact of Community law will, however, be distorted unless EC regulations are implemented and enforced effectively in all parts of the Community.

While regulations are directly applicable, directives require member states to bring into force national laws, regulations and administrative provisions necessary to comply with Community law. Directives thus offer member states the opportunity to determine for themselves the way in which legislation is implemented into national law. Because a directive only imposes an obligation on member states as to the results to be achieved, not the means to achieve it, diversity of national implementing instruments may arise (although in a series of judgments, the European Court of Justice confirmed it is possible for individuals to bring claims against governments, that is to say, for a directive to have vertical direct effect, after the expiration of the deadline for transposition. Following the Francovich judgment, national governments also have certain obligations to compensate individuals for damage caused to them by failure of the State to meet its obligations under Community law.)

The problems associated with implementing Community law are well known. A member state may fail to transpose a directive into national law at all, may do so only partially or inadequately. Even following transposition, the uniform application of Community law is dependent on the interpretation of national statutes by national courts and enforcement by national agencies. The effectiveness of new Community rules and the impact on how single market rules subsequently evolve thus remain in doubt unless effectively implemented and enforced in all parts of the Community.

Gold and Matthews (1993) highlighted the differences between the institutional mechanisms for implementation and enforcement of EC law in their study on health and safety at work, and expressed concern that current mechanisms may not be sufficient to achieve consistently high levels of compliance in all parts of the Community. In part, this reflects a wider problem raised by the principle of subsidiarity. Under subsidiarity, choosing the best means to achieve objectives set out in Community law is the domain of each member state. Such action must not, however, amount to a failure to achieve the original intention of the law and in some cases, such as monitoring compliance with EC rules on state aids, the lowest appropriate level of government will be the EC itself.

The problem of ensuring even-handed implementation and enforcement at the national level was brought more sharply into focus by the emphasis of the Edinburgh summit's declaration on 'subsidiarity'. The Commission's own Sutherland Report (1992) has already acknowledged the potential shortcomings of the current institutional setup and a related report by Dehousse *et al.* (1992) has put forward ideas about the new regulatory mechanisms which would be needed if the single market is to become a reality.

For the authors of the Sutherland Report, there is a risk of fragmentation of the market arising either from divergent interpretation and enforcement of Community law or from the introduction of national rules which segment the market. Subsidiarity does not and cannot be interpreted as permitting such developments. To overcome the failure of some member states to implement and enforce Community law adequately, the Sutherland Report suggested the use of directly applicable regulations instead of directives (for which transposition is required), but also acknowledges that this approach would be difficult for some national legislative structures. Until such time as agreement has been reached on an enhanced role for directly applicable Community instruments, the directive will remain the most commonly used legislative measure.

Since the principle of subsidiarity limits Community activity to objectives which cannot be attained more efficiently at national or regional level, the problem becomes one of how a system can be enforced fairly across all member states and how each country can be convinced that its competitors are in fact enforcing Community rules properly without creating an unfair competitive advantage for firms who do not need to adapt to the rule changes. Yet without even deviating from the letter of the law, there may be strong social, cultural and economic reasons why national government will implement Community rules in a way that is advantageous to domestic actors. Variation in regulatory stringency may provide a source of competitive advantage.

In relation to public procurement, Cox (1993) has shown that variations in the implementation of single market reforms of national arrangements for the award of contracts may distort the impact of new rules across the Community. Single market changes extend the scope of Community public procurement rules to virtually all public and private utility bodies, and revise the threshold levels under which EC law become applicable. Cox, however, suggests a number of factors (such as whether there is a history of national preference or whether effective national remedies are available) which influence the process of contract award in each member state and will determine the effectiveness of an EC enforcement regime for public procurement rules. Given the potential for de facto divergence from single market procurement rules, Cox asserts that it cannot be assumed that the new Community regime for awarding public works will be equally applied in all member states.

While the impact of some rules is dependent on enforcement by national or Community agencies, others are self-enforcing. Diverging from the rules is unlikely to be a viable strategy if such action is ultimately to the detriment of the rule-breaker. Co-operation between firms, conventions and codes of conduct establish expectations that a group of agents will behave in a certain way. These types of collusive behavioural rules are complied with because following the rules is perceived to be likely to bring the most favourable outcome for all actors. They constitute an attempt by firms to control and predict their external environment by introducing regularities in the behaviour of others. Burrows and Hiram (1993), for example, describe how the UK food industry has adopted a strategy of self-regulation to ensure compliance with the Official Control of Foodstuffs Directive. The likelihood of detection and the burden that the law imposes on firms by way of the defence of due diligence make self-regulatory compliant behaviour the most rational response for the industry.

Behavioural rules, established through a process of repeated actions which become habitual and predictable over time, are assumed to provide additional information capable of improving an agent's rational decision-making process. However, to prevent collusive behaviour capable of circumventing Community rules, the Commission must continue to exercise its powers under the Treaty where unilateral action by member states could materially jeopardize conditions required for the evolution of single market rules.

Subsidiarity

While diversity is politically and culturally important for Europe, it also risks conflicting with the effective operation of the single market if such diversity amounts to the application of separate national rules (Sutherland *et al.*, 1992). Subsidiarity is intended to ensure that this degree of segmentation does not occur by indicating those circumstances in which Community action might be preferred.

Stephen Smith (1993) has highlighted the general conditions which might be implied by applying the principle of subsidiarity to the assignment of responsibility for tax policy between the Commission and the member states. Subsidiarity, as defined in Article 3b of the Maastricht Treaty, presumes a preference for decentralization where it may help to ensure that government decisions adequately reflect local preferences and implies that spillovers provide the main economic efficiency argument for centralization of policy. This leads Smith to suggest that the main considerations when determining the functions that should be assigned under Community competence are information gathering and monitoring compliance. Applying the principle of subsidiarity, the competence that the Community exercises should be limited to areas where there are substantial cross-country policy externalities and where compliance with agreements between national governments cannot easily be monitored by national governments.

Smith concludes that implementing the principle of subsidiarity requires criteria capable of identifying those areas where policy-making or implement-ation would be more effective at the Community than the national level. Defining the appropriate limits of Community policy on taxation in terms of subsidiarity remains intractable due to issues of political sovereignty, the diversity of taxation at near optimal levels, and the lengthy process of intergovernmental negotiation which cannot be bypassed.

Begg *et al.* (1993) have focused on a different aspect of the subsidiarity debate: the degree to which subsidiarity can be equated with problems of accountability. They suggest that even where action at the national level may have disadvantages, we should ask whether the disadvantages of Community level action might not be greater. In the final analysis, the balance of advantages and disadvantages is likely to vary from case to case, competence for rule-setting and rule enforcement being distributed across several layers of government according to the comparative advantages in each case (Begg *et al.*, 1993, p. 56). Since the potential costs of centralization (in terms of government failure and diminished accountability) are high, a strong case can be made for governance at the lowest level appropriate.

Centralization at EC level may nevertheless be justifiable provided that the central institutions are designed in such a way as to avoid regulatory capture (where regulatory agencies represent special interests rather than the 'common good'). In the design of EC merger policy, the Community has made explicit attempts to allocate responsibilities between EC and national institutions in accordance with the general principles underlying the notion of subsidiarity. Neven, Nuttall and Seabright (1993) have examined the extent to which centralization accorded by the EC Merger Regulation may be expected to change the character of regulatory capture and found that the procedure used by the Commission, although administratively efficient, is neither systematic nor transparent. They suggest that this may well give rise to certain firms gaining significant bargaining power *vis-à-vis* the Commission, ultimately distorting the impact of the rules in favour of greater tolerance of market power than is consistent with EC competition policy goals.

Neven, Nuttall and Seabright do not, however, conclude that centralization of EC merger policy rules is a mistake. Rather, they suggest that the risk of regulatory capture at the centre can be contained by reforms to increase the transparency of the system and strengthen the role of interests (such as those of consumers) that potentially lose influence through the dominance of firms.

McGowan and Seabright (1993) have examined the tension between Community regulation and subsidiarity. They warn against allowing the current political debate on subsidiarity to lead to a neutering of the Commission's role. McGowan and Seabright also acknowledge, however, that there is a risk of overload on the Community's own resources in trying to do too much and recall the Padoa-Schioppa report (1987) endorsing subsidiarity when it argued that Community effectiveness is undermined by expectations that it contribute to an excessively wide range of policy domains. Monitoring effective national implementation and enforcement of EC rules nevertheless remains a core activity for Community institutions. Without a credible threat of action where member states do not transpose EC law into national legislation, or where national agencies fail to ensure compliance with the Community rules, there is a danger that subsidiarity will lead to sub-optimal levels of regulation. Given that Community resources are likely to remain limited, Commission competence should remain sharply focused on enforcement at a European level. The credible threat of Community sanctions should face those member states neglecting their obligations (McGowan and Seabright, 1993).

4   WHAT DO OTHER ACTORS CONTRIBUTE TO THE PROCESS OF CHANGE?

While regulatory institutions are an essential element in creating the conditions for evolutionary change, no clear picture of how change is occurring can be achieved without also understanding how a variety of other actors influence the way that rules evolve in the single market. Firms, consumers, trade unions, interest groups (such as environmental groups) and individual citizens all have direct and indirect routes by which they seek to influence the form and content of Community rules to their own specific advantage.

Firms

To understand how and why particular forms of evolutionary change occur, the rule framework outlined in the first section of this chapter suggested that there may be a crucial relationship between the internal decisions taken by firms and the external rules of the environment in which they operate (whether regulatory, technological or economic rules).

It has certainly been widely recognized that firms use their knowledge, experience and particular specialization to innovate, develop products, improve processes and organization (Marshall, 1920) and, when they are engaged in similar or complementary economic activities, firms will exchange and develop these ideas, seeking to respond to change in a co-ordinated manner to enhance their own positions.

For Schumpeter (1934) co-operation between firms then becomes an important strategy for influencing the rules. A group subject to the same rules may, for instance, have a common interest in seeking the introduction of new more favourable rules, changes in existing rules or the removal of rules to enhance the competitive potential of the group.

Some aspects of the process by which agents seek to influence the content of new rules, for example by lobbying or through other forms of persuasion are clearly observable. Others are more difficult to identify: strategies to make an adverse rule-change unenforceable or so general or wide in scope as to have little or no impact on existing rule systems (Shipman and Mayes, 1991). Alternatively agents may promote a rule-change which is most desirable, or reduce the need for a rule change at all.

In other instances, there may be powerful reasons why firms seek to influence changes in existing rule systems at the policy formulation stage. Those excluded from potential markets by the old rules, or those inside the rule system who see the potential benefits of new rules as being greater, will have a significant motivation to seek changes.

Particularly in the field of technical standardization the Commission has, in common with the classic model of Community policy-making, frequently turned to industry experts for specific advice (Mazey and Richardson, 1992b). These industry experts are often representatives of the very firms likely to be affected by new Community law. In part this reflects traditional ideas of 'regulatory capture' which govern any industry but it also highlights the complexity of the specific details required in establishing the single market.

While some rules followed by a group of firms will be the result of external factors, such as legislation, others may be self-imposed rules created by the members of the group themselves, such as codes of conduct, conventions or 'gentlemen's agreements'.

In a study of how retail firms respond to change in the single market, for example, Matthews and Mayes (1994) noted that firms tend to adopt these different approaches as compatible elements of a dual strategy in their efforts to influence the evolution of single market rules. Firms exert influence either by lobbying for legislative change, or by co-ordinated behavioural responses in the form of self-enforced rules which determine conduct and create conditions to which the regulator is then obliged to respond. In their efforts to ensure new rules to permit longer shop opening hours, for example, co-ordinated action by retailers in the form of lobbying provided sufficient impetus for a change in German law, while in the UK lobbying, supplemented by a voluntary inter-firm agreement (in the form of a code of conduct to safeguard the terms and condi-tions of employees) was a contributory factor in the partial deregulation of shop opening hours in England and Wales.

The influence of co-ordinated activity by firms is being exerted in a number of respects. In areas where single market legislation relies on the mutual recognition of equivalent technical standards, for instance, the process by which convergence of rules is to be achieved is not spelt out. Agreements between firms may set unenforced or voluntary rules which in practice determine what form convergence will take. Rules devised by national or Community regulatory institutions are thus themselves often influenced by the very firms they seek to regulate. The importance of this linkage in understanding how rules evolve in the single market was highlighted (Matthews and Mayes, 1994) because the commercial behaviour of firms acting together is of a co-ordinated type which has implications for the actual behaviour of other agents and for the evolution of Community rule systems.

Much of the process of integration comes not so much from the regulatory frameworks which are set, but from the competitive and collusive behaviour of firms responding to them.

Consumers

Although Mazey and Richardson (1992b) have noted the role of BEUC (the European Bureau of Consumers' Associations) in the lobbying process, as a co-ordinated group consumers lack the economic and political influence of firms in their attempts to determine the form and content of single market rules at the Community rule-setting or national implementation stages. Where co-ordinated lobbying activity does occur, it is directed towards a desire for common rules to improve product safety. In their examination of the control of foodstuffs directive, for instance, Burrows and Hiram (1993) found consumer groups anxious to use single market rule changes to increase the consumer protection and safety provisions of national rules.

In terms of economic impact, consumers also have another route to influence the evolution of a dominant rule system. Where there is a viable choice of product markets (either because mobility across territorial boundaries to other parts of the Community is practical, or because technology permits distance selling) and where consumers are in possession of adequate information to allow an objective choice between markets, purchasing power may become a significant variable in determining the evolution of a dominant system. Mayes and Hart (1995) describe how Luxembourg's lower excise duty on petrol resulted in a growth in petrol stations just inside Luxembourg and the closure of them nearby in Belgium. The Belgian enclaves in the Netherlands attract Dutch shoppers, while the popularity of cross-Channel shopping trips from the UK to France has grown as the full duty free allowance results in a cost saving greater than the discounted fare. Even where excursions across national boundaries are impractical, consumers may engage in cross-border activities through mail-order, responding to transnational advertising campaigns such as those on satellite television. The potential of consumers to contribute to the evolutionary process of change by choosing to purchase goods in particular markets – notably those with preferable tax rules – does exist.

Trade Unions

Like consumer groups, trade unions have a direct input into the Community rule-setting process via a European level association, the European Trade Union Confederation (ETUC). In addition to the traditional lobbying channels open to interest groups at the Community level, the role of the ETUC was enhanced with potentially far-reaching consequences by the provisions of the Social Protocol to the Maastricht Treaty. Under the 11-state-only Social Protocol procedure, prior to proposing new Community rules the Commission will consult with management and unions at a Community level (UNICE and the ETUC) on the possible direction of Community action. If the Commission then still considers Community action advisable, it will consult on the content of the envisaged proposal. If management and unions can at this stage reach agreement on a non-legislative form of collective agreement, the assumption is that the Commission will not proceed with plans to legislate. Although the system is largely untried (with the exception of the proposed directive on European Works Councils, where the consultation procedure failed to produce an agreement between the management and union representatives) the potential for an enhanced role for the ETUC in the evolution of Community social policy rules may be significant.

Trade unions also have a specific impact on how rules are enforced at the workplace level. Walters and Freeman (1992) showed the role of trade unions in ensuring that employers comply with Community law on health and safety at work. As the Community evolves, the role of trade unions in interpreting and enforcing law at the workplace level, by negotiating with management or by notifying statutory bodies of a breach of the law, is clearly an important factor in determining how new rules will develop.

Interest Groups: the Case of Environmental Groups

Interest groups also influence the rules directly through the policy making process by lobbying Community and member state rule-setters. In addition, they are enforcers of the law in a judicial capacity, bringing cases of non-compliance with the rules before the national courts, and in an administrative capacity, monitoring levels of non-compliance and reporting this to the Commission authorities. Environmental groups provide a useful example of how these tasks are performed at the Community level.

Mazey and Richardson (1992a) have noted that environmental groups, often in conflict with their own national administrations, see the Community as an alternative arena in which to exert influence. Links with Community institutions that are sympathetic towards environmental issues, particularly DG XI of the Commission and the European Parliament, are thus of great importance for environmental groups in the rule-setting process.

During the lobbying process, Mazey and Richardson (1992a) suggest, environmental groups may have a prima facie advantage over firms since they are not inherently competing with each other for market share. Even where there may have been a temptation to adopt the 'Not In My Back Yard' principle, Mazey and Richardson found no evidence that either national or Community level environmental groups have adopted a competitive route to influencing the rule-setting process. The co-operative nature of relations between environmental groups may be an advantage in the lobbying process.

In addition to lobbying during the rule-setting process, groups also fulfill an important role in the implementation and enforcement of Community rules. At one level the enforcement role of interest groups is demonstrated by the way that environmental groups have used the European Court of Justice as a means of forcing recalcitrant member states to implement Community rules on issues such as the quality of drinking water (Mazey and Richardson 1992a).

At another level, the 'whistle-blowing' activities of environmental groups are also important in ensuring compliance with Community rules. By alerting the Commission to instances where member states are failing in their duties to implement EC legislation, groups influence the way that rules are applied in practice. Mazey and Richardson, for example, note that Friends of the Earth were instrumental in bringing to the Commission's attention alleged breaches of Community law concerning environmental impact assessments of the M11 link road and the East London River crossing in the UK. The Commission, Mazey and Richardson suggest, is itself particularly keen to maintain this unofficial monitoring function by groups as a means of filling the 'implementation gap'.

Individuals

All individuals, as citizens of the European Union, have the potential to influence the development of Community rules through litigation in their national courts. The principles of direct effect and supremacy of Community law constitute the means by which EC law can be invoked by individuals before national courts to challenge national law which may be inconsistent in the way that it implements Community measures. Under the direct effects principle, Treaty provisions may be enforced against legitimate expectations of 'private' parties, while most 'public' bodies against which directives may be invoked can hardly be seen as responsible for non-implementation.

The notion that some public authorities may be merely liable-by-association for non-implementation by the State has led some commentators (Steiner, 1993, for example) to conclude that the principle of State liability as applied in Francovich is arguably a more legitimate means of enforcing Community law than the principle of direct effects, since the primary fault for non-implementation must lie with the State. The potential of the Francovich judgment to give individuals a significant instrument to use in the national courts in enforcing Community law must certainly be acknowledged (Snyder, 1993), while the ability of individuals to influence the enforcement process, and hence the way that Community rules evolve in practice, now clearly exists in a judicial context. Yet because national rules on non-contractual liability of public authorities differ considerably from one part of the Community to another, might it be necessary (as Steiner, 1993, suggests) to develop common Community rules governing the liability of public authorities?

5   WHAT CHANGES ARE ACTUALLY TAKING PLACE?

Convergence or Divergence?

The intention of the single market programme is to achieve convergence of national rules in a wide range of policy fields. Faced with national rule systems which are often extremely diverse and which are themselves embedded in arrangements which have evolved over many years, the European Commission has attempted to achieve convergence by imposing only those rules considered essential to ensure basic standards of health, safety and environmental protection, leaving national governments and industry experts to decide the precise content of rules in each member state, and providing a suitable regulatory environment in which national rules can compete and Community-wide rules evolve. A variety of changes are actually taking place. They can considered in the following distinct categories:

(i)   Some Community rules may evolve into national rules

Where Community rules are thought to be appropriate, member states may seek to replicate Community rules as national rules. This may be attractive where Community rules establish a regulatory regime which, over time, is generally seen to be both fair and efficient. Where this is the case, national authorities may seek to create equivalent rules to be followed in the domestic setting.   Wilks and Cini (1991), for instance, have noted that UK Government proposals to revise restrictive trade practices aspects of UK competition policy amount to a 'borrowing' of European Community principles and rules of administration under Article 85 of the Treaty of Rome.

(ii)   Some Community rules may not immediately lead to the evolution of a single market

There should be no presumption, however, that new Community rules will immediately replace the domestic regulatory system or result in the trends indicating the evolution of a single market. Assessing the impact on medical labour created by the First General Directive on the mutual recognition of professional qualifications, for instance, Brazier *et al.* (1992) found that despite the existence of vacancies for qualified doctors in the UK, far from creating a European market for medical labour, absolute levels of inward migration of Community nationals continued to be low. But this does not necessarily mean that there will be a complete absence of change in labour market activity in the long term. By definition, the evolutionary process of change will occur over an indistinct time-scale, the pace of change being determined not only by the complexity of the rules themselves, but by the interaction between a variety of economic, political, legal and social factors. It is to be expected that different rules will be at different stages of the evolutionary process at any fixed point in time.

(iii) Some national rules may evolve into Community rules

One important component of the evolutionary process in single market rules is the assumption that, as a result of competition among rules, some national rules will become commonly accepted as Community-wide rules.

Andrea Williams (1993) has noted that the German idea of Vorsorge (precaution) evolved to form the basis of Community environmental rules. The precautionary principle, embodying very general objectives such as reducing emissions, reducing risks, promoting the use of sustainable resources has proved attractive at the international level because agreements between Community member states by nature necessitate compromise. Proposals for an EC packaging directive which mirror German policy and earlier adoption of the Large Combustion Plant Directive which closely resembles German domestic rules are, Williams suggests, attractive to policy makers because the precautionary principle remains defined only in general terms, leaving governments with a policy to which they can apply their own interpretation. There are wider political objectives to be met by adopting German rules on environmental protection.

Where public and policy pressure in one member state creates conditions in which new rules are adopted, these rules may threaten access to domestic markets by firms from other member states. Weale and Williams (1992) have noted that an important example of this is the German Packaging Ordinance, which makes suppliers of packaged products responsible for the recycling of the packaging. This has led to fears in the European packaging industry outside Germany that the Packaging Ordinance will create new barriers to trade.

Matthews and Mayes (1994) found that, in response to the German Packaging Ordinance, a second round of associated rule changes had also taken place which altered the behaviour of firms both in Germany and in other member states. German retail firms, manufacturers and waste companies set up Duales System Deutschland (DSD) as a private company to collect waste and arranging for its recycling. Although participation in the DSD scheme is 'voluntary', the German retail industry association has declared that after a transitional period stores will exclusively stock products bearing the green dot, which denotes participation in the Duales System.

Because it was financially efficient for a significant number of firms to follow the DSD system, Matthews and Mayes have suggested that retail firms themselves in turn established a self-enforcing behavioural rule, which manufacturers were obliged to comply with or face lost orders. By entering into commercial relationships with DSD in Germany, non-German suppliers of packaged goods were in effect complying with a dominant (German) rule system. Because of the buying power of German retail firms, the Packaging Ordinance has not only altered consumer behaviour in Germany, encouraging the return of packaging to the point of sale, but also altered the actual market rules of the single market, amounting to a fundamental reorganization of the way that retail firms and their suppliers run their entire European operations.

In response to the new rules, Weale and Williams found that the German packaging industry itself was seeking new Community rules equivalent to the Ordinance so as to remove competitive disadvantage when the new law is fully operational. A whole range of national and Community rule changes may have resulted from a single piece of new environmental legislation in Germany.

(iv) Some Community rules may differ from existing national rules

In some instances, Community rules will follow those already tried and tested in other markets. In other cases, the Community will continue to follow an independent line of rule-setting. Community rules to harmonize bank deposit insurance arrangements, have been examined by Richard Dale (1993). The Commission has proposed a policy of harmonization of minimum prudential standards (such as capital adequacy requirements) while encouraging competition among non-harmonized national banking rules but, Dale concludes, the case for harmonizing deposit insurance schemes, even at minimum levels, is not itself proven. By not taking into account the legitimate expectation in some member states that regulators will bail out banks rather than rely on a safety net of deposit insurance, proposed Community rules differ fundamentally from US (or, indeed UK) regulation which is primarily concerned with the moral hazard problem, namely the belief that market discipline cannot be introduced unless those in a position to influence a bank's behaviour (shareholders, depositors and general creditors/subordinated debt holders) are exposed to some degree of risk.

(v)   Some Community rules may be insufficient to facilitate the evolution of a single market

The evolution of a single market through competition and mutual recognition will not necessarily result in a convergence of rules. The result of responses to single market changes may be divergence. Matthews and Mayes (1993) found that in the leasing industry some rules have converged while others have been polarized along 'Anglo-Saxon' and 'Continental' lines. Since many of the incentives to lease come from distortions caused by the segmentation of national rule systems (the three main causes of segmentation being accountancy, banking supervision and taxation rules) firms providing this particular service (the lessors) have a strong incentive to see that the 'advantageous quirks' of their national systems (Matthews and Mayes, 1993) are maintained and not removed by harmonization with the rules in rival national markets.

(vi) Some structural factors will not be addressed by single market rules

In other instances, important elements in determining how the European market evolves are not addressed either by harmonized rules or the prospect of market integration via the mutual recognition route. Matthews and Mayes (1993) noted that the requirement for expertise in local markets, both in terms of technical knowledge and customer networks, in order to establish business successfully in that market means that even if the main regulatory barriers were removed, the commercial division of national markets would seem likely to persist in the leasing industry.

Concluding Remarks

The EC has adopted a variety of routes to the formulation of single market rules. Most of these are intended to create the conditions under which an evolutionary process of convergence towards a system of 'best practice' rules can be achieved in all member states. Although this incremental route to change has proved politically less sensitive than the 'harmonization' strategy attempted by the Commission prior to 1985, the evolutionary route – by definition – takes time to achieve results. It also requires the existence of appropriate regulatory institutions to ensure the adoption of the most appropriate Community law, to 'manage' market relations subsequently and to ensure that EC law is effectively enforced and complied with in all parts of the Community.

But major problems remain. Harmonization of rules can fall short of what is needed for a truly single market and can take a form which is more a statement of the variety which is to be permitted. Mutual recognition is a powerful mechanism but is insufficient to achieve harmonization and can result in a polarization of the market groupings. Many other factors which divide markets are not addressed by the single market process as they reflect institutional structures in the member states and self-regulatory market behaviour.

Even so, in many respects, the single market programme has succeeded in disrupting the status quo in many member states, changing existing behaviour and challenging the appropriateness of existing rules. This alone makes the single market a dynamic and important process with potential strategy gains, co-operation gains, and competition gains for those operating within it. The fundamental issue is the extent to which convergence of national rules and the evolution of a single market rule system have actually been achieved, or are likely to be achieved, via the strategies adopted by the Commission, namely harmonization of minimum standards and competition among rules, through a process of mutual recognition and the removal of remaining barriers to ensure sufficient openness.

REFERENCES

Begg, D., Cramer, J., Danthine, J.-P., Edwards, J., Grilli, V., Neven, D., Seabright, P., Sinn, H.-W., Venables, A., Wyplosz, C. (1993), *Making Sense of Subsidiarity: How Much Centralization for Europe*, London: Centre for Economic Policy Research.

Boulding, K. (1982), *Evolutionary Economics*, London: Sage.

Brazier, M., Lovecy, J., Moran, M. and Potton, M. (1992), 'Professional labour and the single European market: the case of doctors', *Journal of Area Studies*, 115–24.

Brazier, M., Lovecy, J., Moran, M. and Potton, M. (1993), 'Falling from a tightrope: doctors and lawyers between the market and the state', *Political Studies*, **41**, 197–213.

Bulmer, S. (1993), 'The governance of the European Union: a new institutionalist approach', *Journal of Public Policy*, **13** (4), 351–80.

Burrows, N., Hiram, H. with Brown, J. (1993), 'Implementing European Community law: official control of foodstuffs', London: Institute of Advanced Legal Studies Research Working Papers.

Cox, A. (1993), 'Public procurement in the European Community: is a fully integrated market achievable?', *Public Money and Management*, July–September, pp. 29–35.

Dale, R. (1993), 'Deposit insurance: policy clash over EC and US reforms', *Journal of International Securities Markets*, **7** (Spring/Summer), 5–15.

Dehousse, R., Joerges, C., Majone, G. and Snyder, F. with Everson, M. (1992), 'Europe after 1992: new regulatory strategies', Florence: European University Institute Working Paper in Law No. 92/31.

Dosi, G. (1991), 'Some thoughts on the promises, challenges and dangers of an evolutionary perspective in economics', *Journal of Evolutionary Economics*, **1** (1), 5–7.

Giddens, A. (1979), *Central Problems in Social Theory*, Berkeley University Press.

Gold, M. (1993), 'The Formulation of EC Social Policy – preparatory stages', in *Aspects of European Integration: Environment, Regulation, Competition and the Social Dimension*, National Institute Report No. 5.

Gold, M. and Matthews, D. (1993), 'EC health and safety policy', *European Business Journal*, **5** (4).

Hahn, F. (1973), *On the Nation of Equilibrium in Economics*, Cambridge: Cambridge University Press.

Hahn, F. (1984), *Equilibrium and Macroeconomics*, Oxford: Basil Blackwell.

Hayek, F. (1973), 'Economic freedom and representative government', Institute of Economic Affairs Occasional Paper 39.

Leibenstein, H. (1987), *Inside the Firm*, Cambridge MA: Harvard University Press.

Loasby, B. (1991), *Equilibrium and Evolution*, Manchester: Manchester University Press.

Lodge, J. (1989), *The European Community and the Challenge of the Future*, London: Pinter.

March, J. and Simon, H. (1958), *Organizations*, Chichester: John Wiley.

Marshall, A. (1920), *Principles of Economics*, London: Macmillan.

Matthews D. and Mayes, D. (1993), *The Evolution of Rules for a Single European Market in Leasing*, London: National Institute Discussion Paper No. 35.

Matthews, D. and Mayes, D. (1994), *The Role of Soft Law in the Evolution of Rules for a Single European Market: the Case of Retailing*, London: National Institute Discussion Paper No. 61.

Mayes, D.G. and Hart, P. with Matthews, D. and Shipman, A. (1995), *The Single Market Programme as a Stimulus to Change. Comparisons between Britain and Germany*, Cambridge: Cambridge University Press.

Mazey, S. and Richardson, J. (1992a), 'Environmental Groups in the EC: Challenges and Opportunities', *Environmental Politics*, **1** (4), (Winter).

Mazey, S. and Richardson, J. (1992b), 'British pressure groups in the European Community: the challenge of Brussels', *Parliamentary Affairs* **45** (1), (January).

McGowan, F. and Seabright, P. (1993), 'Regulation and Subsidiarity: finding the balance', in *Aspects of European Integration: Environment, Regulation, Competition and the Social Dimension*, National Institute Report No. 5.

McKenzie, G. (1993), 'The EC capital adequacy directive – recipe for integration or disintegration?', *European Business Journal*, **5** (4).

Nelson, R. and Winter, S. (1977), 'Simulation of Schumpeterian competition' *American Economic Review*, **67**, 271–76.

Nelson, R. and Winter, S. (1982), *An Evolutionary Theory of Economic Change*, Cambridge MA: Harvard University Press.

Neven, D., Nuttall R. and Seabright, P. (1993), *Merger in Daylight*, London: Centre for Economic Policy Research.

Nozick, R. (1979), *Anarchy, State and Utopia*, New York: Basic Books.

Nugent, N. (1991), *The Government and Politics of the European Community*, Basingstoke: Macmillan.

O'Keefe, D. (1992), 'Trends in the Free Movement of Persons within the European Communities', in J. O'Reilly (ed.), *Human Rights and Constitutional Law*, Dublin: Round Hall Press.

Padoa-Schioppa, T. (1987), *Efficiency, Stability and Equity*, Oxford: Oxford University Press.

Sah, R. and Stiglitz, J. (1990), 'Technological learning, social learning and technological change', Yale University Economic Growth Centre, Paper 433.

Schumpeter, J. (1934), *The Theory of Economic Development*, Cambridge Mass.: Harvard University Press.

Shipman, A. and Mayes, D. (1991), 'Changing the rules: a framework for examining government and company responses to 1992', National Institute Discussion Paper No. 199.

Smith, S. (1993), 'Subsidiarity and the co-ordination of indirect taxes in the European Community', *Oxford Review of Economic Policy*, **9** (1).

Snyder, F. (1993), 'The effectiveness of European Community law: institutions, processes, tools and techniques', *Modern Law Review*, **56**, 19–54.

Steiner, J. (1993), 'From direct effects to Francovich: shifting means of enforcement of Community law', *European Law Review*, **18** (1), 3–22.

Sutherland, P. *et al.* (1992), 'The Internal Market After 1992. Meeting the Challenge', Brussels: Report to the EEC Commission by the High Level Group on the Operation of the Internal Market.

Wallace, H., Wallace, W. and Webb, C. (1983), *Policy Making in the European Community*, Chichester: John Wiley & Sons.

Walters, D. and Freeman, R.J. (1992), *Employee Representation in Health and Safety at the Workplace: A Comparative Study in Five European Countries*, Luxembourg: Commission of the European Communities.

Watson, S. and Buede, D. (1987), *Decision Synthesis*, Cambridge: Cambridge University Press.

Weale, A. and Williams, A. (1992), 'Between economy and ecology? The single market and the integration of environmental policy', *Environmental Politics*, **1** (4), (Winter), 45–64.

Weale, A. and Williams, A. (1994), 'The single market and environmental policy', Paper for the ESRC Single Market Programme/COST A7 Conference, University of Exeter, 8–11 September 1994.

Wilks, S. and Cini, M. (1991), 'Competition policy – a research prospectus', RUSEL Working Paper No. 3.

Wilks, S. (1992), 'The metamorphosis of European Community policy', RUSEL Working Paper No.9.

Williams, A. (1993), 'The Precautionary Principle and European Decision Making', in *Aspects of European Integration: Environment, Regulation, Competition and the Social Dimension*, National Institute Report No. 5.

Woolcock, S., Hodges, M. and Schreiber, K (1991), *Britain, Germany and 1992. The Limits of Deregulation*, London: Pinter Publishers.

8. The Single Market, European Integration and Political Legitimacy

Albert Weale[*]

Questions of political legitimacy arise from all aspects of European integration. The reason for this is simple. Except under conditions of widespread repression, belief in the legitimacy of the actions of a political authority is a precondition for even minimally successful governance. If, as Lipset (1963, p. 77) once wrote in a famous analysis, 'Legitimacy involves the capacity of the system to engender and maintain the belief that the existing political institutions are the most appropriate ones for the society', how much more difficult might we expect it to be for an emerging and unformed set of political institutions, like those of the European Union, to engender the requisite beliefs across a number of societies than it is for national governments. Thus, unless a belief in political legitimacy can be engendered, the governing capacity of European institutions is called into question.

The purpose of this chapter is to survey, in the light of evidence arising from the UK's Economic and Social Research Council's (ESRC) Research Programme on the Evolution of Rules in the Single European Market as well as other sources, what we currently understand about political legitimacy and European Union. The ESRC Initiative involves a number of related research projects looking at the origins, dynamics and consequences of the creation of a single market in Europe. The projects are primarily empirical, though many of them inevitably raise conceptual and analytic issues, as well as policy questions. My purpose will be to examine what this emerging body of evidence has to say about the problems of political legitimacy in Europe.

Issues of political legitimacy have been given added focus by the events and developments associated with the ratification of the Treaty on European Union (the Maastricht Treaty). The no vote in the first Danish referendum of June 1992, the narrow majority for yes in the French referendum of September of that year, the turn-out of 57 per cent in the European Parliament elections of 1994 (the lowest since direct elections in 1979) and the declining confidence in European institutions as measured by public opinion polls are all elements of what appears to be a declining momentum behind the cause of European

[*] I should like to thank Andrew Cox, Emil Kirchner and Duncan Matthews for detailed and acute comments on an earlier version of this paper. John Peterson was discussant at the Exeter conference, and I am grateful to him not only for his insightful observations, but also for supplying me with a written version. Sarah Leeming took the trouble to supply me with materials from the research projects. The usual *caveats* apply.

integration. Moreover, the sentiments are not restricted to those outside the charmed circle of European policy makers. Jacques Delors is reported to have said of Maastricht that it was too soon to make a treaty on political union, and Professor Andre Szasz, an executive director of the Dutch central bank, has argued that Maastricht contained a lack of clarity about what was intended and why, and an unjustified assumption that monetary union requires economic and political union (both cited in Marsh, 1994).

It is, of course, all too tempting to infer a trend from a modulation, and there is sometimes a regrettable tendency for commentary on European integration to follow short-term developments rather than seek to analyse them in their longer term context. At the same time as the low turn-out in the Parliamentary elections the Austrians voted by a two to one majority to join the Union, and the empirical evidence on the so called 'crisis of legitimacy' in western liberal democracies, which has so often been declared by theorists and practitioners, finds little support in time-series analysis of trends in public opinion (as the forthcoming studies from the European Science Foundation's Belief in Government project will show). Nevertheless, since the maintenance of any political union depends upon a sense of political legitimacy, it would appear that the topic of political legitimacy is at least relevant to our understanding of the dynamics of political union, and it may even be central.

Simplifying somewhat, there are two dominant traditions in political theory of thinking about legitimacy, which I shall term the Lockeian and the Humean (both to remind us of their origins in the works of Locke (1698) and Hume (1752) and to guard us against identifying the theories with the historical work of either). On the Lockeian analysis the notion of consent is crucial. In one way or another, governments earn their legitimacy by securing the consent of the governed. This consent may be expressed in various ways – through elections or referenda or in tacit or explicit form – but, however it is achieved, legitimacy is a child of consent. On the alternative, Humean, view legitimacy is sired from habit out of successful performance. For Humeans citizens acquiesce in the actions of government in order to secure the benefits that governments bring. In some sense this is consent, but as Plamenatz succinctly puts it: 'This consent is not agreement or the granting of a permission; it is acquiescence grounded in the knowledge that government is in the public interest.' (Plamenatz, 1963, p. 302). So whereas the Lockeian theory has the idea of consent at its base, the Humean approach is a theory that rests upon the idea of benefit.

It is only straining the interpretation of these two traditions a little to see the divergence between Monnet and Spinelli over the best way of securing European union as reflecting these two ways of thinking (see Burgess, 1989, pp. 43–63). As is well known (see references cited in Featherstone, 1994), Monnet saw political union as following the administrative integration brought about through supra-national problem-solving bodies. As Burgess (1989, p. 49) aptly puts it, Monnet thought that the state in Europe was obsolete partly because of its collapse in the face of Naziism, but mainly 'because of a perceived discrepancy between changing demands of new technologies and the capacity of the state to meet them'. The consequence of this way of thinking was, as Burgess stresses, a belief in federalism, but a federalism brought about as the outcome of specific achievements that would create the political and institutional context within which popular endorsement of political union would follow. Although Spinelli was prepared to accept this vision of technocratic integration because of its success, it is clear that he felt both that political union had in some sense to precede the technical solution to common problems and that this political union should be based upon the ideas of democracy within the liberal English tradition of political thought (see Burgess, 1989, p. 133). It was these ideas of course that lay behind his 1984 Draft Treaty. Thus, we see a benefit-based theory of political integration in Monnet's theory and a consent-based theory in Spinelli.

How do these two theories stand more generally with respect to political legitimacy and European union? To think about how we might answer this question, consider the following thought-experiment. Suppose that the single market programme had had its intended effects. Suppose, that is to say, that the single market produced an increase of between 4 and 7 per cent of GDP. Suppose further that there were a functional relationship between the economic integration brought about by the single market and the prospects for political union. Then, if the Humean view of political legitimacy were correct, we should expect political legitimacy to have followed in train. The chain of reasoning here is simple. Legitimacy is a product of successful government performance. The token of successful government performance is economic well-being. Hence, any political institutions that are the preconditions for successful economic well-being will acquire legitimacy through those policies that bring about successful economic performance.

One has only to state the thought-experiment to see that it is hypothesis rather than fact. Economic recession has afflicted all Union countries. Almost as soon as the Treaty on European Union was signed by member governments, the process of ratification ran into problems, first with the no vote in the Danish referendum and then with the close referendum vote in France. The Maastricht rebels in the House of Commons did their bit to keep up the excitement. And the convergence criteria for monetary union look for most countries as though they are distant aspirations rather than short or medium term targets.

It follows that there must be something wrong with the assumptions contained in the chain of reasoning that I set out in the thought-experiment. One or more of the following must be false: the Humean theory of legitimacy; the assumptions, including the assumptions about implementability, on which the single market programme rested; the assumption that there is a functional link between economic performance and political union; or the assumption that the institutions of the Community could play the role of political authority envisaged within the theory. In what follows, we shall look at each of these propositions in turn, drawing on empirical evidence from the studies in the ESRC's Initiative.

1 THE HUMEAN THEORY OF LEGITIMACY

Hume's critique of the theory of consent rested upon a simple observation: functioning political systems did not reveal historical incidents in which the consent of the people was secured. Hence, consent could not be the basis of legitimate government. But the relevance of this simple observation to the EU is not entirely clear. If we take an intergovernmentalist perspective, then there clearly has been consent to each stage of the development of the Union, since revisions of the original Treaty of Rome, as well as the Treaty itself, have rested on the unanimous agreement of the participating governments. I suppose that it might be argued that those countries joining as members after the original six had to take the Community as they found it, but this is surely of no greater relevance than the fact that any agreement involves some compromise in one's most preferred outcome in order to accommodate the legitimate interests of other parties to the agreement (whatever some British politicians might say about the wisdom of the rest of Europe conforming to UK understandings). After all, there have been countries who have been granted the right of entry but who have found the terms and conditions on offer too onerous for their individual circumstances.

So, from the point of view of an intergovernmentalist perspective, it would seem that a Lockeian, rather than a Humean, theory was more appropriate. However, the message that I draw from this analysis is that this merely highlights the deficiencies of a simple unqualified intergovernmentalist analysis of European integration. Title IA of the Treaty on European Union speaks of the task of the Union to organize 'relations between the member states and between their peoples' and Article B of the same Title introduces citizenship of the Union in addition to citizenship of the individual member states. The supranationalism of these legal developments is matched in behavioural terms. What we are seeing in the European Union is not simply an organization between governments but the creation of new centres of political activity. Consider Haas's well known definition of integration:

> Political integration is the process whereby political actors in several distinct national settings are persuaded to shift their loyalties, expectations and political activities toward a new centre, whose institutions possess or demand jurisdiction over the pre-existing national states. The end result of the process of political integration is a new political community, superimposed on the existing ones. (Haas, 1968, p. 16).

If this is one aspect of European integration, then we should expect to see behavioural change as integration takes place. We should expect to see changes in the locus of expectations and political activities, with political actors placing less emphasis upon national settings and more upon the European level of decision making. The studies of lobbying within the Community conducted by Mazey and Richardson do show such a pattern (see, *inter alia*, Mazey and Richardson, 1993). As they note, the behaviour of pressure groups is a good indicator of where power is to be found in a social order, since as US lobbyists say, it is best to shoot where the ducks are. Prior to the Single European Act, most European lobbying was conducted via national governments, but the consequences of the institutional changes brought about by the act are that the power of national governments has been weakened and that of European institutions strengthened.

Mazey and Richardson stress that the development of lobbying at the European level is still at an early stage. There is no stable pattern to the process, and the rules of the game are still to be established. The Commission, which is the primary focus of lobbying, is an adolescent bureaucracy pursuing different agenda items in unpredictable ways. The locus of activity can be divided between the Commission and the Parliament, with the latter being the place where interest groups can secure detailed changes to European legislation. Decision rules have been changing and the multi-layered complexity of the decision process has important implications for group strategies, making EC lobbying an activity that requires coordination at various levels. Moreover, despite the desire of the Commission to promote Euro-associations and the tangible support the Commission is able to offer in the form of soft money for conferences and the like, the practical business of policy-making often requires an expertise that only existing national groups can offer. Finally, Mazey and Richardson point out that it is often non-European organizations that have responded to the emerging situation by Europeanising their lobbying activity.

What these studies would seem to indicate is that the political behaviour of lobby groups confirms the expectations of those who see the process of European integration taking a supranationalist form. Expectations and activities are being relocated from the national level to the European level. Of course, it is not necessary to insist that this be a complete supplanting of national activity, merely an added dimension of political behaviour that is significantly increasing in importance. But this uneasy mixture of national and European governance can itself be seen as part of the problem rather than part of the solution. To say that political activity now takes place at the European level as well as the national level is not to offer a way of resolving problems of political legitimacy but instead to provide an occasion for their manifestation. Since, as Helen Wallace (1993, pp. 299–300) has pointed out, lobby group activity raises the question of how the Community balances private and public interests, the *success* of integration on

Haas's criteria in fact give rise to new problems of political legitimacy. We shall have to return to these questions when we consider the problems of institutional reform in the final section.

Within Hume's own account of legitimacy the attitudes of public officials has always been important, and this insight is continued in a modern classic within the Humean tradition, namely Hart's (1961) *The Concept of Law*. An essential requirement according to Hart for the validity of a legal system is that the core of public officials in the broadest sense, including political elites responsible for operating the system, internalize its principles and accept its locus of authority. I know of no empirical evidence that casts direct light upon the attitudes of public officials both at the national and at the European level, but common sense would suggest that in these respects the level of internalized acceptance is high.

One relevant piece of indirect evidence, however, comes from the growth of environmental policy within the European Community. Until the Single European Act environmental policy had no independent standing within the Treaty of Rome, but instead was developed under Article 100 dealing with decision-making competences for completion of the single market and Article 235, the catch-all article that enabled the Community to take on new functions when necessary to achieve the objects of the Treaty. Despite the slimness of the legal basis for environmental policy, it has steadily since 1973 become important within the range of the Community's activity and, even before the coming into force of the Single European Act, it was clear that environmental protection measures were being taken with substantial cost implications. This example appears to imply a substantial degree of de facto acceptance of the competence of the Community in new and emerging fields, at least among public officials and political elites. It could always be argued that the legitimacy of Community environmental competence was more notional than real, since Community environmental policy is plagued by substantial implementation deficits. I review some of the evidence on implementation deficits below, to see what it suggests about the topic of political legitimacy, but, to anticipate a little here, that evidence would not call into question the general claim that public officials have substantially internalized the role of the EU as a source of political authority within its own right.

However, it is difficult to know what sort of implications to draw from this fact. It might be tempting to argue that the emergence of new competences at EC level marked the development of a new form of political legitimacy. On the other hand, this could be straining the interpretation too far. After all, it would be possible to give an intergovernmentalist account of the emergence of new competences like that of environmental protection, since the character of many of the problems is transnational. On this analysis, what drove the development of European environmental policy in the 1980s is the acceptance by the German government in 1982 of the hypothesis that 'acid rain' was due to sulphur emissions from large combustion plants (Boehmer-Christiansen and Skea, 1991, pp. 230–51). Since there is a large import/export trade in sulphur emissions among European countries, governments concerned about the effects of pollution have to find some way of co-ordinating their activities in order to bring about reductions in the volume of emissions. That this is essentially an intergovernmental activity can be seen in the fact that the development of environmental protection in the EC of the 1980s is only one example of international co-operation in the field of environmental protection.

A similar point could be made in respect of the Single European Act itself. As Kirchner (1992) has pointed out, the passing of the Single European Act has been taken by a number of analysts as the opportunity to revive neo-functionalist accounts of European integration, but the inference here again is not straight-forward. Accounts of the national bargaining positions in negotiations leading to the Single European Act suggest that different countries wanted different things from the Act (Garrett, 1992; Moravscik, 1991). If we see the successful passage of the Act as the outcome of a fortuitous series of circumstances in which national preferences temporarily converged, than we should not be surprised if subsequent further developments towards economic and monetary union diverged as the differences of perspective reasserted themselves. In other words, the developments of the 1980s, that so raised neo-functionalist hopes, could be interpreted as representing no more than a political bargain between national governments to deal with problems that they could not deal with themselves. (It should of course be noted that in understanding the full development of the political process surrounding the Single European Act, there are complex methodological questions about intended and unintended consequences.)

The relevance of this discussion in the present context is as follows. On the Humean account of legitimacy a sufficient condition for the validity of a normative political order is the adherence of public officials and political elites to the legitimacy of that order. At first blush, it looks as though policy developments like the growth of environmental policy or the passing of the Single European Act indicate allegiance by the political classes of Europe to an emerging supranational order. Yet, on further inspection, these developments look more like a Lockeian contract among the political classes of Europe to achieve specific purposes than an open ended Humean habit of allegiance to an established (or at least emerging) normative political order.

A third element in this equation is public opinion. For the Humean the state of public opinion gives some indications about political legitimacy, but chiefly in terms of whether there is a general acceptance that government is producing the range of benefits that it should. The distinction was nicely brought out by Almond and Verba in their data in their original five nation civic culture study. This showed substantial variations in the extent to which different national populations 'took pride in' their governmental system, the UK showing 46 per cent, but Germany and Italy showing 7 per cent and 3 per cent respectively. Despite these responses, it could nevertheless be argued that political legitimacy was high, at least in the US, the UK and Germany, since in these societies the bulk of the population were what Almond and Verba (1965, p. 49) called 'allegiants' in the output sense'. That is, they comprised persons who were aware of and evaluated favourably the outputs of government.

The Humean account of legitimacy thus seems to work well in the case of national governments but even here appearances can be deceptive. On the Almond and Verba test, governments secure allegiance by securing benefits, 'outputs', for their populations. But one could argue that this reflects a period of 'normal politics'. In abnormal times, when the boundary of the polity are threatened by war or some other fundamental challenge to political identity, sentiments more visceral than the cool calculation of benefits need to be called into play.

The reason for introducing this qualification relates to the political difficulties likely to be faced in the European integration of nation-states. On the Humean analysis, the political classes will enjoy legitimacy so long as they deliver the goods, but it might be argued that this simple relationship only holds in the context of already formed identities beyond the calculus of costs and benefits. When these identities are threatened with disruption, then we have the problem of Europe in 1992–3 in the attempts to ratify the Maastricht Treaty, 'a document negotiated in a room without windows, into which public opinion had subsequently bulldozed its unwelcome and critical presence' (Wallace, 1993, p. 296). In other words, we cannot simply transpose an understanding of legitimacy suitable to the nation-state to the European level, or, more particularly, we can assume that the same sorts of processes that sustain allegiances in stable nation states will apply to cases where the locus of those allegiances is being changed.

Of course, there is an alternative interpretation of the bulldozer, namely that it simply reflected the social and political strains induced by the economic recession. On this view, we could still retain a Humean view of political legitimacy. We should simply have to alter our expectations about its application at particular times. The benefits of European integration are still there, but will not be unlocked until there is an upturn in the business cycle. Popular discontent with Maastricht was not evidence of Lockeian forces at work, but merely an indication that the timing of the flow of benefits is out of synchronization with the proposed institutional and policy developments.

Time will undoubtedly enable us partially to sort out which of these opposing interpretations is the more accurate. If public sentiment begins to move in a pro-integrationist direction as the European economy picks up, then it may be that we can still tell a Humean story. No doubt, however, the ratio of noise to signal will still be high at that time, so it will not be a straightforward inference to make.

Summarizing this section, we can say that the first premiss of our thought-experiment – that we can account for political legitimacy by appeal to a Humean theory – contains some plausibility, but that it does not hold up unambiguously. There is some evidence, to be seen in the emerging patterns of lobbying, that new supranational loyalties and expectations are being formed within the European Union. The internalization by officials and the political classes of the normative authority of the Union is also evidence for a shifting locus of authority. If the popular backlash against the ratification of the Maastricht Treaty turns out to be the consequence of economic recession, then, as the benefits of European integration begin to flow, the legitimation of EU political and decision making structures should proceed. On the other hand, it is clear from the research that lobbying is not exclusively a supranational process, and that in many ways national organizations have advantages in the pursuit of their interests. The internalization of the normative authority of the EU may simply be a limited *modus vivendi* that national political classes find necessary in order to tackle transnational problems. And the popular backlash on Maastricht may indicate that the roots of legitimacy lie in a Lockeian process, by which authority is ceded by popular mandate, than a Humean process by which government benefits produce allegiance.

So the first premiss of the thought-experiment does not remain entirely unscathed. On the other hand, it is not so damaged as to suggest that we should entirely ignore the other two propositions. The first was the claim that the single market programme would produce substantial economic benefits. The second concerned the putative functional relationship between economic performance and political development. Let us consider each of these in turn.

2   ANTICIPATING AND ASSESSING THE BENEFITS OF 1992

If legitimacy is sired by habit out of successful performance, then clearly the successful performance is a necessary condition for the development of political legitimacy. If the successful performance is missing, then so will be the legitimacy. Are there any reasons for thinking that the legitimacy deficit has its origins in the failure of Europe to secure the economic gains that the 1992 programme promised?

Empirical evidence suggests that of the estimated costs of non-Europe only half are likely to be removed by the single market programme (Mayes, 1991, p. 3). This may suggest that the original Cecchini estimates were over-inflated, but Mayes is careful not to draw this conclusion, arguing that Cecchini was not a prediction about what would happen, but an attempt to estimate the losses due to existing barriers to trade. However, Mayes is willing to echo the criticisms of others to the effect that the Cecchini estimates were wrong on one central respect, namely that they did not take account of the dynamics involved in the process of change. Essentially Cecchini was an exercise in comparative statics, looking at one regime of competition and comparing it with another. As Mayes points out, it did not take into account those dynamic forces that arise in the transition from one regime to another including: the pressure of competition arising from lowering the ability to segment markets; increases in the sizes of firms enabling them to take advantage of scale economies in their global operations; lowering the price of capital, thereby encouraging investment; improving the efficiency of the labour markets by policies in the social dimension; and the effect of the flanking policies for research and development in enhancing growth. Taking these dynamic effects into account, and placing the estimates in the context of broader considerations of economic and monetary union, Mayes suggests that some 70 per cent of the Cecchini estimated benefit could be achieved over a ten year period.

Cox (1992) has also drawn attention to a related problem. As well as the issue of misestimation, there is also the question of whether policy strategies rest upon accurate analytic foundations. Cox argues that in the case of the public procurement directives, which in the Cecchini analysis were thought to be potentially a large source of economic gains, the policy strategy was not well conceived. In particular, he argues that the framing of the directives was based on too simplistic an analysis of market processes, ignoring such phenomena as market concentration, logistical inertia, vertical integration, tender costing, barriers to small and medium size firms, and organizational standard operating procedures (Cox, 1992, p. 144). He suggests in particular that tender costs may well be increased by the directives because firms have to absorb more complicated rules (Cox, 1992, p. 146).

These findings would obviously be consistent with the economic interpretation of the post-Maastricht popular backlash. The economic benefits of the 1992 programme are less than estimated by Cecchini and policy strategies for achieving them may well be misconceived in some cases. In any case we should not expect the benefits would to be fully realized until the late 1990s. Thus, in the context of a severe recession, these benefits would not be sufficient to off-set the down-turn in economic expectations and conditions that affected all west European (and other) economies.

The failure to devise successful policy strategies and the relative slowness with which the benefits have come on stream would be compounded by delays in the implementation of the programme, so that if the benefits would give rise to legitimacy the slowness of the benefits would undermine the legitimacy. There are well-known general reasons why planned programmes do not turn out as intended. Indeed, in the light of the general literature, we should really regard implementation failure as the norm rather than the exception. Moreover, in the case of the EC, there are entrenched features of the policy process that enhance the tendency to implementation failure. The characteristic instrument of policy is the directive, which places implementation in the hands of national governments, who themselves may have reservations about the policy. Directorate-generals within the Commission work in relative isolation from one another, thus increasing the probability that they will adopt uncoordinated, and potentially mutually antagonistic, policies. Bureaucratic incentive structures gives more prizes for the passing of measures and less for their effective monitoring in practice. And, despite populist prejudice to the contrary, the size of the bureaucracy is small in relation to the tasks it has to carry out. Thus, as Matthews and Mayes (1993, p. 76) have pointed out, implementation of EC measures has tended to focus upon their legal form rather than whether behaviour becomes harmonized.

The most recent estimate of implementation delay suggests that there are some sectors of the economy that are especially affected. Tucker (1994) reports failures by national governments to adopt the appropriate legislation in the fields of pharmaceutical products, company law, intellectual property and public procurement. It is significant in this context that implementation here simply means legal transposition, which is quite distinct from behavioural change associated with an alteration of practice. Moreover, Tucker also points out that the strategy of mutual recognition is itself causing problems, particularly for producers in the smaller countries who are facing barriers to trade arising from national quality, health and pest control standards. If legitimacy follows successful performance, the delays in fully implementing 1992 will undermine such success as there might be.

As noted earlier, a Humean theory of legitimacy gives a central place to the attitudes and behaviour of public officials or the political classes. Problems of implementation, even in the relatively narrow sense of legal transposition, are therefore likely to be of importance, and we can see some of these effects by examining Cox and Hartley's work on the implementation of the public procurement directives. Abolishing artificial barriers to trade was given great prominence in the Cecchini studies on the costs of non-Europe, with emphasis being given to the savings that could be expected from more open and competitive procurement procedures. As Cox (1994, pp. 137–8) points out, the EC has evolved since 1985 an extensive programme of legislative drafting to overcome the basic deficiencies of the previous public procurement rules, which provided no effective remedies for aggrieved suppliers. The basic goal of the new rules is the eradication of national preference in favour of more open and competitive structures. More importantly, as Cox points out, the novel element of the new programme is the inclusion of the utilities sectors, covering energy, water, transport and communications, which were previously excluded under the old rules.

Cox looks at the pattern of derogations applied for in the case of energy extraction activities under the Utilities Procurement Directive. Under Article 3 of this directive, countries can apply their own rules for public and private entities involved in the exploration for or extraction of oil, gas, coal or other solid fuels, provided that a certain number of conditions are satisfied concerned with ensuring competition and openness of procedure. Cox (1994, p. 144) cites the case of the French alternative regime which seems more lax than the rules in the directive itself. The effect of such derogations from uniform rules, in Cox's view is to weaken the effectiveness of the single market programme by creating *de facto* barriers to entry for foreign suppliers. But the significant point, in the present context, is not the effect of the derogations, but their cause. The answer was 'the need for the EC to ensure political support for the integration project as a whole, even though this may undermine the search for a Single Market in practice.' (Cox, 1994, p. 135). Here we see the requirements of political legitimacy cutting across the effective implementation of the single market programme.

It can, of course, be argued that energy exploration and extraction is a particular example in which one would expect corporatist pressures at the national level to be at their strongest. The industries are highly specialist, concentrated and capital intensive, and there are in all liberal democracies close and long-standing relationships between the industries involved and the relevant ministries. By the same token, the consumer interest is diffuse, disorganized and technically unsophisticated, so that the standard problem of collective action (Olson, 1965), namely turning latent diffuse interests into organized political action, is especially acute in relation to this sector. Thus, it might be argued that if ever Adam Smith's conspiracy of businessmen against the public interest applied, it would be in this sort of case. However, the present point is that in the context of relatively permanent economic structures, the boundaries of effective action are severely circumscribed by the need to retain the confidence of the political classes influenced by their domestic interested publics.

Within the single market programme there was implicit a theory of political legitimacy. The improved economic performance brought about by the single market would bring benefits to the populations of member states and these benefits would reinforce the legitimacy of Community activity. Moreover, the technical measures in the 1985 White Paper were to be accompanied by the symbolically significant removal of the physical barriers to the free movement of people in the form of the abolition of customs and immigration controls. In theory it should be no more difficult for a citizen of the Union to move between any two member states than it currently is for a citizen of the UK to move between England and Scotland. But just as the symbolic free movement of people between member states has not been satisfactorily achieved, so there are problems of achievement in the rest of the 1992 programme itself, and these may well have implications for the political legitimacy of the Union. The gains from the abolition of barriers to trade may well have been misestimated by Cecchini and in any case the effects of the business cycle will have masked the flow of benefits that were attained. Implementation deficit, which might and probably was anticipated but masked in the exhortatory rhetoric, further contributes to the slowing down of the stream of benefits. So, to the extent to which a Humean theory of legitimacy applies, the benefits were not there in the volume anticipated to effect a shift of loyalties from existing levels of government. It was implicit in the Single European Act and the Maastricht Treaty that popular participation in decision making was not to be introduced, so that the Lockeian theory of political legitimacy was not given a try.

All these conclusions rest upon one premiss, however, namely that there is a direct and positive relationship between the successful implementation of the single market programme and the increasing political legitimacy of the EU. This premiss in turn reflects the basic proposition of the 1985 White Paper, which explicitly stated that the 1992 programme was liberal in inspiration. True. But one can add that it was a particular type of analytic liberalism based upon neo-classical economic postulates, in which the destabilizing effects of economic growth and development are ignored. If, instead, we turn, say, to liberal economic analysis in the Schumpeterian tradition, then economic development is seen as a phenomenon of disequilibrium within which growth is a process of 'creative destruction' (Schumpeter, 1954, pp. 81–86). This has implications for the third element of our thought-experiment which contained the proposition that there is a functional link between the successful implementation of the single market programme and political legitimacy. Perhaps instead we should explore the possibility that the relation is dysfunctional.

3   ECONOMIC PERFORMANCE AND POLITICAL LEGITIMACY: A FUNCTIONAL LINK?

Why should we suppose that the link between the implementation of the single market programme and political legitimacy was dysfunctional rather than functional? Suppose that the Cecchini estimates are right, and that the costs of non-Europe amount to between 4 and 7 per cent of Community GDP. Although reducing barriers to trade would produce gains of this magnitude, then, as Begg and Mayes (1991, p. 63) among others have pointed out, the implementation of the single market would produce losers as well as gainers, particularly regions in difficulty and inflation-prone economies. In other words, the single market programme does not pass the test of the Pareto principle, which says that a policy leading to a reallocation of resources should be adopted provided that it made at least some people better off and no one worse off. It only passes the test of the so called hypothetical Pareto principle, which says that a policy involving a reallocation of resources can be adopted – even when there are some losers – provided that the gains of the gainers are more than sufficient to compensate the losers even though such compensation may not be paid. Herein lies the rationale of flanking policies on social and economic cohesion. If a policy is adopted consistent with the hypothetical Pareto principle, then it may make broader political and social sense not just to allow the losses to lie where they fall, but instead ensure that there is at least some payment from the gainers to the losers. In the absence of such payments the implementation of the single market programme could be dysfunctional for political legitimacy, rather as the maintenance of the gold standard became dysfunctional for political legitimacy in the inter-war period.

These dysfunctional effects would not be serious if we could assume that the integrating economies of Europe behaved according to standard neo-classical principles, in which factors of production move from high cost regions and sectors of the economy to low cost regions and sectors of the economy. But Begg and Mayes (1991) cite convincing evidence and authoritative sources suggesting that incremental smooth marginal transitions are not a feature of the emerging single market, and hence that a laissez-faire policy is inappropriate. To some extent this tension between a neo-classical view and a more structural view can be found in the competing motives of those political actors favouring the single market. But to the extent to which structural change, involving losses for some as well as gains for others, is the dominant mode of implementation for the single market, we would expect some political incentive to develop compensatory policies.

The issue can be approached from another point of view, involving different assumptions but nevertheless leading to similar conclusions. This is a line of argument that has been pursued by Majone (for example, Majone, 1993). Majone notes that one of the fundamental theorems of welfare economics is that under certain conditions a competitive market economy will lead to a Pareto-efficient allocation of resources, that is an allocation in which no person can be made better off without making someone else worse off (Majone, 1993, p. 156). These conditions may not be satisfied for a number of reasons including the existence of market imperfections, information failures or spill-over effects (externalities) like environmental pollution. In these cases we have instances of market failure. The term 'market failure' is intended here to have a quite precise meaning. It does not simply connote the existence of unwanted side-effects from markets (crime, pollution, anomie, and so on). Instead it means the failure of competitive, decentralized markets to achieve an efficient allocation of resources in the Paretian sense. Such market imperfections 'provide a set of rationales for government interventions acceptable, in principle, even to the advocates of a liberal economic order' (Majone, 1993, pp. 156–7).

The typical set of public policy programmes intended to correct for market failures go by the name of 'regulation', usually divided into economic regulation to control the pricing policy of monopolies and social regulation intended to correct for environmental externalities and asymmetries of information between producers and consumers in the form of consumer protection regulation. Regulatory policies of this sort are intended to correct for market failures by creating the conditions within which economic efficiency can be achieved. They may be contrasted with other forms of intervention usually associated with the welfare state intended to achieve a redistribution of resources or ensure that individual citizens have access to specific goods and services (merit goods, like health care and education).

Majone (1993) uses this contrast between social regulation and welfare state policies to suggest that the legitimate sphere for governmental intervention at the European level is in the field of social regulation rather than social policy as traditionally conceived in the welfare state. The reasoning here is both negative and positive. The negative argument relates to the infeasibility of a European welfare state for a number of reasons. The success of the welfare state at the national level itself may preclude European developments. The fears of social dumping and welfare magnets, which would provide rationales for a European state are exaggerated. The budgetary restrictions of the Community are too tight to permit the large-scale spending that welfare states require. The existing variety of welfare state forms imposes constraints on the degree of integration of which they are capable. And it would be difficult to reform some existing redistributive policies, like the CAP, or regional policy, into an efficient form of social policy.

Social regulation, by contrast, has, on Majone's analysis, a number of features that make it a legitimate sphere of EU activity. Activity in the fields of environmental protection, occupational health and safety and consumer protection has shown significant political momentum in revisions of the Treaty of Rome. Similar momentum has been shown in the willingness of the council to pass an increasing number of directives in these fields. More coherence is being introduced into the formulation of directives. Issues of implementation are being addressed, particularly as revealed in proposals for the establishment of European agencies in environment, medicinal products and health and safety at work. And much EU social regulation passes beyond agreement on the lowest common denominator to become innovatory in its own right (for these negative and positive arguments, see Majone, 1993, pp. 159–67). This overall line of argument is clearly consistent with Wallace's (1993, p. 300) observation that the post-Second World War consensus on what constitutes a public good has been disturbed.

In taking up these themes I shall leave aside questions about whether Majone is right to think that elements of a welfare state would be unfeasible at a European level (for a different view see Weale, 1994). Instead I shall consider how much we can realistically expect of environmental policy and social action to off-set the dysfunctions of the single market.

As noted in section 1, environmental policy developed in the EC originally without a basis in the Treaty of Rome. From the late 1960s the environmental policy moved forward in fits and starts, but with a especial concern for the control of dangerous substances and the discharge of pollutants to air and water. In 1986 it received formal legal status in Article 130r(2) of the Single European Act which established the principle that environmental protection requirements should be a component of the Community's other policies and in Article 100A(3) which urged the Commission to take a high level of protection as the basis for environmental measures. Before the Single European Act environmental measures had been passed by the Council principally under the provisions of Article 100, relating to the completion of a common market. After the Single European Act measures of environmental protection could sometimes still be regarded as related to the completion of the single market, in which case they were passed by qualified majority voting in the Council, or alternatively be passed under Article 130r(2), in which case the measure required a unanimous vote. Since the coming into force of the Treaty on European Union environ-mental measures can be passed by the qualified majority procedure.

Among the factors leading to the internationalization of environmental policy are the character of the problems and the widespread public concern in Europe (and elsewhere) about environmental problems. The problem which in the 1980s came to symbolize the trans-boundary nature of pollution was acid rain (more properly designated as acid precipitation). Arising from combustion emissions the increased acidification of rain, snow and mist causes damage to human health, buildings, forests and freshwaters. The anxiety in the 1970s of the Scandinavian countries over the damage to their environment being caused by acid rain has led to an international monitoring programme, which has established that the sources of pollution are often far removed from the effects across national boundaries. Similar findings apply to marine pollution and greenhouse gas emissions (the latter being the ultimate public 'bad'). More obviously, the trans-frontier shipment of hazardous waste has an obvious international dimension. During the 1980s it became apparent to policy-makers in a number of countries that the new scale of these problems meant that they could not be solved by uncoordinated national action, but they needed to be addressed at the international level. Already having a substantial foot in the door, the EU became a natural focus of international action.

McGowan and Seabright (1993, p. 47) have pointed out that the identification of an international regulatory prisoners' dilemma is not sufficient for making the case for delegating powers to the international level, since national governments could simply modify their domestic policies in the light of international agreements. However, McGowan and Seabright note that two further reasons enter at this point to suggest that the delegation of powers from the national to the international level makes sense. Firstly, there are considerable transactions costs in negotiating on international coordination. Secondly, there is the problem of credibility: put simply it is difficult for individual countries to make credible commitments to one another simply by means of international negotiations. There has to be some delegation of authority. If we place this rationale along with the pressure from domestic actors to internationalize regulations to which they themselves are subject, we can see how the EU has come to acquire a legitimate role in environmental protection.

Moreover, it is important to see the EU as being embedded in a wide-ranging network of international organizations. Some of these organizations have played an important role in fostering international policy learning. Thus, the OECD has played an important role in developing the international dialogue about the costs and benefits of environmental regulation, and it is clear that on such subjects as acid rain or the employment benefits that might come from more stringent pollution controls the OECD has played an influential role in relation to the Commission's thinking (see Hajer, 1995).

For these reasons, then, one can understand why the EU might come to be seen to have a legitimate role in the field of environmental protection, and by extension in the field of social regulation more generally. But this is only to state one side of the story. Although there are powerful factors making for the internationalization of environmental protection, there are also reasons for thinking that the national level of decision-making is of continuing significance. And we can illustrate this point in the field of environmental protection.

Just as the character of some environmental problems appears to lead to the need for an international perspective, so the character of other problems, and in particular the relative urgency or priority to be given to different problems, can be expected to vary from country to country. This country-specific feature of the problems becomes most apparent when we move outside the sphere of the developed 'northern' EU states to encompass consideration of all the EU states, north and south. In one of the few comparative studies of Mediterranean environmental policies, Pridham and Cini (forthcoming) pick up on the point about the diversity of environmental problems with which national governments have to deal. Spain, Italy and Greece are characterized as having a 'preponderance of unspoilt, undeveloped natural areas, bordering a semi-enclosed sea, possessing rare flora and fauna and suffering from a poor water supply'. They point out that the Commission recognized the distinctive nature of the problems in 1990. Yet, whatever recognition is given at the European level, it would seem that this distinctiveness would imply distinct national priorities, possibly diverging in considerable respects from the priorities of northern states.

Along with the distinctive character of the problems, there are also other differences that we should expect among European nations. There may well be variations in collective preference about the balance between economic growth and environmental protection depending on the level of economic development achieved. There will certainly be differences in national styles of regulation depending upon the administrative and political histories of the nations concerned. And these administrative variations will be linked to the bureaucratic capacity to formulate and implement environmental protection policies. The question of implementation is particularly significant, for if, following McGowan and Seabright, we see the issue of credibility as crucial in the logic of delegating authority, then doubts about the implementation capacity of various states will make nations less willing to cede control of their own affairs. After all, it does not make sense for a nation committed to a high level of environmental protection to incur the costs and compromises involved in negotiating a proposal through the Council of Ministers only to see its practical effects nullified by a failure of implementation. Pridham and Cini cite evidence where even the capacity to transpose a directive into domestic legislation can be called into question.

If one takes seriously the thought that policy developments rest upon the evolution of policy arguments, then a further constraint on the Europeanization of environmental policy comes into view in the form of the divergent ideological traditions to be found in different nation states. One particular, but instructive, example here is the role of the tax system in relation to environmental policy. Paulus (forthcoming) notes that the neo-classical orthodoxy is that the sole purpose of taxation is to raise revenue in order to finance essential public expenditure, but she also notes that there is now a growing movement of ideas in favour of ecological tax reform and she quotes the Netherlands Scientific Council as saying that the main purpose of public finance is no longer neutral taxation but 'taxation of the things we don't want (for instance environmental damages)'. But what may be a new orthodoxy for the Dutch Scientific council has not been such for British governments in the 1980s where the idea of tax neutrality underwent a considerable revival. Moreover, and this is the relevant point in the present context, the ideological traditions on which such political controversies draw run deep and wide. The same issue of taxation merely for revenue versus taxation for specific social purposes was part of the controversy between Chamberlain as Colonial Secretary and Ritchie as Chancellor of the Exchequer in the 1903 debate within the Conservative Party over imperial preference and tariff reform (Ensor, 1936, pp. 371–6).

Such discussions are related to wider differences of the sort that Albert (1993) discusses as to whether there is a distinctive Rhenish type of capitalism to be set against the Anglo-American variety. There clearly is a line of argument that distinguishes ideological traditions about the role of the state in France and

Germany from its role in Great Britain (Dyson, 1980; Marquand, 1988). Just as we can distinguish different models of the European welfare state, so we can distinguish different ways in which the state can act in the field of environmental protection. In this respect, the limits to integration that Majone identifies in the case of the welfare state is reproduced, to some extent at least, in the field of social regulation. Of course, in the latter case, are the international problems and the regulatory dilemmas pushing for European coordination; but it is important to recognize that state traditions are likely to be recalcitrant. A legitimate role for Europe in the field of social regulation is not something that it can be assumed will develop automatically.

A similar point about ideological diversity can be made on the basis of the work that has been done on the development of social policy within the EC. The term 'social policy' here has to be understood in a specific way. The usual referent of this term is to programmes of income maintenance, health care and education (as well, sometimes, as housing), all of which have a strong element of public expenditure within them. In the present context the notion of social policy means something different, however. In particular it means regulation of employment contracts to ensure for employees certain benefits, notably employment protection, vocational training, equal treatment and health and safety at work.

Recent policy controversies have shown that if some leading European actors have wanted to give legitimacy to the single market by developing a social dimension aimed at the peoples of Europe, they have also encountered the problems posed by the diverse ideological traditions expressed in the fora within which these policies have to be justified. Conversely, it has been difficult for the British government to secure ideological legitimation of the views it has been trying to develop on European social policy.

Duncan Matthews (1992) reveals some of these difficulties in his discussion of the social policy initiatives of the 1986 UK Council presidency. Matthews shows that during the 1986 presidency the then Minister for Employment, Mr Kenneth Clarke, with the support of the Irish and Italian governments, negotiated the adoption of a Council Resolution on an Action Programme for employment growth. Although the resolution itself was cast in rather bland terms, to which all European governments could sign up, Matthews suggests that crucial clues about the character of the document could be derived from the reasons that different governments had for supporting the resolution. In particular, the resolution failed to mention the role of dialogue with the social partners to which the Commission was attached as a way of securing macro-economic goals. For Matthews, then, the UK initiative represented an attempt to produce an alternative strategy for dealing with the problem of unemployment. Matthews reinforces this interpretation by noting the way in which the Commission subsequently tamed the initiative, reinterpreting its emphases to make them consistent with its own strategy.

The role of the UK in this initiative would lead one to interpret the initiative in the light of a more general ideological rift between Rhenish and Anglo-American capitalism. Consistent with this interpretation would be the UK's position on the 1989 Community Charter of Basic Social Rights, which the UK was the only government not to adopt, and its decision to seek an opt-out from the social chapter of the Treaty on European Union which was subsequently incorporated as a protocol of the Treaty. Yet, as Michael Gold (1992) reminds us, things are more complicated than this simple story would suggest. The division over the social protocol could not easily be accounted for in terms of those countries with a statutory framework for industrial relations and those countries with a predominantly volunterist framework, since the Republic of Ireland falls into the latter class but supported the Social Charter. Moreover, despite its opposition to the Social Charter taken as a whole, the UK government was strongly supportive of its health and safety provisions (Gold, 1992, p. 96).

Thus, although there clearly are differences of ideological make-up among countries that make up the EU, such differences are not wholly to be accounted for in ideological terms. To do so would be to confuse the distinctive with the representative. Clearly the predominance of a laissez-faire vision among British Conservatives marks them out from other major parties of the right, but it would be over-generalizing to say that this is a mark of an Anglo-American capitalist ideology. There simply is not the requisite degree of ideological homogeneity within nation states to be able to sustain such an interpretation.

The question with which I started this section began with the observation that there may well be dysfunctions between the successful implementation of the single market programme and the development of political legitimacy at the European level. This possibility therefore raised the question of whether complementary policies could be developed that would off-set the decline of legitimacy created by the implementation of 1992. On the benefit-based view of legitimacy, these complementary policies would provide the basis for political legitimacy that would otherwise be missing. Majone's (1993) claim that the sphere of social regulation could provide a legitimating device for the European tier of government was then discussed. Evidence on both environmental and social policy suggests that, though European developments would not be immaterial, there is enough intellectual, ideological and administrative complexity in the two cases for their functioning as legitimating devices to be uncertain. Thus, if we ask the Humean questions, the implications for our account of political legitimacy are unclear. What happens if we ask the Lockeian questions?

4 POLITICAL LEGITIMACY AND INSTITUTIONAL REFORM

My argument so far has been that a purely benefit-based theory of political legitimacy in the European Union is not without its insights, but also not without its problems. These are not so much problems about the essential terms of the theory, though these certainly exist, as problems about the conditions under which it can be applied to the situation of the EU in the wake of the Single European Act and the Treaty on European Union. In particular, to work with a purely benefit-based approach to political legitimacy involves contentious assumptions about cause–effect relationships. Policies may not produce their intended effects, either because the causal assumptions on which they rest are mistaken so that effects do not follow policies in the way policy-makers intend, or because other, unforeseen, consequences follow in addition to those intended that frustrate the intended effects. Since the vast bulk of the work of the ESRC's Single Market Initiative has been empirical, it has revealed some of the short-comings of the causal assumptions built into the 1992 programme.

That there should be mistaken assumptions as to cause and effect is not surprising. As noted earlier, the Single European Act was agreed by the participating governments for rather different reasons, and the inconsistencies – as Cornford remarked of academic politics in *Microcosmographia Academica* – happily reconciled in the voting. In these circumstances it would have been surprising if the 1992 programme had worked as though there was a coherent, single and unified strategy behind it.

Nevertheless, there was one strategic choice built into the programme, namely a willingness to leave fundamental institutional questions to one side. As Wallace (1993, p. 295) has noted, in the intergovernmental conferences in 1985 and 1991, the participants willingly set aside explicit debate on the fundamental antithesis between intergovernmentalism and integration, preferring to decide incremental additions to the treaties rather than recasting their basic framework. This is not to say that changes like the extension of qualified majority voting to different sectors of policy and the introduction of new powers for the European Parliament are unimportant, but merely to insist that these reforms were conceived as enabling the existing institutions to be able to perform their functions better rather than to replace or supplant those institutions.

There is, however, evidence that the consensus on which this strategy rested no longer holds in the way that it did, and that fundamental constitutional questions about the political order in Europe are now being raised. With the collapse of communism in central and eastern Europe there was bound to have been some reflection along these lines, but there is also reason to believe that this constitutional questioning is itself a response to the realization that political structures and issues are not simply the reflection of economic performance but have an independent existence of their own.

One sign of this constitutional questioning has been the various 'Martin' reports of the European Parliament intended, in the words of Martin (1991, p. 64) to make the European Parliament 'into a real legislative and monitoring body', an ambition which follows the earlier Spinelli initiative of course. But the same sense of constitutional questioning has also emerged in the various proposals for a European constitution that appear to have mushroomed in recent years, including those from the Bertelsmann Foundation, the European Policy Forum, the European Constitutional Group and the No Turning Back Group.

In my earlier exposition of the Humean theory of legitimacy I made the point that although consent was not a central feature of the theory, the theory did nonetheless require there to be an internalization of normative authority by members of the political class. One way of interpreting the flourishing of these constitutional proposals is to say that the basis of that normative authority is now being called into question. This in turn raises the question of whether, for the political classes of Europe at least, the legitimate development of European Union needs to be based upon a Lockeian process of deliberate and explicit consent, rather as the union between Scotland and England in 1707 was based upon an explicitly negotiated constitutional arrangement (not a very satisfactory one I shall say in passing, primarily due to the supine character of the eighteenth century Scots ruling classes – but that is a different matter, since we should not confuse process and substance). In other words, we must ask what would be the terms of a constitutional political contract between the political classes of Europe and perhaps, by extension, among the peoples of Europe?

Joseph Weiler (1992) has raised some of the most relevant questions here. In effect, he identifies four elements of political legitimacy that would need to be addressed in such a contract: the democratic deficit in the decision making institutions of the Union; the inclusion problem; the problem of creeping centralization; and the vision of political community that is being advanced. Weiler does not offer definite solutions to the dilemmas posed by these problems. Instead he seeks to identify what the contours of the problems are in some detail.

The problem of democratic legitimacy is the most well known, and Weiler's contribution here is to note that the Single European Act has made this problem worse rather than better. Before the passing of the Single European Act the parliaments of the member states could exercise at least some notional control over European affairs since the terms of the Luxembourg Accord meant that individual countries could veto proposals where their vital national interests were perceived to be at stake. This in turn meant that national parliaments could exercise some accountability in relation to proposed measures. However, with the introduction of qualified majority voting, it is now possible for European legislation to be passed over the heads of individual governments, and so national parliaments have lost such accountability that they once had.

The second aspect of the legitimacy deficit Weiler borrows from Dahl's question of when a people is entitled to the democratic process (see, for example, Dahl, 1989, ch. 14). This is an aspect of the so called 'inclusion problem'. In outline the problem is easy to state, though its practical implications are considerable. It can be expressed as follows: given that a political community has a rule for taking collective decisions (say the principle of majority rule) how is the class of those entitled to participate according to this rule to be defined? After all, a majority in political community A might decide one thing and a majority in political community B might prefer the opposite. So long as A and B remain distinct communities they can decide differently. But if they form a union, then it will be that one of the majorities in the new unit A plus B will have lost the vote.

In raising this question, Dahl was anxious to maintain that there was no democratic way of settling the inclusion problem without begging the question, since the application of any principle of democracy was itself contingent upon a prior judgment about what constituted the relevant demos that was entitled to decide by majority rule. Although it is possible to state in an abstract way the criteria for the identification of a people, in practice answers to the question are normally supplied 'by history and politics.' (Dahl, 1989, p. 209). For Weiler this problem is important because it suggests that the problem of political legitimacy within the European Union is deeper than simply the problem of the democratic deficit in decision making processes: 'the legitimacy issue does not derive principally from the accountability issue at the European level, but from the very redefinition of the European polity' (Weiler, 1992, p. 24). For Weiler, the Single European Act and the 1992 programme set in train a series of events that detached the benefits of European integration from the processes of consent that would secure legitimacy.

The third element of Weiler's argument is that moves towards European integration risk the dangers of the creeping centralization of competences that are implicit in all federal unions. Thus, the principle of the supremacy and direct effect of Community law within limited fields that was the doctrine of the *Van Gend and Loos* judgment can no longer be relied upon. Weiler then reinforces this argument with a fourth element to the effect that there is a conflict of visions in European integration between (if I can put it in my own terms) the view of union in diversity on the one hand and diversity in union on the other. Read in the most natural way, the upshot of the Weiler analysis is that the problem of political legitimacy may well undermine the achievements of the 1992 programme, since the achievement of political legitimacy for the union that would be required to exercise the required degree of centralized authority over the single market.

Let us for the moment accept that there is a Lockeian dimension to this problem, and say that there is the need to secure processes and procedures that ensure that European governance is exercised in accordance with the consent of the governed. What is the significance of Weiler's analysis in this context?

Consider first the contention that with the passing of the Single European Act national parliaments underwent a loss of control. This aspect of the democratic deficit is undoubtedly right in constitutional theory, but it is, of course, an empirical question as to how important it was in practice. Clearly the practice of national parliaments varied to the degree to which they were able to exercise effective control over the bargains their governments struck at the European level, but there are good reasons for believing that taken in general they were not terribly effective instruments of democratic accountability. Moreover, it is difficult to imagine national parliaments taking on more functions of scrutiny without incurring the problems of overload. As Shirley Williams (1991, p. 160) argues, it would make the EU unworkable to extend the Danish system of parliamentary accountability to all the member states.

It can also be argued that Weiler is being rather too optimistic about the benefits of the system of unanimous decision making. As a rule of social choice, the principle of unanimity has some well known defects, not least that it is a highly conservative rule that allows entrenched interests to protect their position even when this is contrary to the public interest (Sen, 1970, pp. 24–7). This argument has been clearly worked out with respect to Europe by Scharpf (1988), who has shown how super-majoritarian rules have enabled small groups to block potentially beneficial change. On the assumption that the single market does produce net benefits, then a change away from the principle of unanimity towards a less conservative system of concurrent majorities was clearly an essential element in helping to secure that gain. I am not here simply asserting the claims of the public good against those of political freedom of choice, but merely noting that a decision rule that prevents the members of a political community dealing with structural impediments to the promotion of their collective interests cannot itself enjoy much legitimacy.

There is one important institution that Weiler neglects in his discussion, namely the party system. It is not just in theory that political parties are the means by which preferences are articulated and aggregated. Instead as Budge and Keman (1990) have shown the processes of party competition are effective in determining government policy. Bogdanor (for example, Bogdanor, 1990) has long stressed that democratic accountability at the European level requires a European party system. Of course such a system cannot be conjured up from nowhere, and it was clear in the 1994 European elections that the election was still being fought in a series of national campaigns. But it does suggest that more efforts of constitutional design ought to go into thinking about the role of parties.

What these considerations suggest is that, although the strategy of leaving fundamental institutional questions to one side in the intergovernmental conferences of 1985 and 1991 enabled a further development of European integration, that strategy only postponed, rather than eliminated, those questions. Indeed, to the extent that the achievement of the single market raises questions about suitable flanking and compensatory policies that cannot be dealt with satisfactorily within the present institutional arrangements, the strategy of neglecting institutional questions may only have increased the need to redesign them at a later stage.

In this context, I shall end on a personal note. I agree with Weiler that there is an irreducibly Lockeian element in the construction of political legitimacy at the European level. What this may suggest is that the processes by which European political institutions are constructed are as important as the structures that are suggested. Would it be too much to ask that, at the next revision of the treaties, the processes of negotiation be more open and democratic?

REFERENCES

Albert, M. (1993), *Capitalism against Capitalism*, London: Whurr Publishers.

Almond, G.A. and Verba, S. (1965), *The Civic Culture*, Boston: Little, Brown and Company.

Begg, I. and Mayes, D. (1991), 'Social and economic cohesion among the regions of Europe in the 1990s', *National Institute Economic Review* November, pp. 63–74.

Boehmer-Christiansen, S. and Skea J. (1991), *Acid Politics; Environmental and Energy Policies in Britain and Germany*, London and New York: Belhaven Press.

Bogdanor, V. (1990), *Democratizing the Community*, London: Federal Trust for Education and Research.

Budge, I. and Keman, H. (1990), *Parties and Democracy*, Oxford: Oxford University Press.

Burgess, M. (1989), *Federalism and European Union. Political Ideas, Influences and Strategies in the European Community, 1972–1987*, London and New York: Routledge.

Cox, A. (1992), 'Implementing 1992 public procurement policy; public and private obstacles to the creation of the single European market', *Public Procurement Law Review*, 2, 139–54.

Cox, A. (1994), 'Derogation, subsidiarity and the single market', *Journal of Common Market Studies,* 32 (2), 127–47

Dahl, R.A. (1989), *Democracy and Its Critics*, New Haven and London: Yale University Press.

Dyson, K. (1980), *The State Tradition in Western Europe*, Oxford: Martin Robertson.

Ensor, R.K. (1936), *England 1870–1914*, Oxford: Clarendon Press.

Featherstone, K. (1994), 'Jean Monnet and the "Democratic Deficit" in the European Union', *Journal of Common Market Studies*, **32** (2), 149–70.

Garrett, G. (1992), 'International co-operation and institutional choice; the European Community's internal market', *International Organization*, **46** (2), 533–60.

Gold, M. (1992), 'Social policy; the UK and Maastricht', *National Institute Economic Review*, February, pp. 95–103.

Haas, E.B. (1968), *The Uniting of Europe; Political, Social and Economic Forces, 1950–1957*, Stanford, California: Stanford University Press, second edition.

Hajer, M. (1995), *The Politics of Environmental Discourse; Ecological Modernization and the Regulation of Acid Rain*, Oxford: Oxford University Press.

Hart, H.L.A. (1961), *The Concept of Law*, Oxford: Clarendon Press.

Hume, D. (1752), 'Of the Original Contract' in *Essays, Moral, Political, and Literary*, T.H. Green and T.H. Grose (eds), London: Longmans, Green and Co. (1889), pp. 445–60.

Kirchner, E.J. (1992), *Decision Making in the European Community*, Manchester and New York: Manchester University Press.

Lipset, S. M. (1963), *Political Man*, London: Mercury Books.

Locke, J. (1689), *Two Treatises of Government*, P. Laslett (ed.), Cambridge: Cambridge University Press (1960).

McGowan, F. and Seabright, P. (1993), 'Regulation and Subsidiarity; Finding the Balance', in D.G. Mayes, (ed.), *Aspects of European Integration*, London: National Institute of Economic and Social Research.

Majone, G. (1993), 'The European Community between social policy and social regulation', *Journal of Common Market Studies*, **31** (2), 153–70.

Marquand, D. (1988), *The Unprincipled Society*, London: Jonathan Cape.

Marsh, D. (1994), 'Partners dance to different tunes', *Financial Times*, June 18/19, p. 8.

Martin, D. (1991), *Europe; An Ever Closer Union*, Nottingham: Spokesmant.

Matthews, D. (1992), 'The 1986 UK presidency; an assessment of its impact on social policy initiatives', National Institute of Economic and Social Research Working Paper, no 10.

Matthews, D. and Mayes, D.G. (1993), 'The evolution of rules for a single European market in leasing', National Institute Discussion Paper, no. 35.

Mayes, D.G. (1991), 'Introduction', in D.G. Mayes (ed.), *The European Challenge*, New York and London: Harvester Wheatsheaf.

Mazey, S. and Richardson J.J. (1993), 'EC policy making; an emerging European policy style?' in J.D. Liefferink, P.D. Lowe and A.P.J. Mol (eds), *European Integration and Environmental Policy*, London and New York: Belhaven Press, pp. 114–25.

Moravscik, A. (1991), 'Negotiating the Single European Act', in R.O. Keohane and S. Hoffmann, (eds), *The New European Community* Boulder, San Francisco and Oxford: Westview Press, pp. 41–84.

Olson, M, (1965), *The Logic of Collective Action*, Cambridge, Mass.: Harvard University Press.

Paulus, A. (forthcoming), 'Possibilities of Using Taxes for Ecological Purposes', in M. Faure, J. Vervaele and A. Weale (eds), *Environmental Standards in the European Union*.

Plamenatz, J. (1963), *Man and Society,* London: Longman.

Pridham, G. and Cini, M. (forthcoming), 'Enforcing Environmental Standards in the European Union; Is There a Southern Problem?', in M. Faure, J. Vervaele and A. Weale (eds), *Environmental Standards in the European Union*.

Scharfp, F. (1988), 'The joint decision trap, lessons from German federalism and European integration', *Public Administration*, **66** (3), 239–78.

Schumpeter, J. (1954), *Capitalism, Socialism and Democracy,* London: Allen and Unwin, fourth edition.

Sen, A. K. (1970), *Collective Choice and Social Welfare,* San Francisco: Holden-Day Inc.

Tucker, E. (1994), 'Foot-dragging slows down path to single market', *Financial Times*, Thursday June 16, p. 2.

Wallace, H. (1993), 'European governance in turbulent times', *Journal of Common Market Studies*, **31** (3), 293–303.

Weale, A. (1994), 'Social Policy and European Union', *Social Policy and Administration*, **28** (1), 5–19.

Weiler, J. (1992), 'After-Maastricht; Community Legitimacy in Post-1992 Europe', in W.J. Adams (ed.), *Singular Europe; Economy and Polity of the European Community after 1992,* Ann Arbor: University of Michigan Press, pp. 11–41.

Williams, S. (1991), 'Sovereignty and Accountability in the European Community', in R.O. Keohane and S. Hoffmann (eds), *The New European Community,* Boulder, San Francisco and Oxford: Westview Press, pp. 155–76.

9. The External Impact

Christopher Brewin

It would appear that as the interest and concern on the part of non-members grow, so does the sensitivity of the European Community about this increased interest and concern. In fact, within the Community there exists some uneasiness about 'groundless fears', often expressed by non-members, of possible protectionism by the Community. Some even consider these outside opinions as an unwarranted interference in the internal affairs of the Community.

In contrast, many outside the Community have a different perspective. While recognising that the formation of the European Community will be a delicate, integrative exercise requiring very careful handling of many politically charged issues within the Community, they are conscious of the enormous impact such protectionism would have not only upon their relations with the Community itself but also upon the future of the world economy and the legal framework that governs world trade and investment. On this score it is legitimate for all those directly and indirectly concerned, to maintain a keen interest in the way this integrative process is being implemented and to express their views on the future course of the single European market – as far as that process may affect their position in the world economic system, as well as the prospects of its viability. (Owada, 1989)

One characteristic of this entire process is its openness. There are many opportunities for formal and informal consultation at all stages of drafting and subsequent review. A second characteristic is that the inter-relationships between the institutions are still evolving, with a consequent impact on the legislative process. (Amcham, The EC Committee of the American Chamber of Commerce in Belgium, 1991 p.iii)

Indeed our evidence suggests that interest groups beyond the EC – both in 'aspirant' states such as Sweden, but more particularly groups from the US and Japan – *now see the EC policy process as of central relevance to their attempts to manage their public policy environment.* (Richardson/Mazey, ESRC end of award report, emphasis added)

1 INTRODUCTION

1.1 External Impact

One way of demonstrating the impact of the Commission's Single Market programme on the Community's Northern, Southern, and Eastern neighbours, and on Europe's global competitors, is to list some of the measures which each of them took on their own account.

The EFTA countries agreed as a bloc to adopt 130 EC regulations and 800 standards, and to adapt 630 directives to their national legislation. The Austrians led three other EFTA governments to apply for membership. Turkey developed procedures to harmonize existing and new legislation with European norms, and applied in 1987 for membership. The 'completion' of the Common Commercial Policy meant that the new regimes of Eastern Europe had to conclude 'Europe' agreements with the EC rather than bilateral agreements with its individual member states.

The United States, instead of continuing President Reagan's downgrading of their Mission in Brussels to the European Communities, mounted a wide-ranging campaign through both government and business channels which moved from a negative phase to a positive framework-agreement on mutual consultation procedures in the 1991 US–EC Declaration. This declaration was followed up by sectoral agreements, notably on competition policy. It was the model for a similar-sounding EC–Japan Declaration as all explicit *national* discrimination against imports from Japan was replaced by Community-wide agreements.

1.2 External Origins

Conversely, there would not have been a Commission programme without the two separate external pressures of an American campaign against protectionist barriers in services and the scale of Asian penetration of the market for manufactures both in Europe and in competing for market share elsewhere.

Thus Lord Cockfield himself explains the remarkably short gestation of the Commission's White paper, *Completing the Internal Market* issued in June 1985 (Commission, 1985) as due to preparatory work done in the UK Department of Trade and Industry before he went to Brussels. This characteristically systematic work was itself a consequence of his conversations in 1982 with Malcolm Baldridge, the US Secretary of Commerce. Both the Reagan Presidency and Mrs Thatcher's government were ideologically committed to *deregulation* of business, and each calculated that their own financial sectors would benefit from dismantling national protectionism in services. However this is not to say that the Single Market was an American idea. Baldridge himself seems to have regarded it as threat to the GATT Uruguay Round which he saw as the instrument of deregulation, dismissing the Single Market as utopian: 'Forget it, we live in an age of reality, not of dreams.'

In any case, the Anglo-Saxon commitment to international deregulation was insufficient in itself to persuade what in 1985 became twelve disparate member states to agree to majority voting in carrying through such a complicated legislative programme. A more important external influence was the perception shared by all Western European governments, including Scandinavian and Alpine governments, of the loss of global competitiveness in manufactures to Japanese and other Asian industries. The Cecchini studies put credible numbers backing up the widespread perception that computers consisted of American software and Japanese hardware, and that Africans preferred Japanese cars and TV sets.

Taking 1963 as the base year, the shares of Community countries in third country markets, compared with those for exports of OECD countries to the same third countries, were less than 80 per cent (Cecchini, 1988, p. 85).

The pan-European Round Table of major Industrialists, chaired by Per Gyllenhammer of Volvo, combined the external threat with a demand for internal change. They blamed low investment in European industries on high corporate taxation in Western Europe and Scandinavia, which reinforced the attraction of moving production to lower-cost countries. In contrast to their low profile at the signing of the treaty of Rome, big industrialists became the champions of the single market. In important sectors from cars to communications, they were willing to forgo the security of contracts from their home governments for the greater efficiency antici-pated from reducing the number of firms from twenty to three or four groups organized on a Continental scale.

In other words, behind the apparent technicality of the Single Market rules lay a change in the public values promoted by European elites. A reduction of corporate taxation would translate into less public money for welfare recipients, national industrial champions, and sectoral groups like miners, steelworkers and farmers. Although global competitiveness was not in 1985 strictly within Community competence, the aim became to recover competitiveness with outsiders in both the European and world markets.

The means were both cheap and internal. They were cheap in that rules controlling public subsidies cost little in themselves, reduced public investment, and were accompanied by cosmetically small R&D programmes and redistributive regional and structural policies. They were internal in that firms operating on a European scale would produce goods cheaper than either merely national firms or firms outside the Community. As Cecchini put it,

Imports originating elsewhere in the EC will gain in competitivity in relation to items produced nationally or *imported from outside* the Community. (Cecchini, 1988, p.93)

The Internal Market Programme thus may be seen as a response by European elites to an external problem. It had the additional advantage to national elites that its status as a European programme reduced potential confrontation with electorates and special interest groups.

1.3 Internal Development Takes Precedence

Given its limited resources, the Commission's concentration on this internal solution meant that it was not in the early stages interested in possible external solutions of the kind advocated by American theorists and adopted by the US Government.

Where the US Government demanded that the Japanese invest their trading surplus in US government bonds, property, and local production facilities, the Commission did not have the authority or internal cohesion to copy such a blatant example of power politics. Secondly, the Commission did not take seriously the arguments of 'interdependency' theorists that 'consultation mechanisms', such as those advocated by the Trilateral Commission, would enable the Big Three to manage the shifts in the relative positions of Asia, America and Europe (Nye, Biedenkopf and Shiina, 1991). Thirdly it rejected a protectionist Community Preference in industrial goods, as advocated by Jacques Fauvet of Peugeot in vivid rhetoric,

> The question is why the Europeans did not better arm their negotiators. They left like the Bourgeois de Calais barefooted and lightly clad to ask Tokyo for permission to create a Single Market. (Agence Europe, 7 December 1991).

Fourthly, the Delors Commission was not tempted by enlargement to Northern, Southern and Eastern Europe as the means to give European manufacturers a home market that would include all of Europe, Africa and the Soviet Commonwealth. The Commission position that *'internal development takes priority over enlargement'* was reiterated by President Delors in the speech suggesting the creation of a free trade area with EFTA countries as an alternative to membership (Commission, 1989). With respect both to Turkey before 1989 and Eastern Europe after 1989, the Commission saw enlargement as too great a threat to the achievement of Monetary Union and too big a drain on its resources for redistribution under the rubric of social cohesion.

In view of the international ambitions of the second Delors Commission (Ross, 1995, p. 514), it is worth stressing how small a part was anticipated for negotiation with third countries in the original programme. The external dimension was barely discussed in public presentation of the '1992' programme (Commission, 1986). Moreover, little evidence of lobbying on behalf of external interests can be adduced in the first two years of the

Internal Market programme. Lord Cockfield's idea was to set Europe's own
house in order by deliberate timetabled removal of anti-competitive barriers.
His personal style was hostile to interference, to caucuses, and to lobbyists.
His officials in DGIII were sometimes at odds with those dealing with
external relations in DGI. In my own brief encounters with officials in
DGIII, I was told that as it was up to each service whom they consulted, they
would obviously bring in DGI whenever there was an impact on third
parties. However they preferred not to inform DGI too early, because DGI
always demanded to be at every meeting! An example of the tension
between the style of the directorates can be seen in relations with EFTA.
DGIII was interested in detailed work on rules of origin, and joint use of the
Single Administrative document for all movements of goods. De Clercq as
External Relations Commissioner was preoccupied with questions of
principle, telling the EFTA representatives at Interlaken in May 1987 that
the Community would give priority to its own autonomy, to realising the
Internal Market, and requiring that gains be balanced on both sides. In his
autobiography he complained that 'the confusion was not helped any by the
partnership ideas launched by Delors in 1989' (De Clercq, 1990)

This precedence to internal developments was even more marked in
Opinion 1/91 of the European Court of Justice. The Court rejected that part
of the EEA treaty which would have given its judges a role in jurisdiction
over internal market rules in EFTA countries. European lawyers did not
protest that the Court's new requirement of acknowledged supremacy within
territorial boundaries as a precondition of its jurisdiction would have ruled
out all the early judgements of the Pescatore Court – given that there was no
clause in the treaty explicitly endowing European law with supremacy or
even priority.

External relations erupted onto the Single Market agenda quite suddenly
in 1988 when external governments – principally the Americans – became
alarmed by the dynamism of the 1992 programme. The term, 'Fortress
Europe' is not a quaint reference to medieval history. The allusion is to the
economic *machtpolitik* of Schacht and Hitler. This disproportionate reaction
did not last, but the reasons for it can be sought in two distinct dialectics.

The first, *the external effects of internal harmonization*, affected
particularly the Community's European neighbours. The research on which
this chapter is based concentrated on Switzerland as representative of EFTA
countries, Hungary as representative of Central and Eastern Europe, and
Turkey as representative of countries associated to the Community under
Article 238.

The second, the increased saliency of what Christopher Stevens has called
the 'pyramid of privilege' (Stevens, Kennon and Ketley, 1993) in the
Community's external relations, was more important to non-European

countries. My study concentrated on the effects on the Community's consultation procedures with its two biggest single trade partners, Japan and the United States of America.

2   EXTERNAL EFFECTS OF INTERNAL HARMONIZATION OF THE RULES

The difficulty of maintaining patterns of traditional economic co-operation with the developing European Single Market was well articulated by members of the Swiss Federal government. In its 1990 report the Swiss Federal Council noticed the

> increasing tendency of the EC to *develop its external relations on the basis of harmonization of legislation* rather than in accordance with the principles of traditional international co-operation. (Swiss Federal Council, 1990)

Traditional international co-operation meant, for Switzerland, the agreements reached by the procedure of meetings twice a year between its trade diplomats with officials of DGI, attended by observers from the member states. Discussions were pragmatic in the sense of trying to remedy grievances expressed by important interests on both sides without getting enmeshed in profound juridical questions of rights.

What this meant in practice can be illustrated by the negotiation on behalf of Swiss beer interests for access to the huge German market. Within the Single Market, producers of beer from any member state have the right, enforceable through the Courts, to sell in Germany any beer which meets the standards of their home market. Swiss exporters are however obliged to obey the medieval German 'purity law'. Swiss officials did not ask for the right to sell in Germany any beer containing chemical additives produced in Switzerland. The most they thought they could get was a derogation which would permit Swiss brewers to sell the new non-alcoholic beers in Germany, without any right enforceable against the German state through German courts. For its part the Commission negotiators sought in parallel negotiations improved access to Swiss roads between Germany and Italy for the juggernauts which could circulate as of right within the Community, but whose movements through Switzerland were restricted. The Swiss were inclined instead to offer to pay for two new rail tunnels through their mountains as their way of enhancing European unification without compromising their environmental concerns.

The conflict between the right of states to decide the content of law within their jurisdiction, and the increasing magnetism of the Community can be further illustrated from the service sector. If the Swiss wanted to sell insurance in the Community, then Swiss law within Switzerland had 'autonomously' to adhere rigorously to the detailed requirements set out in the relevant Single Market directives drawn up in fora from which the Swiss were excluded. Even after adapting so completely, and a negotiation which pre-dated the Single Market by a decade, their participation was only allowed by the EC member states subject to a denunciation clause.

A third important consequence of the possibility of national economies becoming one European economy is that foreign direct investment is more likely to set up production facilities within the territory of the European Union than to risk exclusion by setting up outside its borders. In the words of the 1990 Report of the Swiss Federal Council,

> Non seulement la position concurrentielle des entreprises suisses pourrait se voir affaiblie, mais encore la position de la Suisse en tant que pays d'accueil d'investissements directs en provenance de la CE.

This is in line with one of the arguments deployed by the Austrian and Swedish governments in seeking membership – namely that even companies owned and managed by their own nationals would prefer to invest in new facilities within Community borders. The reasoning behind this fear seems to have been composed of two elements. One was the cost of surmounting the Common External Tariff, which was nothing new and in any case low. The second was fear of European protectionism in the future.

In its dealings with other European governments, the European Community and its negotiators were prepared to abandon the Common External Tariff, which was not defended as an important symbol of its own existence, or as instrument of some future protectionism. A free trade area was offered to EFTA states, and the longstanding aim of a Customs Union with Turkey remained on the agenda. However they did not offer free, or reciprocal, access to the Single Market. The conditions can be grouped into five categories.

The Commission disliked the sectoral access agreements of the kind sought by Swiss negotiators. 'Cherry-picking' they claimed invariably caused problems with individual member states obliged to defend their own industries – like Portuguese resistance to textile imports from rich Switzerland and poor Hungary.

Secondly, Commission negotiators thought other rich European countries should pay for the benefits of access to the Single market in two distinct ways. The first was an obligation to take their fair share of the redistribution costs to the poorer states of Europe. The EFTA states already had their own procedures for this in the longstanding EFTA aid to Portugal. The second was to offer agricultural concessions for 'Southern' products.

Thirdly, they had no qualms about expecting their European neighbours to harmonize their internal legislation with that of the Single Market. Just as Nordic identity in the past had induced post-war harmonization within Scandinavia, so the pan-European sense of identity held by Commission officials held that it was in everybody's interests for Turks and Hungarians to adopt their standards, their competition rules and rules of origin. The EFTA countries participated either as members or observers in the standard-setting bodies – CEN, CENELEC and ETSI – and in some EC management committees on R&D in return for financial participation. However, as non-members, they obviously did not participate in Council legislation, and Swiss demands to be present on management committees in the financial sector were rejected.

Fourthly, the increasing saliency of Single Market legislation meant that its officials were dealing with rafts of similar issues separately with the Austrians, Swiss, Swedes, Finns, and Icelanders on successive days. On grounds of practicality they preferred to group neighbouring states into 'blocs'. This was reluctantly accepted by Hungary, Czechoslovakia and Poland, and resolutely resisted by the Swiss.

Finally, as the superpower confrontation collapsed, the EC wanted to institute closer 'political dialogue' with their neighbours in Scandinavia and the Alps, with Turks, with the new regimes of Eastern and Central Europe.

The Community and its European neighbours thus had a range of bilateral and multilateral options in regularizing the ways in which outsider states and their enterprises might secure influence, consultative rights, or access to information with respect to Single market norms. Below I will examine in more detail the diplomacy with respect to the options considered with each group of neighbours ranging from membership, extending the customs union, Association agreements under Article 238, participation in pan-European standards bodies, bilateral global framework agreements, sectoral agreements, or simply unilateral adaptation to Single Market norms.

However, from the perspective of non-European competitors, this range of possible 'deals' open to European neighbours was itself part of the problem.

3   INCREASING EC TRADE DISCRIMINATION

While the Internal Market Programme aims at *unifying* conditions of competition within the EC area, the long-term trend in the Communities' external trade relations has been towards *diversifying* conditions of access to its market. (GATT, 1991, p. 7).

The fears of Fortress Europe which erupted suddenly in 1988 took the Community institutions by surprise because, I have argued, the programme itself was not an attempt to resolve European problems by resort to Schachtian economic *machtpolitik*. De Clercq in London, Delors himself, the Commission in October and the Rhodes Council in December all rejected the charge along such lines as

> The Community will seek a greater *liberalization* of international trade: the 1992 Europe will not be a fortress Europe, but a partnership in Europe. (European Commission statement of October 10th, 1988)

However, the chant of liberalization was always accompanied by a protectionist chorus. The Single Market could be open to outsiders on the basis of reciprocal benefit. The significance of this formula is that it rejects the free trade formula of equal opportunity. At the Punta del Este conference inaugurating the Uruguay Round of the GATT, Europe's trade partners refused to accept the objective of 'balanced results' defended by the Community. Nevertheless the Commission's World Partner paper in October specified 'openness on the basis of mutual benefits' (Commission, 1988a). After internal debate on third country access to financial markets, that phrase was specifically endorsed by the European Council meeting in Rhodes in December. 'Europe', said Delors, was 'neither a fortress nor a sieve (passoire)' (Agence Europe, 4 December 1988).

Although the Community was justified in rejecting comparison with Hitler's Europe, it is as well to look at the shared long-term fears which explain why the atmosphere was so bad at the Montreal midterm review of the Uruguay Round. These had as much to do with the increasing size of the Community, and its increasing differentiation between outsiders, as with complaints about the detailed content of the directives. I shall deal with all three points in turn. Academic treatment of this issue has not been helped by the dearth of factual studies on the international trade effects of the completion of the common commercial policy. The consequences of the Common Agricultural Policy have received much more attention. Francis Jacobs, presently an Advocate-General, has made the point that,

> In general, the relationship of the completion of the internal market to international trade has been neglected. (Jacobs, 1994)

I have used the GATT's two-volume study of 1991, and the annual volumes on unfair trade practices produced by the USA and Japan.

3.1 Increasing the Size of Community and the GATT

In a book on rules it is appropriate to recall that the GATT is based on a rule intended to prevent European states from discriminating between nations in trade terms. The most-favoured nation rule outlawed the Imperial Preference of the 1930s which the Japanese had attempted to counter with their Asian Co-Prosperity sphere. In GATT terms the Community exists by virtue of Article XXIV, allowing common markets to behave as though they were a single sovereign state. It had not been foreseen that a common market would be able to discriminate through 'association' with its Mediterranean, Northern or Eastern European neighbours and ex-colonies.

However by 1985 the enlargement of the Community to Iberia meant that what had begun as an exception to the rules had become the world's largest single market. By virtue of its importance, it could not be excluded from the GATT, and under its rules other countries had no right to prevent its further enlargement provided they received bilateral compensation for loss of trade. For example, in 1985 the Americans refused to accept that the general reduction in Spanish tariff protection on entry into the Common External Tariff outweighed the damage consequent on the new tariff imposed on its soybean exports to Spain. Some Commission officials thought that appeasing the USA on this issue would be followed by increased American demands in the future (Brewin and McAllister, 1986).

In the ten years since 1985 the outside world has had to accept further enlargement and increasingly differential treatment accorded to groups of states. In 1987 came the unsuccessful Turkish application from what was then the most populous country in Europe. In 1989 'inner-German' trade arrangements were transformed by full German unification. In 1990 the European Economic Area increased the size of the internal market to include 360m consumers. Although it did not immediately extend the Customs Union, it was quickly followed by enlargement to Austria, Finland and Sweden. After 1989 the 'third-generation' Europe agreements offered a further potential increase in the European market. Indirectly, these agreements helped the case for compensating 'special' arrangements with Latin America, Asia, and Mediterranean countries.

The consequences of the Community's size for the GATT regulatory framework can be illustrated by three examples. When the Community in 1985 wanted to sell butter to Russia in defiance of a GATT agreement, it was the GATT rule that had to be changed. The bad atmosphere at the interim Uruguay Round meeting in Montreal in December 1988 was partly due to the Community stress on reciprocal or mutual benefits, 'the balance of mutual advantages that is the golden rule of GATT negotiations' (Commission, 1988b). Thirdly, when the Community was criticized in 1991 by the novel trade policy review procedure, the authors were informed by the Community's blunt negotiator in Geneva, Tranh van Trinh, in words that could not be recorded in the official minutes, that if GATT wanted to continue in existence it should not make trouble for the Community.

Moreover, each increase in the size and integration of the Community increased the saliency of the past history of Community protectionism. Where the Commission saw each enlargement as bringing barriers down to Community levels, and each special agreement as reducing its own barriers, the rest of the world tended to see actual as well as potential Community protectionism. The Community's agricultural policy harms its competitors both through protection of the European market and export subsidies. There are Community quotas on textile and steel imports, and there have been national quotas on Japanese car imports. Thirdly, the agreement in the European Council to the replacement of two thousand national quotas by Community quotas under the Single Market programme was linked to fierce debates on how much the defensive mechanisms of the 1984 Trade Policy Instrument should be strengthened. These procedures are intended to deter 'forward pricing' by external producers – that is setting prices below cost in order to increase market share to levels at which those prices will yield profits, a legitimate procedure for domestic producers. Finally, if there had been no threat of protectionism, Austrian, Swedish, Swiss and Japanese producers and investors would not have invested to the same extent in local production facilities within the territories of the Community. Let us now move to the specific features of the 1992 programme that led outsiders to surprise the Commission with the force of their fears of fortress behaviour.

3.2 Protectionism and Liberalization in the Single Market

All the Community institutions intended the Single Market programme to be liberalising. They claim that as the world's largest trader, its interests lie in reducing protection. The replacement of national tariffs and safeguard clauses by the Community versions has been in accordance with its obligation under Article XXIV GATT to increase free trade on balance. As the French government pointed out in its 3 September 1993 memorandum advocating more retaliatory instruments of trade policy, the 1984 New Trade Policy Instrument has only been used twice, and only eight anti-dumping measures were in force. Although there are difficulties in including international companies run from outside Europe in research programmes, there is some acceptance of the doctrine that international competition is as much between companies as between countries. For the forty signatories of the GATT code on technical barriers, there is free access to the internal market. After 1991 type-approval procedures allowed for recognition of external validation where there were equivalency and either bilateral or multilateral agreement with the country or organization concerned (Commission, 1992). In all the years since 1986, the Community's imports from the rest of the world have risen faster than total world imports (Christopherson, 1991, p. 27). This is not to say that price and quality now determine trade within Europe without reference to national origins. Directives cannot be expected to sweep away what may be categorized as cultural norms – especially the preference by individuals, companies and government purchasing agents for goods and services that will keep employment at home. Moreover it is not easy to disentangle the consequences of completing the internal market from the Uruguay Round and other international agreements which predate 1985. The last major difficulty in drawing up a balance sheet is the considerable sectoral variation in the protectionist tendencies of member states. The car agreement restricting Japanese imports to their present levels for a decade, is a compromise between those member states whose manufacturers enjoyed protection and those who were either free traders or lacked manufacturing plant on their territory. In the banking sector by contrast the Americans took the view that it was the Commission whose drafting of reciprocity in the Second Banking directive was potentially protectionist. The compromise here was to allow a greater say to the member states to reassure the United States that their interests would be safeguarded by the UK and Germany.

In general terms, the approach of mutual benefits is less protectionist than a doctrine of European benefit in negotiating with less powerful countries. It acknowledges the role of negotiation to mutual advantage in a similar spirit to those of the GATT rounds. On the other hand, free traders are quite right to point out that reciprocity of benefits is not a free trade criterion to the extent that reciprocity of opportunity enables all traders to operate under the same rules. I have selected a few examples of explicit discrimination without attempting an overall balance-sheet, or a comparison with the protectionist practices of the USA and Japan.

On public procurement, the November 1989 text of the Commission's proposal for contracts in public telecommunications reads

> Lastly, taking account of the EEC's commercial interests *vis-à-vis* third countries, the directive provides that an offer may be discarded if the Community content does not reach the 50% level.

There has been much dispute with the United States about the legitimacy of the explicitly discriminatory clause permitting large contracts to be given preferentially to a European contractor whose bid is less than 3 per cent above an external rival. The huge subsidies to Airbus from participating states have engendered much diplomatic activity from the United States. The timetable for ending national discrimination against Japanese goods, and the nature and permanency of Community discrimination against Japanese car imports and transplants has similarly been of particular concern to Japan. Both the USA and Japan were concerned by the aborted European attempt to adopt the lower MAC-packet family of standards for the new generation of high-definition TV to protect European production and sales to Africa. TV has also been central to discrimination justified as protecting European culture in the long dispute whether a specified proportion of programmes shown on TV networks should be required to originate in Europe.

It is impossible in this chapter to describe the long diplomacy associated with these examples of discrimination; my purpose is limited to illustrating why groups of countries needed to obtain information on directives and standards, or seek to influence their content, or claim that the effects on themselves justified a right of consultation on Single Market matters.

4 THE SINGLE MARKET, THREE GROUPS OF EUROPEAN NEIGHBOURS AND THE TWO BIGGEST NON-EUROPEAN COMPETITORS

4.1 Switzerland and the EFTA Countries

I do not take pleasure in being impolite to my EFTA friends, but the fact remains that they do not have a European policy. (Per Kleppe, EFTA Secretary-general, 1991, p. 71)

Geneva is the location of the EFTA Secretariat, and Switzerland also chaired its meetings at the time my research proposal was written. However, there are major differences of interest and principle between the EFTA countries. For example, the Swiss do not share the Icelandic and Norwegian interests in fisheries policy, and have assiduously protected their sovereignty and neutrality which might be compromised by the trade sanctions inherent in a common trade policy, common economic policy, or common foreign policy. The Alpine and Scandinavian states of EFTA are held together by the magnetism exerted by the Community – a metaphor which refers as much to currents of repulsion as attraction. These currents were increased by the dynamism of the Single Market process. It induced three phases of negotiation, which are set out below before more a more detailed discussion of each.

First were sectoral agreements under the 1984 *Luxembourg process.* In 1985 thought was given to harmonising EC and EFTA rules of public procurement, on which EFTA rules were more numerous on paper. However the EFTA office concluded, and this will delight neofunctionalists, that first there had to be harmonization of standards and the rights of capital, services and workers to move freely. In October 1987, the Scandinavians and Austrians began discussions among themselves on the implications of this more general approach, which became M. Delors' offer of 'partnership' on 17 January 1989.

In March 1989 the *Oslo process* set up meetings of high-level officials from the Community and the EFTA side who became negotiators after June 1990 for the 'fullest possible' realization of what became the European Economic Area. Dissatisfaction with this *twin-pillar framework agreement* persuaded five governments to propose negotiations for full membership; all except Switzerland have now reached the stage of seeking popular ratification of accession agreements.

4.2 The Luxembourg Process

In 1984 the few remaining tariffs between EFTA and the EC were dismantled. As discussed above, customs matters, transport, and trade co-operation can be discussed in the framework of a Comité mixte. Equality was asserted by having two secretaries, one Swiss and one provided by DGI. Within this framework trade diplomats have made progress on questions of rules of origin (June 1988 Tampere Convention), rules of competition such as subsidies, safeguards and dumping. The adoption of the Single Administrative Document for example, saved Swiss industry $123m a year in customs costs.

Common rules on standards have been developed in voting in the pan-European standards organizations, CEN, CENELEC, and ETSI. Representatives of EFTA states have votes on the same terms as EC states; however additional clout lies with the Community because in the event of disagreement EC members vote separately on their own standards, thus presenting others with a fait accompli to which they must adapt if they wish to sell goods in the Single Market. The November 1988 Tampere Convention provided for mutual recognition of test results and proofs of conformity. There has been mutual information on all draft technical legislation since November 1990. By 1989 there was a total of 180 bilateral agreements. In the case of Switzerland these covered participation in EUREKA and EC research projects, COST, ESPRIT II, BRITE, RACE, COMMETT II, ERASMUS.

Swiss industrialists, who employ some six million EC citizens, are at least as well informed as any in the EC. They are European members of UNICE, the employers' organization, and receive early drafts of directives as full members of relevant trade and agricultural associations. The Commission seems to have no difficulty in fining Swiss firms for participating in illegal cartels. The first Euro-information centre for small businesses outside the territory of Member states was set up in Geneva. From 1991 all EFTA countries have been linked to the BC-NET giving access to consultancies.

Parallel to this web of mixed committees, consultation and information mechanisms has been the development of a common legal space in commercial law. Since 1988 the Lugano convention has provided for enforcement of judgements by the others' courts in civil and commercial matters. It has not worked smoothly as the EFTA countries retaliated against the Community's indifference to decisions delivered by their courts; moreover EFTA courts have no possibility of recourse anywhere to a system of preliminary judgements to secure uniformity.

Finally in 1984 the Luxembourg Convention committed its signatories 'to play a more important part in the world'. However despite Norwegian enthusiasm, the Swiss excluded any reference to foreign policy, limiting themselves to consultations in GATT and the OECD on economic and monetary safeguards, and on Third World development.

4.3 The Oslo Process

There was lively debate in Oslo before diplomats of the lightly institutionalized EFTA countries agreed

> to explore various options and ways and means to strengthen the institutional links between the EFTA states and the EC. (#11 of Declaration by the EFTA Summit, Oslo, 14–15 March 1989)

Opinion ranged from the Austrian enthusiasm for membership through a willingness to explore a more global framework 'Partnership' agreement to the Icelandic reluctance to change anything.

For Switzerland, adopting the rules of the Community meant doubling the volume of its total legislation, amending without debate one-third of existing legislation, and with the Cantons and the Federation having little choice in how they adopted EC legislation. Six of the popular referendum initiatives proposed between 1973–87 would henceforth be inadmissible. The Cantons feared that changing from a turnover tax to VAT might well increase the federal share of revenue.

On the side of the Commission, there was considerable doubt whether the Swiss were prepared to accept that the Single Market was leading towards pan-European government. President Delors said bluntly to the European Parliament, 'These Swiss have got to stop viewing the Community as an ordinary international organization' (Agence Europe 15 February 1992).

The Oslo process was undertaken not to bring the EFTA countries of 32 million to full membership, but to avoid membership applications from delaying the internal market process for the 320 million of the Twelve. This remained the Commission priority until it was forced to accept membership applications at the Edinburgh summit even before all internal frontiers had been abolished. At the end of the process, M. Delors summed up his three objectives thus:

> Firstly, *extending the benefits of the single market to the EFTA countries*, with the rights and obligations conferred by it, as well as the limits. Agriculture is therefore not included within the agreement for the present. Secondly, *there are the beginnings of a partnership* between the Community and EFTA. And thirdly, setting out an important marker for the establishment in the medium term, of the architecture of the wider Europe. The provisions and machinery of the agreement will ensure that the Community will remain *fully autonomous* when it comes to decision-making. At the same time they will allow EFTA to be *adequately informed and involved* in order to assert its interests just when decisions of interest to the European Economic Area have to be taken. (Delors, 1992)

This tough stance limited partnership to 'informing and involving' others only at the point when the fully autonomous Community was making laws which others would have to obey. It was little different from the Association status which the EFTA countries had wanted to avoid when they began the Oslo process in response to M. Delors' speech offering partnership. Especially as this term was that used after 1989 to encapsulate Western Europe's relationship with the East in the new architecture, it is worth setting out the difference between the unitary concept preferred by EFTA and the two-pillar concept of the Commission.

4.4 Unitary Partnership

In October 1990, EFTA ministers reduced their demands for derogations in return for 'a genuine common decision-making mechanism'. By this they meant a unitary decision-making structure for legislation, with representatives from EFTA as well as member states on the committees which managed the implementation of directives, and judges on a joint judicial body. However, the EFTA negotiators were divided among themselves with respect to the implications for their own sovereignty. Thus Swiss negotiators were more reluctant than the Norwegians to accept that national judges from all 19 countries would have to seek preliminary rulings from a supranational court on EEA law. On the other hand, the same attachment to national sovereignty meant that they were much keener than the Swedes to have the formal right to be represented on EC management committees in

the same way that as states they were represented in international organizations like the Bank of International Settlements. In 1990 there was strong
pressure from Zurich and Basel for Swiss membership of around 100
committees (30th report). This claim was then reduced in the second
working group to about 40 committees and then the fifteen relating to
financial services, the Swiss being especially interested in who would
manage the safeguard clauses in the event of economic turbulence. In
contrast Swedish lawyers were much more pragmatic in accepting the
Community insistence on its own autonomy. Where a non-member country
provided financial resources, as in research, or knowledge as on standards,
then nationals might be invited to appear as experts or serve as members.
The Pompidou Committee on drugs was chaired by a Swedish national.

4.5 Two-pillar Partnership

However, within a few months of the opening of formal negotiations, the
Community view of partnership prevailed. The metaphor of 'two pillars'
carries the implication that each side shall decide autonomously. There
would be no overarching authority. Moreover there was to be no delay in
reworking directives on the internal market to take account of the fact that
EFTA states had more voluminous legislation in both the competition and
environmental fields. As the EFTA lawyers familiarized themselves with
EC legislation, they could make suggestions of detail, but in principle their
task was to adapt their domestic legislation to that which had already been
decided by the Twelve alone. Although EFTA states were not committed to
automatic acceptance of *future* EC legislation, the Swiss ambassador to the
EC, Dr B. de Tscharner protested that

> The Community should contemplate future developments in terms of dialogue and co-
> operation with its partners, and not in a spirit of fait accompli'. (Agence Europe, 5
> March, 1992)

The Court's Opinion 1/91 rejecting the opportunity to bring all trade in the
European Economic Area within a unitary legal framework can be understood as
in accordance with this two-pillar approach.

In comparison with the bloc to bloc negotiations with the Lomé Associates, two
differences may be noted. Once the EFTA Secretariat had been upgraded to be
the locutor of the Commission, it had more clout than any equivalent
organization of the ACP states. Secondly it was agreed that the external actions
of the Community would be the subject of informal discussions and a six-
monthly review with the Political Director from the EU Presidency country.
However, as with Lomé, the interests of individual nations within the blocs could

become all too important – as in the dossier on fishing rights in Nordic waters. Veli Sundbäch, the chief negotiator on the EFTA side put the point thus,

> There was another slightly disturbing element in the negotiations, which became more and more apparent towards the end when final compromises were drawn. Our negotiating partner on the EC side was the Commission, but it had to take into account the wishes of the member states. (EFTA, 1991 p. 3)

He further complained that on the final day in Luxembourg the EC side celebrated with champagne before the EFTA states had decided to accept the final terms – an interesting instance of the asymmetry between the two sides. However the EC side did not exploit their power to the extent of carrying out their threat that rejection of the EEA in a referendum would lead the EC to negotiate everything from the beginning. The rejection of the EEA by the Swiss-German cantons and the Norwegian government did not result in the EC tearing up all previous bilateral agreements.

4.6 Membership

The December 1992 referendum also prevented the Swiss government from applying for membership. According to the Swiss ambassador to the EC, this had become the real objective from the autumn of 1991 (Agence Europe, 5 March, 1992). The impossibility of influencing legislation decided in advance by the Twelve seemed to meet the criterion for preferring membership over bilateral negotiations set out by a working group of the Federal Ministry of Foreign Affairs. Swiss interests would be better served by membership

> dès que la Suisse ne sera plus en mesure de négocier avec la CE des accords vraiment équilibré. Le traité EEE constituera à cet égard un test très important. (Federal Council, 1990)

It is now time to turn to the negotiations with Turkey, which like other states 'Associated' with the European Community, has long been frustrated by a contradiction which stems from the nature of building a Community without a Constitution.

4.7 Turkey

The Community's self-image is that it provides a better alternative to basing international relations on power. The reality faced by weaker 'Associated' states is that it is confronted by a commercial policy which is the product of such fraught internal decision-making that it finds it very difficult to take account of the interests even of states linked to it by formal institutions.

On the one hand, in seeking to bring trade under the rule of law, the Community seeks to institutionalize relationships – what might be labelled the Monnet approach. The Fourth Lomé agreement with ex-colonies associated with the EC, negotiated by DGVIII, contains the most elaborate provisions for any or all of the ACP states to exercise rights of consultation on any matter they choose. Article 181, 1 says that

> Consultations shall take place, where the Contracting Parties concerned so request, in order to take account of their respective interests. (OJL 229 17 August 1991)

Annex XIX lays down procedures for completing the process within three months. Consultation is also the subject of articles 12, 24, 30g, 32b, 41, and 178.

On the other hand, the Community is seeking to become an 'ever-closer Union', asserting European autonomy in trade, monetary and perhaps defence matters, – what might be called the de Gaulle approach. However it lacks any institution comparable to the French presidency of the Fifth Republic which can subordinate sectoral and state interests for the sake of securing co-operation from important or needy outsiders.

Association agreements have long illustrated the two-pillar approach discussed above. The Community side defines its own position as a powerful inflexible bloc which then listens to the demands and complaints of Associates in ministerial Councils, Committees of officials and impotent joint Parliamentary Committees. The ACP countries have scarcely used their right to be consulted on Single Market matters. The Turks decided not to press the 'comitology' issue on Single Market matters as their experience of an Association Council had already convinced them that such consultation rights were not fruitful. Their view of the EC commitment to the rule of law has been jaundiced by the German refusal to honour the commitment to make free movement of workers effective from 1986. The Turkish government refuses to attend the meetings on 'illegal' textile quotas where its industrialists are told what they will receive.

Finally although the industrialists (TUSIAD) and Chambers of Commerce combined in 1964 to set up a research and lobbying organization, the IKV, which has had a Brussels office since 1984, it does not have the resources required for influence on the Community process through effective lobbying. Its dialogue is limited to contacts with the few officials in the Commission, the Council and Parliament who have long taken an interest in relations with Turkey. Turkish firms have tended to regard fines and anti-dumping actions as part of the price to be paid for exporting to the EC. The Turkish Standards Institute is informed of European standards in advance of their publication, but does not itself participate in the voting in CEN/CENELEC. There was no Turk on the Round Table of European industrialists until 1991. It was the success of the enlargement of membership to Iberia that convinced the Ozal regime that membership might prove a better option than Association. Like the new regimes in Spain and Portugal, the new Turkish government wanted to shift from a protected import substitution regime to industrial competitiveness funded by large foreign investment. Like Spain, Turkey's agricultural potential is such that it could immediately take as much as a tenth share of the high-priced European market. The Turkish government responded to the Commission's Internal Market programme by requiring every Turkish Ministry after 1986 to assess the compatibility of Turkish legislation with EC legislation. The EC Press Office in Ankara was upgraded to the status of a full delegation. In 1987 the Turkish government applied for full membership within ten years to be followed by a seven-year transition period to 2004. When the Council supported the Commission's deferral of membership, both sides agreed that there be a Customs Union by 1996. This goes beyond the links of the EEA in that it implies a Common Commercial Policy. The State Planning Organization after 1988 sent ten delegations to DGIII to inform itself on Single Market directives. Turkish interest in the Community can be gauged from the fact that there are more journalists accredited to EC institutions than from most member states.

4.8 Hungary

I have in mind a special type of membership which would allow affiliate members to contribute to the formulation of policies in domains considered of joint Community interest ... be consulted in the enlarged sessions of the Council of Ministers, or the European Parliament, on themes with a major trans-European dimension, such as transport, telecommunications, energy, research and culture ... co-operate closely in matters of foreign policy, tie their exchange rate to the ECU ... avoid the risks of an ad hoc intergovernmental approach. (Commissioner Andriessen, Prague, 10/06/91, Agence Europe, 10 June 1991)

The new regimes of Central and East Europe were less interested in specifically Single Market matters than in financing the shift to a social market, trading with the West instead of the East. More than half the potential exports to the EC from the countries 'returning to Europe' were in textiles, steel, and agricultural products – precisely the declining industries which had been deliberately omitted from Lord Cockfield's programme even though they had all long been within the Commission's competence. The pretension of a European Single Market was a bad joke to exporters of Hungarian hens who now faced CAP protection and subsidized exports in their established markets in the DDR and Austria. While the Hungarian meat exporters' Association had its own man in Brussels, Single Market matters were left to government officials.

The Commission seconded its own men to the Hungarian Ministry of International Economic Relations, rather as Montagu Norman had a Bank of England official in the Hungarian Finance Ministry in the 1920s. However whereas the bankers of the 1920s had underwritten loans, the Commission was in the business of offering advice and negotiating the Europe Agreements.

Under the PHARE programme run by consultants appointed by the Commission on behalf of the group of 24, the European Community saw its role as paying for Western consultants to provide information and advice. Except for loans to support the balance of payments, money was not handed to the new democratic regimes to use for restructuring as they thought fit. As in the ACP countries, a couple of locally recruited project officers vetted elaborate contracts. As most of these projects were initiated by Hungarian and Brussels consultancies, it is easy to understand how both the Commission and the Government could assert that it was the other side which wanted the particular contracts agreed. In comparison with what the Germans were prepared to pay to integrate the DDR, or what the Americans paid to preclude Communist regimes in Western Europe, the PHARE programme amounts to the message, 'We owe them nothing'. A small part of this advice related directly to the Single Market.

The Europe agreements did not promise future membership, but on the other hand downplayed the discredited status of 'Associate.' They offered what Commissioner Andriessen above called 'affiliated' countries eventual access to the Western market on condition that the Eastern regimes maintained market regimes and political pluralism, to which respect for individual and group rights was added. The trade aspects of these agreements came into force on an interim basis in March 1992. At a time when the Commission was unable to supply copies to Customs officials until legal interpreters had completed checking the text, several missions of non-member countries were able nevertheless to show me that they had copies. The strengthening of the Common External Policy associated with the 1992 programme here had the important consequence of precluding the intergovernmental 'co-operation' agreements of previous years. Also, as with Northern Europe, hard-pressed DGI officials were keen to group countries in ways unknown to geographers or historians. The Visegrad bloc takes its name from the town where the new Hungarian, Czech and Polish leaders had their first meeting.

4.9 The United States

Although the Community owed its existence to Monnet-style co-operation with the United States, the first country to accord it diplomatic recognition, its sense of identity has often required Gaullist resistance to American leadership. Americans are used to taking a leading role in committees deciding European defence and monetary policy in organizations like NATO and the Bank for International Settlements. The EC in its intergovernmental aspect as European Political Co-operation has since 1974 informed the State Department of its forthcoming agenda before meetings, presumably so that the USA can then exert influence indirectly through the British, Dutch and German governments. In common with other 'friendly nations', the US is given more information than European MEPs or citizens about the outcomes of EPC ministerial discussions. It is not therefore surprising that Secretary Mosbacher demanded an American presence on EC committees dealing with Single Market matters like telecommunications and banking. It is all the more significant therefore that DGI was able to mobilize sufficient support to exclude American participation on the basis that the EC in its 'communautaire aspect' was both autonomous and more than a mere international organization.

However, American government and industry remained keen to exert influence on the Single Market programme. The new dynamism of the Commission, combined with an American deficit in trade with Europe between 1985 and 1989, persuaded Bush as vice-president and then President to reverse Reagan's downgrading of the US Mission to the Community. This is not the place to consider policy disputes over Uruguay, Airbus, rules of origin, agricultural subsidies, quotas, and so on, but procedural agreements in themselves indicate the enhanced status of the Delors Commission from the perspective of Washington. The only permanent external mission of the USTR was established in Brussels. Mrs Carla Hills became famous for her well-publicized weekly visits to the Berlaymont. Her notes-verbale stimulated the Commission delegation to the USA to use similar procedures with American Senators and Governors. The longstanding links between the House of Representatives and the European Parliament became an important avenue of mutual understanding. In 1985 the Commission President was allowed to attend G7 meetings, and thereafter to present policy papers. In 1989 Bush in Boston and Secretary Shultz in Berlin welcomed the leading role of the Community in the new Europe. In 1990 the Delegation in Washington was accorded full ambassadorial status. In 1991 DGIII concluded an Agreement on biennial talks on competition and antitrust policy. In 1992 the US-EC Declaration regularized consultation procedures at Presidential, Ministerial and official levels. This was a markedly different status from the December courtesy call paid since 1982 by the US Secretary of State on his way home from the NATO ministerial meeting. In 1993 DGXV agreed with the US Treasury to institute an early warning system on monetary movements.

While procedures may not alter the long-term greater importance to Washington of its bilateral relationship with Tokyo, where the US deficit is much greater, they do add up to a more equal relationship with Europe than in the past. In terms of this paper, the size of the US commercial stake in Europe, where companies of US parentage have nine million employees (European firms employ three million Americans), served to modify the effect of recent 'Buy American' nationalism. Their lobby organization, AMCHAM, successfully argued that bullying tactics of the kind used against Japan would be counter-productive in influencing the European Community.

The EC Committee of the American Chamber of Commerce in Brussels reorganized itself in 1985 and became the sole conduit for 14 American Chambers of Commerce in Europe. By 1991 its staff of 14 serviced 18 subcommittees and 57 working groups representing 130 industrial and service companies. Among them are the leading consultancy firms used by the Commission to draft proposals, Ernst & Young, Arthur Andersen, and Price Waterhouse. Those willing to speak to its working groups, and write introductions to its papers, include the leading officials of the Commission and influential members of the Parliament. Its *Countdown 1992*, produced twice a year, became the most informative guide to the Single Market programme, supplemented by *The Business Guide to EC Initiatives* and *The EC Information Handbook*. The Commission officials I interviewed could show me examples of information supplied as white papers by the EC Committee which they used because of its quality (yellow, green and pink papers are for internal use within AMCHAM). This well-funded lobbying has its uses, but suggests the need for limits on a form of influence which gives an advantage to American business over Turks and Hungarians, and probably over industrialists and consumers of member states.

4.10 Japan

The low profile adopted by the Japanese Mission in Brussels contrasts strongly with that of the US Government and of US business. The quality of the representatives sent by the Ministry of Foreign Affairs and the Ministry of Trade and Industry shows the importance they attach to understanding the Community. The list of visitors from the Diet to the European Parliament includes future ministers and prime ministers. As the range of Community competence has developed, so the range of Japanese ministries keeping themselves informed by being represented in Brussels has also increased.

Despite their strong ideological preference for dealing with sovereign states like themselves, committed to the most favoured nation principle of the GATT, the Japanese have shown extraordinary interest in what to them is a dangerous oddity, whose structure is inimical to the legal basis of the world trading order. A Eurobarometer poll conducted in Japan in August 1991 found that 29 per cent of the public and 62 per cent of managers had heard of the 1992 programme. (*Target 1992*) There were fifty speakers on the TEAM 92 Speakers' panel in Tokyo. The cultural asymmetry between European interest in Japan is as great as the payments asymmetry which for the year ending in March 1992 rose to $28.4bn (Agence Europe 13 April 1992).

Thus while those on the Japanese desk in DGI may not speak Japanese, Japanese in the JETRO or from the Association of machine manufacturers are expected to know comparatively far more of European history, culture and languages. Japanese sensitivity to this disparity is shown by their appreciation of M. Delors' referring to books on Japan when he visited Tokyo before signing the EC–Japanese Declaration; what they did not know was that he had primed the Delegation from the European Parliament to recite a litany of complaints about the drop in imports of European luxuries. The EC–Japan cultural centre set up in Tokyo in 1986 and the experimental centre for industrial co-operation dating from 1987 show that both sides are aware that their undeveloped relationship has cultural roots.

For whatever reason, the stance of both the Japanese government ministries and of industry has been low-profile. A typical reaction is expressed in the policy of localization expressed by NOMURA,

> In Europe, Nomura will function totally as a European financial institution, 'prospering together with our clients', and supplying surplus capital from trade in the global framework to the regional market.

It is consonant with this low profile that although the Japanese have the financial resources needed for effective lobbying, their preference for using European consultancies rather than, say, NOMURA, makes it difficult to assess the extent to which they take an independent line rather than following behind the Americans. Although they are members of European associations, on standards, they have preferred adaptation, rather than attempting to influence their formulation. This is all the more remarkable in that some standards, as in the MAC-packet family of TV standards, were drawn up to hamper access for Japanese goods. Like the Turks, the Japanese state has been reluctant to compromise its understanding of legal rectitude by seeming to put its authority behind agreements with the Community which are incompatible with free trade principles. While the French Assembly and the GATT published details of the MITI's commitments in July 1991 on 'consultation' on cars, these are not to be found specifically in the annual list of unfair trade practices published by JETRO.

The immediate consequences of the Single Market therefore have been to make the Commission the principal locutor of Japanese trade interests, rather than the nation states individually. However, despite the free trade preferences of Commissioners Brittan and Bangemann, the use of market access as bargaining chips intended to bring down the trade deficit has been much in evidence in the short term. Both these points are implicit in the title of the 1992 Commission document on 'A consistent and global approach: a review of the Community's relations with Japan', endorsed on 15 June by the Council.

However there is in the EC–Japan Declaration of 1991 an awareness which is picked up in the MANO report of December 1992 that relations could be improved by concentrating less on trade disputes and more on common political interests. Bluntly, if Arabs did not buy goods and services in Europe with yen obtained for oil, both the trade deficit and the multilateral trading system would become difficult to sustain. Both the MITI and the Foreign Ministry seem willing to respond to joint approaches to common problems like aid to the USSR, policies on the global environment, relief of debt, more substantive controls on chemicals and nuclear waste, and joint investment in aeronautics and satellites.

5 CONCLUSIONS

The external impact of the Single Market programme has been both considerable and variable. All the neighbours of the EC have had to make major efforts to adapt their own legislation and standards to the new directives. For the EFTA countries in particular this required a huge bureaucratic self-education in taking on board 12,000 pages of the acquis. More than a thousand EFTA officials had to understand how the Community works in their field of expertise in order to negotiate the European Economic Area. To a lesser extent, American-owned businesses in Europe and Japanese corporations had to inform themselves of, and adapt to, the phenomenon of a completed internal market and external commercial policy.

External influence over the content of directives and standards has been less obvious. Some EFTA countries and the American government and its business interests were willing and able to devote the necessary resources to attempting to have their say with the Commission, Council and Parliament. The Japanese were able to do the same, but for the most part were unwilling to be seen to attempt to influence an external legislative process.

However in all these cases, external governments and firms remained the demandeurs, with no rights to speak or vote except as second-class members of the European standards bodies, or on other matters in which a financial contribution gave the right to a say. The Delors 1989 notion of 'a new more structured partnership with common decision-making and administrative institutions' proved to be subordinate to the concern for creating a state-like autonomous union. The Single Market and its flanking policies increased the saliency of the Community, but not its institutional capacity to subordinate national and sectoral interests to the needs of its weaker neighbours. Moreover, the logic of creating the Single Market proved incompatible in the short run with enlargement. Iberian enlargement in 1985 had not been undertaken because the EC needed more vegetables, but out of a sense of solidarity in helping Spain and Portugal establish a democratic process and market economy – an identity which had been unimaginable twenty years earlier. Public opinion was not prepared to make the short-term sacrifices for the sake of the political and economic stability either of Turkey or of Eastern and Central Europe. With respect to the fourth option, protection extended in territory and to industrial as well as agricultural products, the jury is still out. Meanwhile, much of the foreign direct investment in Europe has been a hedge against Community Preference in industry.

Finally, this story demonstrates the European capacity to think of national and European interests in incompatible intellectual frameworks at the same time. The process of adopting the Single Market programme either through the Court route of Cassis de Dijon or through the Commission/Council legislative route would have been impossible without the institutionalization known as the Community method. Yet the power political framework is much more convincing than the identity framework in understanding why the rich EFTA countries were acceptable as members but not the Turks or Czechs. Similarly pressure from the established bloc leader, the USA, was acceptable where pressure from the Japanese would not have been.

Perhaps the best analogy for Europeans of the 1990s is with America of 1940. Dealing with a weak presidency, a mass of conflicting agencies, a Senate close to the interests of local states, a Supreme Court capable of independent action, proved very frustrating for the British Ambassador, Lord Halifax. Yet by 1948 the USA was able to get states as diverse as California and Montana to contribute 1.6 per cent of its GNP, 10 per cent of the Federal budget to make some of its neighbours and potential competitors safer economically and politically.

REFERENCES

Amcham, (1991), EC Committee of the American Chamber of Commerce in Belgium, *Business Guide to EC Initiatives*, Autumn.

Brewin, C. and McAllister, R. (1986), 'Review of the activities of the European Community in 1985', *Journal of Common Market Studies*, **23** (4).

Cecchini, P. (1988), with Michel Catinat and Alexis Jacquemin, *The European Challenge: 1992: the Benefits of a Single Market*, Aldershot: Wildwood House.

Christopherson, H. (1991), in Finn Laursen, (ed.), *Europe 1992: A World Partner*, Maastricht: European Institute of Public Administration.

Commission (1985), *Completing the Internal Market*: White Paper from the Commission to the European Council. COM(85)310 Brussels, 14 June.

Commission (1986), *Explaining the Single Market*.

Commission (1988a), Europe 1992: Europe World Partner, *Agence Europe*, Doc 1530, 25 October.

Commission (1988b), 'Uruguay Round: main aspects of the Community's position on Montreal Conference', 5–7 December 1988, *Agence Europe*, Doc 1536, 9 December.

Commission (1989), 'The broad lines of Commission Policy', *Agence Europe*, Doc 1542/3, 26 January.

Commission (1992), 'Explanatory Memo on laws relating to EC type-approval of motor vehicles', *Agence Europe*, Doc 1767, 1 April.

Delors, J. (1992), *Target 1992*, November/December.

De Clercq, W. (1990), *Europe: Back to the Top*, Brussels: Roularta Books, 1990

EFTA (1991), *EFTA BULLETIN*, 3 April.

GATT (1991), *Trade Policy Review: The European Communities*, vol.1. Geneva: GATT, June.

Jacobs, F. (1994), 'Foreword' in Eeckhout, *The European Internal Market and International Trade*, Oxford: Oxford University Press.

Kleppe, P. (1991), 'EFTA and the EC's internal market' in F. Laursen (ed.) *Europe 1992: World Partner*, EAP\EIPA.

Nye, J. Jr., Biedenkopf, K. and Shiina, M. (1991), *Global Co-operation after the Cold War: a reassessment of Trilateralism*.

Owada, H. (1989), The implications for Japan – EC relations', *Business in the Contemporary World*, **1** (4), Summer.

Ross, G. (1995), 'Inside the Delors Cabinet', *Journal of Common Market Studies*, **32** (4), December.

Stevens, C., Kennon, J. and Ketley, R. (1993), 'EC-South African trade', *International Affairs*, **69** (1), January.

Swiss Federal Council (1990), *Federal Council Report on Switzerland's Position in the Process of European Integration*, November .

10. Mutual Trust, Credible Commitments and the Evolution of Rules for a Single European Market

Giandomenico Majone

1 INTRODUCTION

As sociologists from Simmel to Luhmann have argued, trust is a basic social mechanism for coping with system complexity. It facilitates cooperation, simplifies transactions and makes available the knowledge and experience of others. Also, recent research in game theory and in industrial economics emphasises the importance of trust, and of the reputation system on which trust is based, for sustaining cooperation in a world of self-interested individuals, and for governing contractual relations more complex than simple spot-market transactions.

The significance of mutual trust for a system as complex as the single European market could not have escaped the attention of the drafters of the founding treaties. Article 5 of the Treaty of Rome expresses the requirement of Community loyalty in the following terms:

> Member States shall take all appropriate measures, whether general or particular, to ensure fulfillment of the obligations arising out of this Treaty or resulting from action taken by the institutions of the Community. They shall facilitate the achievement of the Community's tasks.

> They shall abstain from any measure which could jeopardize the attainment of the objectives of the Treaty.

Analogous prescriptions are contained in article 86 of the treaty establishing the European Coal and Steel Community, and in article 192 of the Euratom treaty.

Mutual trust is clearly crucial for a system which depends on the loyal cooperation of the member states, and of their administrations, for the formulation and implementation of common rules. In fact, the European Court of Justice has interpreted article 5 in a way that, going well beyond the principle of international law that *pacta sunt servanda*, approaches the principle of *Bundestreue* or 'federal comity' of German constitutional law (Due, 1992; Scharpf, 1994).

In the interpretation of the Court, article 5 gives expression to a general principle of mutual trust and cooperation not only between member states and Community institutions, but also among national governments. In the same spirit, the Commission's White Paper on the *Completion of the Internal Market* (Commission of the European Communities, 1985) lists mutual trust as the first element of the new approach for the mutual recognition of diplomas.

Thus, the starting point of this paper – the strategic significance of trust in a system as open-ended and interdependent as the Community – is hardly new. Unfortunately, the current debate on this issue tends to be legalistic, and seems to assume that trust can be elicited by preaching or imposed by judicial fiat. Still lacking are systematic analyses of the cascading effect of distrust on many problematic aspects of the integration process – from excessive centralization and unnecessary uniformity to the paradox of over-regulation and under-implement-ation – as well as concrete proposals for improving an increasingly unsatisfactory state of affairs. This paper is a first attempt to make some progress in both directions. Much more work remains to be done in preparation of the forth-coming Intergovernmental Conference on institutional reform.

2   DISTRUST AND THE PARADOX OF CENTRALIZATION

If trust is so important in reducing social complexity and sustaining co-operation then its lack must have serious consequences for the evolution of a system like the European Union. In this and the two following sections I examine the implications of distrust through the prism of several issues which figure prominently in the current debate on institutional reform: centralization, over-regulation, non-compliance, subsidiarity and mutual recognition. The general argument is that in all these cases, distrust – toward the European institutions and among the member states themselves – has impeded the development and/or the implementation of efficient solutions.

Let us begin with what may be called the paradox of centralization. Member states strive to preserve the greatest possible degree of sovereignty and policy discretion. This is shown, for example, by their stubborn resistance to the extension of supranational competences in the areas of foreign and security policy, taxation and macroeconomic management, and by their refusal to give the European Commission a direct role in implementing EC policies. At the same time, however, these states have been willing to delegate important regulatory powers even in areas not mentioned by the founding treaties and for purposes not essential to the smooth functioning of the internal market.

Thus, of seven areas of significant policy development at present – regional policy, research and technological development, consumer protection, education, culture, environment and health and safety at work – only the latter is explicitly mentioned in the Treaty of Rome, and then only as a field where the Commission should promote close cooperation among the member states (Article 118, EEC).

Environmental policy is a striking illustration of the paradox of centralization. In the two decades from 1967 to 1987, when the Single European Act (SEA) finally recognized the competence of the Community to legislate in this area, well over 100 directives, regulations and decisions were introduced by the Commission and approved by the Council. Budgetary crises, intergovernmental dissensions, and the Europessimism of the 1970s and early 1980s hardly affected the rate of growth of Community environmental regulation. From the single directive on 'the approximation of laws, regulations, and administrative provisions relating to the classification, packaging and labeling of dangerous substances' of 1967 (Directive 67/548/EEC) we pass to 10 directives/decisions in 1975, 13 in 1980, 20 in 1982, 23 in 1984 and 17 just in the six months preceding the passage of the SEA (Johnson and Corcelle, 1987). Today European environmental regulation includes more than 200 pieces of legislation. In many member states the corpus of environmental law of Community origin outweighs that of purely domestic origin (House of Lords, 1992).

Moreover, while the first directives were for the most part concerned with product regulation, and hence could be justified by the need to prevent that national standards would create non-tariff barriers to the free movement of goods, later directives increasingly stressed process regulation (emission and ambient quality standards, regulation of waste disposal and of land use, protection of flora and fauna, environmental impact assessment), aiming at environmental rather than free-trade objectives.

Why did the member states accept such a massive transfer of regulatory powers to the supranational level? After all, in the Community system the Council of Ministers, which represents the national interests, must approve all Commission proposals. In order to control transboundary pollution, countries have to cooperate, of course, but international cooperation can take many forms. As Coase (1960) showed, problems caused by negative externalities could be solved efficiently through decentralized arrangements. If national regulators could credibly commit themselves to take into account the international repercussions of their decisions and to implement in good faith intergovernmental agreements, international market failures could be managed in a decentralized fashion, without delegating regulatory powers to a supranational authority. An international secretariat would suffice to facilitate the exchange of information and to reduce the costs of organising cooperation.

The problem with international regulatory agreements is that it is often difficult for the parties concerned to know whether or not an agreement is properly kept. The main reason for this is that economic and social regulation is unavoidably discretionary. Because regulators lack information that only regulated firms have and because governments are reluctant, for political reasons, to impose excessive costs on industry, bargaining is an essential feature of regulatory enforcement. Regardless of what the law says, the process of regulation is not simply one where the regulators command and the regulated obey. A 'market' is created in which bureaucrats and those subject to regulation bargain over the precise obligations of the latter (Peacock, 1984). Since bargaining is so pervasive, it is often difficult for an outside observer to determine whether the spirit, or only the letter, of an international agreement has been violated.

When it is difficult to observe whether the parties are making an honest effort to enforce a cooperative agreement, the agreement is not credible. Hence, many international market failures cannot, in practice, be corrected in a de-centralized fashion because of problems of trust and credibility. Notice, too, that international regulatory failures may occur even in the case of purely local market failures. For example, problems of safety regulation for construction of local buildings create non transboundary externalities and thus, according to the subsidiary principle, should be left to the local authorities. However, if safety regulations specify a particular material produced only in that locality, they may amount to a trade barrier and thus have negative external effects. In such a case, local regulation of a local market failure creates an international regulatory failure.

Similarly, local authorities have sometimes controlled air pollution by requiring extremely tall smokestacks on industrial facilities. With tall stacks, by the time the emissions descend to ground level they are usually in the next city, region or state, and so of no concern to the jurisdiction where they were produced.

These examples illustrate a dilemma of regulatory federalism which the principle of subsidiarity cannot resolve in the absence of mutual trust and a sense of comity. Local or national governments may be more attuned to individual preferences, but they are unlikely to make a clear separation between providing public goods for their citizens and engaging in policies designed to advantage the locality or the country at the expense of its neighbours. Centralization of regulatory authority at a higher level of government can correct such externalities, and possibly capture economies of scale in policy making. But its cost is the homogenization of regulation across jurisdictions that may be dissimilar with respect to underlying preferences or needs (Noll, 1990).

In sum, the paradox of centralization can be explained, in part, by the fear that national governments may use regulation to promote their own interests rather than common regulatory objectives (for a more complete analysis of the paradox see Majone, 1992). On the other hand, it should be noticed that the optimal assignment of regulatory responsibilities among different levels of governments need not coincide with existing jurisdictional boundaries. There may be significant externalities and a need for joint action between some, but not all regions within a country or group of countries.

Hence the optimal solution may be found neither at the European nor at the national level, but at some intermediate level comprising a group of states (or regions within different states) facing the same problem. The scope of the externality would determine the membership of the group. Self-regulating organizations encompassing several states ('regional compacts', such as the Delaware River Basin Commission) have been used in the United States since the 1960s and in some cases even earlier (Derthick, 1974). More recently, institutional arrangements encompassing American states and Canadian provinces have been created in order to control pollution in the Great Lakes region.

By pooling their financial, technical and administrative resources these consortia of states or regions are in a better position to deal satisfactorily with their regulatory problems than either by acting alone or by relying exclusively on centralized regulation which cannot be closely tailored to their specific needs. The 'regional compact' model combines flexibility with economies of scale in policy formation and implementation. Its adoption on this side of the Atlantic would have far-reaching consequences for the future of European regulation. Instead of the traditional dichotomy of centralized or national regulation, with its artificial separation of rule making from enforcement, we would have a system of different, but compatible, regulatory regimes coordinated and monitored by a small regulatory body at the European level. Among the tasks of this body would be providing technical and administrative assistance, facilitating the diffusion of ideas and policy innovations, and acting as 'regulatory of last resort' where regional regulators failed to achieve their objectives.

Ten years ago a major study of European environmental law and policy noted that '[i]t is striking that the Community has not yet used the concept of regionally differentiated standards as a distinct harmonization strategy' (Rehbinder and Stewart, 1985, p. 221). This is still true today, even if a few environmental directives allow member states to set regionally differentiated standards in zone designated by them in accordance with Community guidelines. The model suggested here goes much beyond these timid attempts to tailor regulation to the specific needs of different regions of Europe. However, it assumes that member states are prepared to grant their own regions the freedom to deal directly with other regions and with the European institutions. Once more we run into the problem of trust.

3 DISTRUST AND THE PARADOX OF OVER-REGULATION AND UNDER-IMPLEMENTATION

The Brussels authorities are accused not only of centralizing tendencies but also of producing too many, and too complicated, rules. A recent report of the French Conseil d'Etat uses expressions like 'normative drift', 'luxuriating legislation' and 'regulatory fury'. It notes that by now the Community introduces the corpus of French law (and presumably of other national laws as well) more rules than the national authorities (Conseil d'Etat, 1992).

At the same time, it is common knowledge that many European rules are not faithfully implemented, or not implemented at all. The implementation deficit has become so serious over the years that the member states now realize that non-compliance threatens the credibility of their collective decisions. The European Council meeting at Dublin in June 1990 first gave the issue of non-compliance a high political profile in its final declaration. At the Maastricht summit, the heads of state and government stressed again the need for Community rules to be accurately transposed into national law and effectively implemented, while the Treaty on European Union contains new powers for the European Court of Justice to fine member states which fail to comply with judgments of the Court.

Despite this new awareness of the seriousness of the problem, the question raised by Joseph Weiler some years ago is still pertinent: how can there be a compliance problem given the strict control by the member states of the legislative process? (Weiler, 1988). Even more puzzling are the complaints over over-regulation since the Council, not the Commission, is the ultimate legislator. To be sure, many factors are involved both in over-regulation (Majone, 1994a) and in non-compliance (Krislov, Ehlermann and Weiler, 1986). A full analysis of these phenomena is beyond the scope of this paper; here I limit myself to arguing that distrust must be included among the explanatory variables.

In order to understand non-compliance one must keep in mind not only that member states are not enthusiastic about strict surveillance of their own markets in the interest of Union objectives, but also that their determination to implement European rules vigorously is weakened by the suspicion that other national governments may not behave in the same correct way (Vervaele, 1992). Without concrete measures to increase the level of mutual trust, therefore, the obligation of Community loyalty contained in article 5 of the Rome Treaty remains a dead letter and cannot serve as a basis for a system of effective enforcement.

In the preceding section I argued that the mutual distrust of the member states is responsible, in part, for a higher level of centralization than is strictly necessary for the smooth functioning of the internal market. But member states also mistrust European institutions and this attitude has significant, if paradoxical, consequences both for the quantitative growth of Community rules and for the poor level of enforcement. The immediate consequence is that the Commission is kept on very tight rein: it is chronically understaffed; closely monitored through an intricate system of 'regulatory' and 'management' committees which can block its proposals and transmit the file to the Council, which can overrule the Commission; and obliged to rely almost exclusively on the national bureaucracies for implementation of the measures it elaborates.

These drastic methods of control are only partially successful in limiting the regulatory discretion of the Commission (Majone, forthcoming) but produce several undesirable, and probably unanticipated, consequences. Consider first the budget constraint.

By national standards, the Community budget is quite small: less than 1.3 per cent of the gross domestic product of the Union or about 4 per cent of the combined expenditures of the central governments of the member states. It is also very rigid, since compulsory expenditure represents almost 70 per cent of the budget. These limited resources are insufficient to support large-scale initiatives in areas such as industrial policy, energy, transport or research and development, not to mention social policy or macroeconomic stabilization (Majone, 1993). However, the budget constraint has only a limited impact on regulatory activities. This is because the real costs of regulation are borne by the organizations and individuals who have to comply with it. Compared to these costs, the cost of producing the rules is negligible.

The structural difference between regulatory policies and policies involving the direct expenditure of public funds is especially important for the analysis of EC policy making since not only the financial, but also the political and administrative costs of implementing European rules are borne by the national administrations rather than the Commission. Thus, the attempt to restrict the scope of supranational policies by imposing a tight budget constraint has unwittingly favoured the expansion of a mode of policy making that is largely immune to budgetary discipline. Given the constraint, regulation turned out to be the most effective way for the Commission to maximize its influence.

Moreover, by denying the Commission any significant role in implementation the member states have encouraged a tendency to focus on the quantitative growth of European legislation (so that, for example, the number of directives approved by the Council is viewed as an important indicator of success) rather than on effective compliance and actual results. Over-regulation cannot be blamed only on the Commission, however. Many regulations and directives are introduced at the demand of individual member states, the Council, the European Parliament, The Economic and Social Committee and a variety of private and public interest groups, rather than by autonomous initiative of the Commission. While responsiveness to such demands may increase the legitimacy of the Commission, it also contributes to the apparently unstoppable growth of EC regulation.

The consequences of uncontrolled and unco-ordinated demands for EC legislation are aggravated by institutional factors. Because the Commission is a collegial body, central control over the regulatory activities of the different Directorates General (DGs) is weak. Lack of central coordination leads to serious inconsistencies across and within regulatory programmes, absence of rational procedures of setting priorities, and insufficient attention to the cost-effectiveness of individual rules. One method of limiting regulatory growth would be to set up an office with the power to oversee the entire regulatory process and to discipline the activities of the DGs by comparing the social benefits of proposed measures with the costs imposed on the European economy by the regulatory requirements.

Such an office or 'regulatory clearing house' (somewhat similar to the US Office of Management and Budget) should be established at the highest level of the Commission. A centralized review process would help the Commission's president screen demands for EC regulations and shape a consistent set of measures to submit to the Council and to the European Parliament.

Also the phenomenon of regulatory complexity can be usefully analysed from the perspective of this paper. Many students of EC policy making have pointed out that Community directives usually contain many more technical details than comparable national legislation.   The explanations that such regulatory complexity is due to the technical perfectionism of the Commission lacks plausibility: the Commission, as noted above, is chronically understaffed, has no in-house research capabilities, and is largely composed of generalists, not of technical experts.

Rather, regulatory complexity is in part another manifestation of the cascading effect of mutual distrust. Doubting the commitment of other governments to implement European rules seriously, and being usually unfamiliar with different national styles of administration, national representatives often insist on spelling out mutual obligations in the greatest possible detail. On the other hand, a vague and open-ended directive not only gives a member state wide latitude for wrongful or self-interested application, but also prevents the possibility of invoking it by an individual before a national court (Weiler, 1988).   Thus, regulatory complexity may also serve the objectives of the Commission by providing partial compensation for its exclusion from the implementation process.

Also the labyrinthine system of committees of national experts, created to assist the Commission and at the same time to limit its discretion, favours regulatory complexity by introducing a strong technical bias into the Community regulatory process. In many cases, national experts have significantly increased the quality of Commission proposals (Weiler, 1988; Dehousse *et al.*, 1992; Winter, 1993). In fact, what is known about the *modus operandi* of these committees suggests that debates there follow substantive rather than national lines. A good deal of *copinage technocratique* develops between Commission officials and national experts interested in problem solving rather than in defending national positions (Eichener, 1992). By the time a Commission proposal reaches the Council of Ministers all the technical details will have been worked out – but little or no attention will have been paid to issues of cost-effectiveness or practical implementability. This technical bias, combined with the reluctance of the

Council to engage in difficult and time-consuming policy control, and with the lack of central oversight at the Commission level, may be another factor contributing to regulatory complexity.

Empirical evidence on this point is scanty at best, but the hypothesis has also theoretical support. Some economists have argued that an explanation of regulatory complexity does not need to rest on the peculiar interests of the regulators but on the economic interests of third parties, namely, specialists in various aspects of regulation such as lawyers, accountants, engineers or safety experts. Unlike other interest groups, these experts care more about the process than the outcome of regulation. They have an interest in regulatory complexity because complexity increases the value of their expertise. Thus 'red tape' may not be simply evidence of bureaucratic inefficiency or ineptness. Rather, in part, rule complexity is a private interest that arises because a complex regulatory environment allows for specialization in various stages of rule making, as well as in 'rule intermediation' (Kearl, 1983; Quandt, 1983).

4   MUTUAL TRUST AND MUTUAL RECOGNITION

The new approach to harmonization and technical regulation outlined in the Commission White Paper on *Completing the Internal Market* (COM (85) 310 final) represents the most important attempt so far to reduce both over-regulation and regulatory complexity at the European level. As is known, the main elements of the new approach are the mutual recognition of national regulations and standards, and the delegation of quasi-legislative powers to European standardization bodies. Here I focus on the first element, and more specifically on the crucial importance of mutual trust for the success of the strategy of mutual recognition.

Since the free movement of workers is an essential condition for a common market, the idea of the mutual recognition of 'diplomas, certificates and other evidence of formal qualifications' can be found already in article 57 of the Treaty of Rome. The idea was in fact implemented fairly early in certain fields where national legislations were already similar, so that no complex harmonization was needed: in 1976 for medical doctors, in 1988 for nurses, in 1978 for dentists and veterinary surgeons, in 1983 for midwives and in 1985 for pharmacists. Little progress, however, could be made in other fields, notably law, architecture, engineering and the pharmaceutical profession, where national practices differed widely. Also, experience showed that the large measure of discretion retained by the member states often impeded the harmonization process. The national governments only implemented the minimum requirements of the directives, retaining the power to decide which diplomas of other member states complied with the relevant Community directive (Zilioli, 1989).

In the 1985 White Paper, the Commission announced its intention of applying the *Cassis de Dijon* philosophy also to professional mobility. The new strategy aimed at a general (rather than sectoral) system of recognition based on the following elements: mutual trust between the member states; comparability of university studies across the member states; mutual recognition of degrees and diplomas without prior harmonization of the conditions for access to, and the exercise of, professions; and the extension of the general system to salary earners.

These principles find concrete application in Directive 89/48 on 'a general system for the recognition of higher education diplomas awarded on completion of vocational courses of at least three years' duration'. Unlike the older sectoral directives, the new directive does not attempt to harmonize the length and curricula of professional education, or even the range of activities in which professionals can engage. Instead, the directive introduces a system by which the states can compensate for such differences, without restricting the freedom of movement. Mutual trust and loyal cooperation among the member states are supposed to replace the impossible task of harmonizing vastly different national systems of professional education and licensing. Each state is supposed to trust other states' courses of study as being generally equivalent to its own, and a competent national authority must accept the evidence provided by another member state.

Mutual trust as a substitute for legally binding harmonization is an admirable principle, but it remains to be seen whether the appeal to a common cultural heritage shared by the different national systems of education is sufficient to limit the traditional right of the states to control the education of citizens and residents and to regulate the professions. The scattered empirical evidence so far available is not very encouraging.

The problem is that instead of proposing concrete measures to increase mutual trust, the Commission tends to invoke general principles such as the common cultural heritage of European universities. In the 1985 White Paper it argued that 'the objectives of national legislation, such as the protection of human health and life and of the environment, are more often than not identical', so that 'the rules and control to achieve those objectives, although they may take different forms, essentially come down to the same thing, and so should normally be accorded recognition in all Member States' (Commission of the European Communities, 1985, p.17).

The limits of such *a priori* reasoning are shown, for example, by the judgment of the Court of Justice in the 'wood-working machines' case (Case No. 188/84 ECR, 1985, p.419). In this case the court was confronted with two different national approaches to safety: German regulation was less strict and relied more on an adequate training of the users of this type of machinery, while French regulation required additional protective devices on the machine. The Court ruled against the Commission which had argued that both regulations were essentially equivalent, and found that in the absence of harmonization at Community level, a member state could insist on the full respect of its national safety rules, and thus restrict the importation of certain goods.

Advocates of mutual recognition often do not seem to realize how demanding the principle is. An American scholar has noted that the mutual recognition approach may require a higher degree of comity among member states than the commerce clause of the US Constitution requires among individual states. The commerce clause has been interpreted by the US Supreme Court to allow each state to insist on its own product quality standards – unless the subject matter has been preempted by federal legislation, or unless the state standards would unduly burden interstate commerce (Hufbauer, 1990, p. 11).

The crucial importance of trust between national administrations is demonstrated by the failure of early attempts to harmonize national regulations for the approval of new medical drugs. The old EC procedure included a set of harmonized criteria for testing new products, and the mutual recognition of toxicological and clinical trials, provided they were conducted according to EC rules. In order to speed up the process of mutual recognition, a 'multi-state drug application procedure' (MSAP) was introduced in 1975. Under the MSAP, a company that had received a marketing authorization from the regulatory agency of a Member State could ask for mutual recognition of that approval by at least five other countries. The agencies of the countries nominated by the company had to approve or raise objections within 120 days. In case of objections, the Committee for Proprietary Medicinal Products (CPMP) – a group which includes experts from Member States and Commission representatives – had to be notified. The CPMP would express its opinion within 60 days, and could be overruled by the national agency that had raised objections.

The procedure did not work well. Actual decision times were much longer than those prescribed by the 1975 Directive, and national regulators did not appear to be bound either by decisions of other regulatory bodies, or by the opinions of the CPMP. Because of these disappointing results, the procedure was revised in 1983. Now only two countries had to be nominated in order to be able to apply for a multi-state approval. But even the new procedure did not succeed in streamlining the approval process since national regulators continued to raise objections against each other almost routinely (Kaufer, 1990). These difficulties finally induced the Commission to propose the establishment of a European Agency for the Evaluation of Medicinal Products and the creation of a new centralized Community procedure, compulsory for biotechnology products and certain types of veterinary medicines, and available on an optional basis for other products, leading to a Community authorization. Both the agency and the centralized procedure have been established by Council Regulation No 2309/93 of 22 July 1993.

The Regulation justifies the creation of the new agency and the centralized procedure by the need 'to provide the Community with the means of resolving disagreements between Member States about the quality, safety and efficacy of medicinal products'. The problem with the old decentralized procedure was that differences among national schools of medicine and differently perceived needs for new drugs led to divergent interpretations of drug approvals despite the fact that they had been prepared according to a standardized European format (Kaufer, 1990). Thus, mistrust may reflect insufficient understanding of different regulatory philosophies and of national styles of policy making.

However, it is likely that the decentralized procedure did not work also because some national regulators lacked, or were thought to lack, the scientific and technical expertise, financial resources and policy infrastructure needed to deal effectively with complex regulatory issues. Community assistance may be needed in order to help all members achieve a level of competence sufficient to support mutual trust and effective cooperation. As a recent study of new regulatory strategies in the EC argues, 'the "Europeanization" of expertise upon which a mutual recognition of risk assessment and consensus building may be built presupposes the setting up of an infrastructure which not only ensures continuous cooperation between the Community and national administrations, but also an ongoing involvement of those communities of experts on which national administrative authorities rely' (Dehousse *et al.*, 1992, pp. 15–6).

5   THE FOURFOLD PATH TO TRUST AND CREDIBILITY

The analysis developed in the preceding pages suggests several reforms – some quite radical, others more incremental and in part already implemented on an *ad hoc* basis – to improve cooperation among national and supranational institutions. The protracted and acrimonious debates which have accompanied the ratification of the Maastricht Treaty have at least made clear that the future of the Union lies not in further centralization but in an ever closer cooperation among the different levels of institutions and governance.

The reforms suggested here are inspired by the following principles. First, mutual trust and credible commitments cannot be achieved by contractual means or by other legal obligations, but only by changing the motivations of all the relevant actors. Second, a lasting reform of the present system cannot be limited to the European institutions, as much of the current debate seems to assume, but also embrace national and sub-national governments, as well as non-governmental actors. Third, in a phase of transition like the present one, clarity about objectives and about the best strategies for achieving them is more important than attention to what is politically or legally possible today: to reform is precisely to remove the constraints of the past. Finally, it should be noted that although the proposals made here address only some of the issues currently being debated, they form a reasonably coherent and self-contained subset. Moreover, they could be easily expanded to cover other issues such as the democratic deficit of European institutions and how to achieve transparency and political accountability without compromising the efficiency objectives of the internal market programme (Majone, forthcoming).

After these preliminary remarks, we are ready to consider separately the four ways to increase trust and credibility.

Greater Political Independence

The fear that governments may use regulation strategically, to pursue short-term political advantages rather than regulatory objectives, is arguably the main source of mutual distrust and lack of policy credibility. The consequences, as we saw, are more centralization and greater uniformity of norms than is necessary for market integration. Under the present institutional arrangements, however, a plea for more decentralization and greater normative flexibility is easily seen as an open invitation to grant further discretionary powers to the member states thereby placing market integration in jeopardy.

The way out of this dilemma is to grant more independence to national (and, as I argue below, supranational) regulators so that their commitment to a set of objectives decided at the European level is not compromised by domestic political considerations or by ministerial interference. Independence changes the motivation of regulators whose reputation now depends more on their ability to achieve the objectives assigned to their agencies than on their political skills. With independence, a problem-solving style of policy making tends to replace the more traditional bargaining style. Also, it is not difficult to show that greater independence implies more, rather than less, public accountability (Majone, 1994b).

By now the independence of central banks enjoys widespread political support in most countries of Europe. Also, the Treaty of Maastricht, although generally opposed to further delegation of policy making powers to the supranational level, assigns sweeping powers to the European Central Bank (ECB). The ECB can make regulations that are binding in their entirety and become European member states' law, without the involvement of the Council or of national parliaments. The Bank has a single objective, monetary stability, and the freedom to pursue this objective in complete independence of the other European institutions and of the national governments. Moreover, since the governors of the central banks of the member states are members of the ECB Council, they too must be insulated from domestic political influences in the performance of their task; they can no longer be players in the old game of pumping up the economy just before an election (Nicoll, 1993).

The recent rise of (more or less) independent regulatory agencies throughout Europe (Majone, 1994b) shows that the perceived advantages of independence are not confined to central banks. Among the justifications for such agencies are the need for expertise in highly complex matters, combined with rule making and adjudicative functions that are inappropriate for a government department; and the usefulness of the agency model whenever it is hoped to free public administration from partisan politics and party political influence. Agencies are also said to provide greater policy continuity and stability than cabinets because they are one step removed from election returns (Baldwin and McCrudden, 1987).

While these advantages of agency independence are acknowledged in theory, old habits of ministerial interference continue to persist in practice. Even in Britain, after more than a decade of privatizations and deregulation, government departments still preserve important regulatory powers so that the operations of agencies often are dependent on prior decisions of the Minister laying down the principles to be applied. In France the Minister of the Economy maintains important powers to regulate economic competition despite the creation in 1986 of the supposedly independent Conseil de la Concurrence. The Minister remains the final decision maker in matters relating to mergers and acquisitions, and the power of investigating anti-competitive practices is still in the hands of the administration.

Even the powerful Bundeskartellamt of Germany must occasionally yield to ministerial decisions. Thus, in 1989 the agency opposed the merger of Daimler Benz with the Messerschmitt-Bölkow-Blohm Company. Despite the clear danger of a distortion of competition in several important markets, the Minister of the Economy overrode the Bundeskartellamt allowing the merger to take place, subject to some conditions, in the name of industrial policy.

The relative ease with which agency autonomy can be disregarded in the name of political considerations extraneous to the logic that led to the creation of independent bodies in the first place, show how precarious the position of national regulators still is. Until the respect of agency independence becomes part of the different national political cultures, the national and international credibility of their regulatory policies will continue to remain open to doubt.

Networking

Credibility can be developed through team work. Although people may be weak on their own they can build resolve by forming a group (Dixit and Nalebuff, 1991). The same is true of organizations. A regulatory agency which sees itself as part of an international network of institutions pursuing similar objectives and facing analogous problems, rather than as a new and often marginal addition to a huge national bureaucracy, is more motivated to resist political pressures. This is because the regulator has an incentive to maintain his or her reputation in the eyes of fellow regulators in other countries. A politically motivated decision would compromise his/her international credibility and make cooperation more difficult to achieve in the future.

Professional associations of regulators working in the same policy area (antitrust, regulation of financial services, environmental protection, occupational health and safety, and so on) have been in existence for many decades in the United States and Canada. The experience of these countries shows that such regulatory networks serve a variety of useful functions, including the exchange of information and the comparative evaluation of new policy ideas and instruments. Professional associations of regulators are also beginning to develop at the international level – for example, the International Organization of Securities Commissions, IOSCO. The need of close professional links is even more urgent in Europe than in North America since, as was seen in section 4, lack of familiarity with the regulatory philosophies and administrative practices of other countries breeds distrust and impedes the practical implementation of the principle of mutual recognition.

The European Commission should obviously plan a key role in facilitating and coordinating the work of EU regulatory networks, and in ensuring that their activities are consistent with European objectives. The network model is perhaps easiest to visualize in the field of competition. An over-worked and under-staffed DGIV has already advocated a move toward a decentralized system of enforcement via proceedings before national courts. However, it has been rightly pointed out that it would make more sense to transfer responsibility for enforcement to the national competition authorities than to national courts and private litigants. These authorities perform a role which is analogous to that of DGIV, and they possess the kind of experience and expertise which courts of ordinary jurisdiction often lack. Moreover, there already exist direct links between Commission inspectors and national competition authorities as regards any investigations carried out by the Commission. In fact, under Regulation 17, the relevant national competition authority must be associated with enquiries and investigations, and its officials must be present if a search of premises is carried out (Harding, 1994, pp. 7–9).

There is no reason why the network model could not be extended to other areas of economic and social regulation. In fact, at an informal meeting of the Council of Ministers in October 1991, it was agreed that member states should establish an informal network of national enforcement officers concerned with environmental law. The recent creation of a number of European agencies (see below) may be seen as a further move in this direction. However, the logic of the model suggests that not only national regulators but also their counterparts in the Commission should be independent. Although European commissioners are not supposed to pursue national interests, usually they are politicians who, after leaving Brussels, will continue their careers at home. This makes national pressures often difficult to resist. In a number of well-publicised cases such pressures have produced flawed or at least inconsistent decisions. Again, competition policy, including the control of mergers and of anti-competitive state aid, provides the clearest examples. Several analysts have argued that Europe will never have a coherent competition policy without a cartel office independent both from the national governments and from the Commission. Commissioners would still be able to reverse an independent agency's decisions, as the German government does in the case of some of Bundeskartellamt's rulings. But the political costs of doing so would be high, and the interference plain for all to see.

Less Legislation, Better Implementation

The paradox of over-regulation and under-implementation was discussed in section 3. It was pointed out that at present the Commission is motivated to pay more attention to rule-making than to the effective enforcement of the rules it proposes. This is because, with a few exceptions like competition rules and fisheries, the Commission plays no direct role in implementation. Future reforms must correct this bias. Closer cooperation among independent national regulators or among groups of countries, or regions in different countries, would make more decentralized rule making possible; but it would also increase the need for greater powers of inspection of national or regional regulatory activities.

Even in areas like competition policy and environmental protection where many rules will continue to be set at the European level, there is a strong case for some form of centralized oversight of the measures taken by the member states to monitor and enforce compliance. This is because, to repeat a point already made, EC regulations lose credibility if they are not consistently implemented throughout the Union. Consistent implementation would require the creation of European inspectorates, but the reluctance of member states' governments to accept such a concept is almost universal.

A second-best solution, the idea of an 'audit' inspectorate to examine the policies and performance of national regulatory authorities, rather than seek to supplant them, has received much favourable attention recently. The audit inspectorate would publicly report its findings to member states, the Commission and the European Parliament. It would report not only on actual outcomes, but also on shortcomings in administrative arrangements, such as inadequacies in training and resourcing, leading to insufficient regulatory activities.

The issue of independence arises also in this context. The 1992 Report of the House of Lords Select Committee on the European Communities on *Implementation and Enforcement of Environmental Legislation* (House of Lords, 1992) rightly points out that the functions and powers of a European inspectorate should be carefully distinguished from the Commission's own duty to enforce

Community policies in the event of failure to do so by the member states. Thus, in the case of environmental policy, the inspectorate should not be part of DGXI. Rather, 'the logical home for an environmental inspectorate on the lines indicated is the European Environmental Agency, with whose functions the inspectorate would neatly dovetail' (ibid., p. 41). Institutional separation from the Commission would enable the inspectorate to scrutinize the Commission's own role, notably in providing assistance to the member states through the Structural Funds or the Cohesion Funds. Indeed, the use of such funds in the countries of southern Europe has sometimes produced serious consequences for the environment.

For analogous reasons, European inspectorates in such fields as the regulation of medical drugs, veterinary and plant control and health and safety at work should be organized within the corresponding new European agencies (Office of Veterinary and Phytosanitary Inspection and Control, European Agency for the Evaluation of Medical Products, Agency for Health and Safety at Work) rather than as offices of the Commission. Also, existing European inspectorates in the areas of competition, agriculture and fisheries – now housed in DGIV, DGVI and DGXIV, respectively – should be insulated from the Commission, possibly in connection with the transformation of the corresponding DG into an independent agency, see above.

Improving Regulatory Capacities

As was shown in section 4, early attempts to introduce the mutual recognition of toxicological and clinical trials for approval of new medical trusts failed because national regulators raised objections against each other almost routinely. We suggested that in this as in other cases, mutual distrust may also have been caused by the perception that some regulators lacked the resources and expertise needed to deal competently with complex regulatory issues.

It is a fact that regulatory capacities vary a good deal across the European Union. For example, until the last 1980s several member states lacked independent competition authorities or legislation on mergers. Even today most countries do not have a fully-fledged environmental protection agency or a specialized environmental inspectorate. Decentralization, both of rule making and of enforcement, remains problematic as long as such differences in regulatory capacity persists. Here, then, is a potentially fruitful field of co-operation between Community institutions (in particular the new European agencies) and national administrators.

The practice of regulatory federalism in America provides some useful suggestions in this direction. For example, when the Occupational Safety and Health Act (OSH Act) was passed in 1970, few states had comprehensive laws dealing with safety and health at work and fewer still had adequate programmes to enforce them. In spite of this, the OSH Act did not provide for the complete federalization of this area. The objective of assuring safe and healthy conditions at the workplace was to be reached, in part, by 'encouraging the States to assume the fullest responsibility for the administration and enforcement of state occupational safety and health laws', by means of federal grants and approved state plans (OSH Act, Section 2(b)(11)).

The Act incorporates special mechanisms for utilizing state resources. The most important of these are the provisions for 'state plans' contained in Section 18(b) through (g). While the Act generally preempts state enforcement once the federal government regulates, Section 18(b) provides that states desiring to regain responsibility for the development and enforcement of safety and health standards under state law, may do so by submitting and obtaining federal approval of a state plan which meets the requirements set forth in Section 18(c). Approval of a state plan by the Occupational Safety and Health Agency (OSHA) permits the state to re-enter the field of occupational health and safety regulation.

The Secretary of Labor (in whose Department OSHA is located) is to approve a state plan only if it demonstrates the availability of adequate financial resources and the existence of a sufficient number of trained personnel. States are entitled to receive federal funding for developing the plan and implementing it after approval. For the first three years after initial approval, all state plans are considered 'developmental'. During this period, when federal and state governments have concurrent jurisdiction, the Secretary evaluates the state plan at least every six months. States must submit annual activity reports and inform the public of its rights to file written complaints during this three-year period. This procedure known as CASPA (Complaints About State Plan Administration) provides information which OSHA uses to determine whether a developmental plan should be rejected or certified as operational.

Thus, the American implementation plans have three attractive features: (a) states retain the possibility to act if they see fit; (b) in order for them to do so, they must meet precise standards; (c) such a flexible solution takes due account of the fact that not all states enjoy a similar regulatory capacity; some of them need federal assistance in order to meet national standards. Could such a model be transposed at the EC level? The setting is of course radically different here. Far from being the exception, decentralized implementation tends to be the rule. Yet, to require member states to draw up an implementation plan and to set up the means that are necessary to make it operational would force them to address the implementation issue more systematically than is currently the case. Resources for the structural funds could be used to assist those member states lacking sufficient resources to develop the plans and the requisite structures.

It is clear, however, that such a system can work only if the Community is technically equipped to assess the adequacy of implementation plans, to monitor the activity of national regulators, to provide guidance – all activities that, by its own admission, the Commission is currently not in a position to carry out satisfactorily, but which could be entrusted to the new European agencies. Despite the practical difficulties, the proposed scheme is quite in line with the subsidiarity principle: member states would retain their primary responsibility, while the Community's main task would be to assist and supplement their action (Dehousse *et al.*, 1992, pp. 63–5).

6   CONCLUSION: REFORM BEGINS AT HOME

The Treaty on European Union contains two important political signals: first, the member states are not prepared to accept an unlimited expansion of Community competences and, second, the Commission has been weakened. The 'three pillar' structure of the Union signifies a refusal to 'communitarize' foreign policy and immigration matters. Even the new competences established by the treaty in fields such as education, culture, public health or consumer protection are replete with reservations: the Community can encourage cooperation among the member states, support and supplement their action, but harmonization of national laws is often excluded. As far as the Commission is concerned, not only were most of its proposals postponed or rejected, but its institutional status was weakened. One cornerstone of its power, the right of initiative, has been watered down in monetary policy where it only enjoys the right to put forward recommendations. It is also bound to play a lesser role in the new co-decision procedure. Furthermore, some declarations attached to the treaty (declarations on transparency and access to information and on the cost-benefit evaluation of Commission proposals) suggest that its legitimacy has been questioned (Dehousse *et al.*, pp. 8–10).

The Intergovernmental Conference on institutional reform scheduled to begin in 1996 should draw all the conclusions that logically follow from these premises. If the future of the Union lies not in more centralization but in closer cooperation among the different levels and institutions of governance, then the member states must be prepared to take concrete measures to improve mutual trust and the credibility of their commitment to the common objectives. This will require, *inter alia*, greater determination to resist the pressures coming from domestic distributional coalitions, and the temptation to gain short-term political advantages at the expense of policy consistency. Given the nature of the democratic process, these conditions are best met by delegating regulatory powers to politically independent institutions. I have argued that such delegation would not only increase policy credibility, but also greatly facilitate cooperation among national, subnational and European authorities. A similar institutional development at the EC level, resulting in a bigger role for the European agencies, would also make it possible to undertake activities, such as monitoring and certain types of research, best done at that level, without increasing the size of the Commission.

In the post-Maastricht era institutional reform must begin at home. Unless the national governments are willing to rethink their role in the economy and to show concretely their commitment to the common objectives, the only alternatives are more centralization or a progressive weakening of the economic and political foundations of the Union.

REFERENCES

Baldwin, R. and McCrudden, C. (1987), *Regulation and Public Law*, London: Weidenfeld and Nicholson.

Coase, R, (1960), 'The problem of social cost', *The Journal of Law and Economics*, **3**, 1–44.

Commission of the European Communities (1985), *Completing the Internal Market*, COM(85) 310 final. Luxembourg: Office for Official Publications of the European Communities.

Conseil d'Etat, (1992), *Rapport Public 1992*. Paris: La Documentation Française, Etudes et Documents No. 44.

Dehousse, R., Joerges, C., Majone, G. and Snyder, F. (1992), *Europe After 1992: New Regulatory Strategies*, Florence: European University Institute, EUI Working Paper Law No. 92/31.

Derthick, M. (1974), *Between State and Nation*, Washington D.C.: The Brookings Institution.

Dixit, A. K. and Nalebuff, B.J. (1991), *Thinking Strategically*, New York: W.W. Norton.

Due, O. (1992), 'Article 5 du Traité CEE: une disposition de caractère fédéral?', in *Collected Courses of the Academy of European Law*, **2** (1), 23–32. Dordrecht: Martinus Nijhoff Publishers.

Eichener, V. (1992), *Social Dumping or Innovative Regulation?* Florence: European University Institute, Working Paper SPS No. 92/28.

Harding, C. (1994), 'The relationship of the Community and state on the enforcement of Community law and policy', paper presented at the E.S.R.C./C.O.S.T. A7 Conference on *The Evolution of Rules for a Single European Market*, Exeter, 8–11 September 1994.

House of Lords, Select Committee on the European Communities (1992), *Implementation and Enforcement of Environmental Legislation*, London: HMSO.

Hufbauer, G.C. (ed.) (1990), *European 1992*, Washington D.C.: The Brookings Institution.

Johnson, S. and Corcelle, G. (1987), *L'Autre Europe Verte: La Politique Communautaire de l'Environnement*, Bruxelles: Editions Labor.

Kaufer, E. (1990), 'The regulation of new product development in the drug industry', in G. Majone (ed.), *Deregulation or Re-regulation?*, London: Pinter, pp. 153–75.

Kearl, J.R., (1983), 'Rules, rules intermediaries and the complexity and stability of regulation', *Journal of Public Economics*, **22**, 215–26.

Krislov, S., Ehlermann, C.D. and Weiler, J. (1986), 'The political organs and the decision-making process in the United States and the European Communities', in M. Cappelletti, M. Seccombe and J. Weiler (eds), *Integration Through Law*, **1**, Berlin: Walter de Gruyter, pp. 3–110.

Majone, G. (1992), 'Market Integration and Regulation: Europe after 1992', *Metroeconomica*, **43** (1–2), 78–102.

Majone, G. (1993), 'The European Community between social policy and social regulation', *Journal of Common Market Studies*, **31**, 153–75.

Majone, G. (1994a), 'Understanding regulatory growth in the European Community', Florence: European University Institute, mimeo.

Majone, G. (1994b), *Independence vs. Accountability? Non-Majoritarian Institutions and Democratic Government*, Florence: European University Institute, Working Paper SPS 94/3.

Majone, G. (forthcoming), 'The European Community as a regulatory state', to appear in *Collected Courses of the Academy of European Law*, Dordrecht: Martinus Nijhoff Publishers.

Nicoll, W. (1993), 'Maastricht revisited: a critical analysis of the treaty on European Union', in A.W. Cafruny and G.G. Rosenthal (eds), *The State of the European Community,* vol. 2, Boulder, CO.: Lynn Rienner Publishers, pp. 19–34.

Noll, R.G., (1990) 'Regulatory policy in a federal system', paper presented at *Conference on Regulatory Federalism*, Florence, European University Institute.

Peacock, A. (1984), *The Regulation Game*, Oxford: Basil Blackwell.

Quandt, R. (1983), 'Complexity in regulation', *Journal of Public Economics*, **22**, 199–214.

Rehbinder, E. and Stewart, R. (1985), *Environmental Protection Policy*, Berlin: Walter de Gruyter.

Scharpf, F.W. (1994), 'Community and autonomy: multi-level policy-making in the European Union', *Journal of European Public Policy*, **1** (2), 219–42.

Vervaele, J.A.E. (1992), *Fraud against the Community*, Deventer and Boston: Kluwer.

Weiler, J.H.H. (1988) 'The White Paper and the application of Community law', in R. Bieber, R. Dehousse, J. Pinder and J.H.H. Weiler (eds), *1992: One European Market?*, Baden-Baden: Nomos, pp. 337–58.

Winter, G. (1993), 'Drei Arten Gemeinschaftlicher Rechtssetzung und ihre Legitimation', in G. Brüggemeier (ed.), *Verfassungen für ein Ziviles Europa*, Baden-Baden: Nomos, pp. 45–72.

Zilioli, C. (1989), 'The recognition of diplomas and its impact on educational policies', in B. De Witte (ed.), *European Community Law of Education*, Baden-Baden: Nomos, pp. 51–70.

Index